REEL
PATRIOTISM

General Editors David Bordwell,
Donald Crafton, Vance Kepley, Jr.
studies in film **Supervising Editor** Kristin Thompson

Film Essays and Criticism
Rudolf Arnheim
Translated by Brenda Benthien

Post-Theory: Reconstructing Film Studies
Edited by David Bordwell and Noël Carroll

*Reel Patriotism: The Movies
and World War I*
Leslie Midkiff DeBauche

*Shared Pleasures: A History of Movie Presentation
in the United States*
Douglas Gomery

*Lovers of Cinema: The First American Film
Avant-Garde, 1919–1945*
Edited by Jan-Christopher Horak

*The Wages of Sin: Censorship and the
Fallen Woman Film, 1928–1942*
Lea Jacobs

Settling the Score: Music and the Classical Hollywood Film
Kathryn Kalinak

Patterns of Time: Mizoguchi and the 1930s
Donald Kirihara

The World According to Hollywood, 1918–1939
Ruth Vasey

REEL
PATRIOTISM

THE MOVIES AND
WORLD WAR I

Leslie Midkiff DeBauche

The University of Wisconsin Press

The University of Wisconsin Press
114 North Murray Street
Madison, Wisconsin 53715

3 Henrietta Street
London WC2E 8LU, England

Library of Congress Cataloging-in-Publication Data
DeBauche, Leslie Midkiff.
Reel patriotism: the movies and World War I /
Leslie Midkiff DeBauche.
264 pp.   cm. — (Wisconsin studies in film)
Revision of the author's thesis presented at the
University of Wisconsin–Madison.
Includes bibliographical references and index.
ISBN 0-299-15400-9 (cloth: alk. paper).
ISBN 0-299-15404-1 (pbk: alk. paper).
1. World War, 1914–1918—Motion pictures and the war.   2. Motion
pictures—United States—History.   3. War films—United States—
History and criticism.   I. Title.   II. Series.
D522.23.D43   1997
940.3—dc20   96-45979

for my mother
Kathleen Black Midkiff

and in memory of my father
Francis Morris Midkiff

CONTENTS

Illustrations   ix

Acknowledgments   xi

Introduction   xv

1   The U.S. Film Industry and the Coming of War,
    1914–1917   3

2   The Films of World War I, 1917–1918   35

3   Programming Theaters and Exhibiting Movies in Wartime   75

4   The Film Industry and Government Propaganda on
    the Homefront   104

5   The U.S. Film Industry at the End of World War I   137

6   The War Film in the 1920s   159

7   Conclusion: Practical Patriotism   195

Notes   201

Selected Bibliography   234

Index   240

ILLUSTRATIONS

1.1. Advertisement for *Joan the Woman* in the *New York Times*, 20 December 1916   15

1.2. Advertisement for *Joan the Woman* in *Moving Picture World*, 3 February 1917   18

1.3. Advertisement for *Joan the Woman* in *Moving Picture World*, 10 February 1917   19

1.4. Advertisement for *Joan the Woman* in *Moving Picture World*, 24 February 1917   19

1.5. Advertisement for *Joan the Woman* in *Moving Picture World*, 3 March 1917   20

1.6. Geraldine Farrar as Joan of Arc   25

1.7. Joan of Arc in the posters of the War Savings Stamps campaign   26

2.1. Three images from *To Hell with the Kaiser*   37

2.2. Patriotic Fox advertisement in *Moving Picture World*   39

2.3. Advertisement for *Over the Top* in *Exhibitor's Trade Review*   47

2.4. Advertisement for *Johanna Enlists* in *Motion Picture News*   51

2.5. Promotional materials from *The Little American*   60

2.6. Advertisement for *The Little American* in *Motion Picture News*   62

2.7. Advertisement for *The Little American* at the Evanston Strand Theater   66

2.8. Advertisement for *The Little American* at the Studebaker Theater   67

2.9. Promotion of *The Little American*   69

2.10. Image from the press book for *How Could You, Jean?*   72

2.11. Image from the press book for *How Could You, Jean?*   73

3.1. "Smiles" films advertising   84

3.2. "Smiles" films advertising   85

3.3. Advertisement for *Our Allies in Action* in the
      Milwaukee Journal   92
3.4. Advertisement in the *Milwaukee Journal* featuring
      local folk   94
3.5. Advertisement in the *Milwaukee Journal* featuring
      Rita Jolivet   95
3.6. Advertisement in the *Milwaukee Journal* highlighting
      Red Cross contributions   96
3.7. Advertisement in the *Milwaukee Journal* announcing
      community singing   97
3.8. Advertisement for *Hearts of the World* in the
      Milwaukee Journal   98
3.9. Advertisement for *The Unbeliever* in the
      Milwaukee Journal   99
4.1. A U.S. Food Administration certificate   106
4.2. Movie stars enhanced their public images by working
      for the war effort   117
4.3. Famous Players-Lasky advertisement demonstrating
      practical patriotism   121
4.4. Advertisement for *The Unbeliever* in the *Detroit Free Press* 129
4.5. James Montgomery Flagg's illustration of a soldier   130
4.6. Raymond McGee, star of *The Unbeliever*   131
5.1. Advertisement in *Moving Picture World* placed by
      Harold Edel   150
5.2. Advertisement for *Shoulder Arms* in the
      Indianapolis News   152
6.1. Luring the audience   162
6.2. Advertisement in *Moving Picture World*,
      7 December 1918   163
6.3. Advertisement in *Moving Picture World*,
      23 November 1918   164
6.4. "Remember Belgium"   166
6.5. The Hun and the girl in a still from *The
      Unpardonable Sin*   167
6.6. Prepared advertising for *What Price Glory?*   175
6.7. *40,000 Miles with Lindbergh*   181
6.8. Aviation and autobiography sell *Wings*   183
6.9. *Legion of the Condemned*   187
6.10. *Lilac Time*   188

ACKNOWLEDGMENTS

I HAVE INCURRED many debts of gratitude as I worked on this book; I can only begin to settle those accounts. My words of thanks are hardly sufficient payment for the many kinds of help I was given or for the generosity of the givers.

My dissertation committee at the University of Wisconsin–Madison gave the first draft of *Reel Patriotism* a very careful reading. I thank Tino Balio, John Milton Cooper, Jr., Donald Crafton, Vance Kepley, Jr., and my chair, David Bordwell. Their interest in my study coupled with their criticisms kept me fascinated in the topic of World War I over the many years this work has been in progress.

Librarians at the Library of Congress's Manuscript Reading Room and Motion Picture Division, the National Archives, the Billy Rose Theater Collection, the Wisconsin State Historical Society, and the Brigham Young University Library brought me the documents I asked for and found for me treasures I never suspected. Ed Duesterhoeft, director of the Microforms Reading Room at the University of Wisconsin–Madison Memorial Library, made years of reading microfilm pleasant. Maxine Fleckner Ducey at the Wisconsin Center for Film and Theater Research provided films, photographs, and press books that helped to shape my ideas. I also thank Lawrence Suid for sharing with me documents relating to the promotion of *The Unbeliever.*

Fellow graduate students Julie D'Acci, Matthew Bernstein, Karen Greenler, Mary Beth Haralovich, Denise Hartsough, Donald Kirihara, and Richard Neupert listened to my ideas, asked me tough questions, and helped to give my often amorphous thoughts form. Linda Henzl helped me type and retype my manuscript, and I am grateful for her patience and her speedy fingers.

The University of Wisconsin–Stevens Point is a teaching college where four courses a semester is the norm. Thus, finding time for research and writing is a challenge. As I began to revise and expand my dissertation, the University Personnel Development Committee funded research trips to the Library of Congress and attendance at Le Giornate del Cinema Muto in Pordenone, Italy. I have been helped immeasurably by the Interlibrary Loan Department, especially Christine Neidlein and Colleen Angel. Doug Moore of University News Service printed my illustrations and encouraged my work over several years. My department, the Division of Communication, granted me course release and cheered my progress. Cathy Ladd gave computer advice, friendship, and the name of her hair cutter. Dean Gerard McKenna of the College of Fine Arts and Communication suggested ways to balance teaching and writing. No faculty member has a more supportive dean.

Students, including Jason Fare and those taking my War Film class, have also helped me write this book. They asked thoughtful questions, engaged in lively discussions, and forced me to be clear. Three graduate students gathered research for this work. Jacqueline Braun y Harycki, Ann Duser, and Russell Haines were efficient, conscientious, and willing to join in my quest.

Colleagues at the University of Wisconsin–Stevens Point have taken time out of their own too busy lives to help me. Susan Brewer walked me through my arguments with good humor and incisiveness. In the struggle to teach, to write, and to live sanely, she is a most valued comrade. Theresa Kaminski and Jon Roberts read the manuscript at various stages, and shared bibliography, books, and their superior grammar with me. Members of the Friday Afternoon Writing Group helped me refine Chapter Six. Sally Kent listened as I read whole paragraphs over the phone. Leslie McClain-Ruelle, Valentina Peguero, Barbara Dixson, and Leslie Wilson have helped to make UW–SP a warm and stimulating place to work. Thanks to all.

My friends have provided support, taken me out to lunch, and shared the breakthroughs as well as the stumbling blocks. Their faith in me has been sustaining. The hospitality of Susan Braden and Ann Dymalski made research trips to Washington seem like holidays. Gail Allen, Kate Anderson, Joanne Bernardi, Ginnie Bondeson, Cristie Cecil, Cindy and Rod Clark, Jim Haney, Mary Lou Harris-Manske, Kathy and John Hartman, Susan Henry, Janice Orr, Mary Jo Patton, Alice Randlett, the entire Webb Family, and the Monthly Mystery Club charted my progress and shared my enthusiasm.

I am lucky to have had Kristin Thompson, a scholar and writer I admire, edit my work. She sent me back to archives and arguments, back to sentences and words in pursuit of accuracy, clarity, and thoroughness. The trip has been rigorous but invigorating, and I am grateful. Paul Boyer's and Thomas Doherty's careful readings of my manuscript helped me clarify my ideas and spruce up my prose. Raphael Kadushin and Sylvan Esh at the University of Wisconsin Press helped me fine-tune my work and guided it through to completion.

The support of my grandmothers, Kate Key Black and Peter O'Keefe Midkiff, my mother and father, my sister Claire, and my brothers, Brian and John Midkiff, has been vital. Their confidence made me more confident. Rose Tiesling, Jackie and Dennis DeBauche, and Sue and Pat Glime likewise encouraged my efforts. My thanks.

None have been more generous with their love and forbearance than my own family. Dillon taught me to untangle knotty data with "walking logic," Harry reminds me by his example how much fun research is, and Sally points the way to further study by wondering about the image of hedgehogs in the films of World War II. My husband Joe has turned renovating our old house into a metaphor for careful scholarship, graceful prose, and bringing the past back to shining life. Would that I were as skilled at my craft.

INTRODUCTION

LIKE A MAJORITY of Americans during the three years before the United States intervened in World War I, George Kleine, a Chicago-based film producer and distributor, did not support joining the conflict.[1] In September 1915 he wrote to Chicago's Union Trust Company, one of the banks he patronized, expressing his disapproval of a loan that institution proposed making to England and France.[2] As late as 6 April 1917, the day President Woodrow Wilson signed the declaration committing his country to fight in the Great War, Kleine sent a telegram to Congressman Fred Britton congratulating him on his antiwar stand. "You know our circle of friends all American born of various ancestral origins / No one wants war almost all bitterly opposed / Never has Congress, an administration, or a press so misrepresented the popular will."[3]

Nevertheless, when the United States entered the conflict, Kleine, like most Americans, supported the government's war effort. On 23 June 1917 he wrote Secretary of War Newton Baker expressing interest in bidding on the distribution rights to government-produced documentaries.[4] A year later, in September 1918, he made a much more generous offer to George Creel, chairman of Wilson's Committee on Public Information.

> I am prepared to deliver my eighteen film exchanges to the United States for the distribution of its films, the government to receive the gross receipts less actual depreciation. . . . If the interests of the government require it, I would accept no further films for distribution from private producers, and refrain from further production myself, for the period of the war.[5]

Kleine gave those of his employees who entered the service letters of introduction to a Paris bank, "and this house has kindly consented to keep a fatherly eye on them." Kleine authorized the bank to advance these men up to two hundred and fifty francs, and more in case of an emergency.[6] He also took time to approve sending a clip from the three-reel drama *The Star*

Spangled Banner, which his company distributed, to the parents of Captain Edward F. Fuller who had appeared in it and later died in action.[7] In fact, Kleine cooperated with the government throughout World War I. He bought Liberty Bonds and encouraged his employees to do likewise.[8] He received the help of the United States Marine Corps in the production and marketing of two films, *The Star Spangled Banner* and *The Unbeliever,* and in turn he urged the use of these films in the Corps' recruitment drives.[9] He maintained a steady correspondence with various departments in the government, offering his help in the distribution of films and his advice about the best ways to market their propaganda in an efficient manner.[10]

George Kleine's motivations for these actions were both professional and personal. He believed, for instance, that the newsreel film of the war would be popular with audiences, and, judging from the tenor of his correspondence, he had a genuine interest in the men and women who worked for him. As a citizen and a businessman, Kleine was representative of many of the individuals in the United States film industry during World War I. He was concerned about the well-being of his employees and his country, but he was also concerned about the prosperity of his company. George Kleine's behavior manifested the primary tenet of practical patriotism: it was appropriate and reasonable to combine allegiance to country and to business. In fact, it was understood that enlisting in the war effort on the homefront would likely benefit the film industry's long-term interests.[11]

When the United States entered World War I in 1917, the film industry seized the opportunity to convey the government's messages to the American people. A number of federal departments and agencies routed educational programs and propaganda through the variety of channels the film industry made available. Throughout the nineteen months of American involvement in World War I, the government's needs to garner support for the war effort, to conserve food, to raise money, and to enlist soldiers were met through the production of short instructional films, the public-speaking activities of movie stars, the civic forum provided by movie theaters, and the administrative expertise offered by film industry personnel. Film industry personnel were assigned by their trade association, the National Association of the Motion Picture Industry, to work directly with government agencies.

The film industry also had much to gain from working closely with the United States government. In trade journals and in private correspondence, individuals representing all of its branches alluded to this belief.

The dates that bracket my study, 1914 and 1929, suggest there were causes and effects on the homefront of the film industry's enlistment in the war. The war posed a direct challenge to the conduct of business as usual: the film industry might even have been deemed "nonessential" by the government and shut down for the course of the war, or it might have been subjected to government influence, which could easily have involved altering its product and disrupting distribution channels and timetables. The movies could have been decried as a frivolity not fitting to a nation at war. These threats were successfully countered in part through cooperative association with the government. Even more, the goodwill of both the moviegoer and the government, which accrued to the film industry on account of its war work, served as a selling point in the 1920s when its major companies began to trade their stock on Wall Street, and it provided a buffer against national censorship when movie stars became embroiled in scandal. In addition, the war itself provided film producers with material for narrative films throughout the 1920s.

Like George Kleine's rationale for supporting the war effort, my reasons for writing this book are both professional and personal. *Reel Patriotism* began as a dissertation which looked at the relationship between the United States film industry and the federal government in 1917 and 1918. I wanted to know how the industry produced, distributed, and exhibited its films at this juncture in its development, and I was curious about what difference the war made to the way the industry operated. Pretty dry stuff; still, I finished my degree and got a job. I began teaching students who were usually baffled by the finer points of the film history I presented and for whom movies from the silent era looked weird. As my fascination with the films of World War I grew, the desire to excite these students, or at least help them to understand the pleasure of going to the movies and the importance of films and theaters in the lives of people like their own great-grandparents, pushed me deeper into American history. *Reel Patriotism* is the result of melding perspectives on film production, distribution, and exhibition with those of cultural history.

Each of the chapters in this book contains a case study: *Joan the Woman* (Cardinal Film Corporation, 1916), *The Unbeliever* (Edison, 1918), *Shoulder Arms* (First National, 1918), *Wings* (Paramount, 1927), and the films of Mary Pickford made in 1917 and 1918. These movies, some influential, some controversial in their time, merit examination today because they evoke the workings of an industry poised to dominate the leisure time of Americans, and because they illustrate the complex interrelationship between film history and social history. In the profile of filmmaking and movie-going that follows, I muster documents that address production decisions, advertisements heralding sales strategies, and both trade and popular press reviews of the movies from the years between 1914 and 1929.[12] Chapter One describes the corporate expansion taking place within and among the companies constituting the film industry in the years before 1917, showing *Joan the Woman* as a film shaped by the competing pressures of a business in flux and a country verging on war. Chapter Two surveys the range of films produced during 1917 and 1918. Chapter Three highlights film exhibition in Milwaukee, Wisconsin, during the eighteen months of United States involvement in World War I, and in doing so shows how the needs of an industry with a mass-produced and nationally distributed product met the realities of a specific and potentially unreceptive market. Chapter Four describes the network created by the National Association of the Motion Picture Industry linking film personnel with governmental departments to coordinate the dissemination of information to the American public through movie theaters.

While the film industry did not change the basic ways it produced, distributed, and exhibited films during World War I, it did adapt standard practices to meet the needs and pressures of the times. In addition, the war accelerated certain changes that were taking place within the film industry. Chapter Five examines the war-related and non-war-related influences that culminated in the oligopolistic structure the industry adopted. Chapter Six describes the way World War I found its way into film narratives spanning a range of genres in the 1920s.

Douglas Gomery and Robert C. Allen point out that film history accounts for change and stasis over time. My work looks at the years 1914–1929, a period during which the film industry was determining the course it would, in essence, follow until 1948. By 1917 the classical Hollywood style and mode of production were functioning, and industry structure was, at the least, envisioned. Still, it was a young industry whose footing in American popular culture was still being established, and World War I posed a threat of major proportions. That these threats did not materialize is in part because they were recognized and met by individuals like George Kleine, companies like Famous Players-Lasky, and institutions like the National Association of the Motion Picture Industry, all of whom formulated and followed a principle of practical patriotism.

REEL
PATRIOTISM

1

The U.S. Film Industry and the Coming of War, 1914–1917

The war now in progress in Europe will undoubtedly affect the film situation here. . . . Inasmuch as we have in the past suffered from an overimportation of cheap features so-called the situation is not without its compensating advantages.

editorial, Moving Picture World, *15 August 1914*[1]

THE EUROPEAN WAR had been "in progress" for less than two weeks when *Moving Picture World*'s editor made his assessment. The apparent callousness of his equation of death and destruction for the belligerents with more favorable distribution conditions for U.S. film companies belies the shock most Americans felt as the war began. It makes clear the concerns of the rapidly developing film industry, however. While President Wilson worried in private that the conflict would "vitally change the relationships of nations," *Moving Picture World*, speaking publicly to its readership of theater-owners and film exhibitors, welcomed the possibility of change.[2] Among the warring nations were France and Italy, two strong competitors in the lucrative American film marketplace.

War between the Central Powers and the Allies would inevitably affect the United States, of course. The assassination in June 1914 of Archduke Ferdinand, heir to the throne of Austria-Hungary, by a Serbian nationalist, brought the forces of the Triple Entente—Britain, France, and Russia—into combat with the Triple Alliance, comprising Germany, Austria-Hungary, and Italy. In 1914, one-third of American citizens were either foreign-born themselves or the children of foreign-born parents, and disbelief at the events in their homelands soon gave way to a battery of responses.

The first antiwar protest, the Woman's Peace Parade, took place in New York City on 29 August, and by December the pleas of a growing number of organizations promoting peace clashed with an outcry for mili-

3

tary preparedness.[3] Positioned between these two camps were the many Americans, who, for a variety of reasons, were isolationists.[4]

Despite Wilson's desire for neutrality and his plea for Americans to be "impartial in thought as well as in action," the war's impact was felt in the United States in a number of ways. First, the U.S. economy had to contend with the negative impact of belligerent nations cashing in their American securities in exchange for gold. The New York Stock Market shut down in late July and did not reopen until November 1914. This banking crisis led to business layoffs and exacerbated unemployment, with the national unemployment rate rising to 11.5 percent by late winter.[5] In addition, the British strategy of choking off German trade affected producers in the United States, particularly cotton growers in the South.[6] It was not until the spring of 1915 that orders for war materiel began to have generally positive effects on the American economy.

Thus, whatever "compensating advantages" might have accrued from limiting the importation of foreign movies, the film industry also faced a challenge. Its consumers—already a national audience in 1914—divided along multiple fault lines in their response to the "sanguinary conflict."[7] This lack of consensus, evident right up to April 1917, and coupled with the disruption of international trade and the effect of the European war on the United States economy, was not without ramifications in the sensitive machinery of the film industry.

From 1914 to 1917, film producers, distributors, and exhibitors in the United States created the structure and developed the practices which would sustain them through the 1920s. Trends like business consolidation, established in a whole range of industries prior to the war, were generally accelerated.[8] Equally important for the growth of the film industry, the years 1914–1917 saw the establishment of a national film distribution system. In 1914, W. W. Hodkinson formed Paramount, which proved more efficient than earlier companies in distributing movies throughout the States. Adolph Zukor, one of the principal corporate players in the production of the film that is the focus of this chapter—*Joan the Woman*—was also a central figure in shaping this young, vital industry. Early on his Famous Players combined with the Lasky Company and other smaller film production studios. Then, in 1916, he gained control of Paramount.

World War I occurred toward the end of a demographic transition in the United States. According to historian Robert H. Wiebe, between the 1870s and 1920 this country changed from a society of "island communities" inhabited by individuals who believed in their own local autonomy to an urban society: "An age never lent itself more readily to sweeping uniform description: nationalization, industrialization, mechanization."[9] Those people joining in the migration from a rural to an urban setting forged new identities within very different communities. Professional associations, trade groups, and labor unions offered the new middle class of working persons in the city an alternative to church and family as modes of identification.

The film industry, following in the wake of this migration and adapting its business strategies along the way, offered these people a new form of entertainment for their leisure time. As producer, distributor, and exhibitor of a mass-produced and nationally marketed product, the film industry was one of the strands helping to weave the still outlying, island communities together with the newly vital urban-industrial centers. World War I facilitated this coming of age by generating a greater sense of national community and by providing the film industry with the opportunity to play a central role in this new community. Borrowing battlefield rhetoric, the industry would prove itself during the war—it would go "over the top" in helping the government, securing its own place in the entertainment economy, and amusing as well as informing its audiences. The history of the production, distribution, and exhibition of *Joan the Woman* demonstrates the volatility within in the American film industry in the years before the United States entered World War I, and the ways in which business considerations and political conditions affected artistic decisions made by Cecil B. DeMille, the film's director.

Joan the Woman (1916)

Joan the Woman, Cecil B. DeMille's ten-reel special, provides a useful vantage point for looking at the complicated relationship connecting World War I, the development of the U.S. film industry, and the phenomenon of the feature film.[10] It bears traces of the dynamic changes taking place within the film industry as the country moved ever closer to war in the latter part of 1916 and the spring of 1917. *Joan the Woman* debuted in Washington, D.C., at the National Press Club, on 22 December 1916. Jesse Lasky and Cecil B. DeMille attended, and so did Jeanie Macpherson, "author of the scenario, [who] enjoyed the novelty of being the only woman in the gathering."[11] *Joan* opened in New York City, at the

44th Street Theater, on 25 December 1916; it closed there on 14 April 1917, the week after the United States entered the war. The film starred the popular opera singer Geraldine Farrar, in her fourth film appearance, as Joan of Arc. It was directed by DeMille, produced by the Lasky Company, and distributed by Lasky/Cardinal.

Joan the Woman was the result of a set of influences, including the European War. Its preproduction, production, and postproduction work occurred as Zukor's Famous Players and the Jesse L. Lasky Feature Play Company, Inc., which employed DeMille, were merging their enterprises, absorbing smaller production companies like Morosco and Pallas, and taking control of Paramount's nation-wide distribution system.[12] This corporate expansion created pressures that affected production decisions concerning *Joan the Woman*, such as the budget and the length of the film. The film was also shaped by the narrative conventions of the classical Hollywood style current in 1916, by prevailing fashions in filmmaking, and by the political beliefs of DeMille and Macpherson.

Joan the Woman told the story of the Maid of Orleans, beginning when her country was besieged by the English and ending with her death in flames at the stake. DeMille and Macpherson, however, embellished the peasant girl's history in a way that would become conventional in classical Hollywood film, by adding a love-story subplot. In their version, Joan falls in love with an English soldier who, although also in love, hands her over to the men who will execute her. *Joan* also included a frame story, a timely prologue and epilogue set in the trenches of World War I in which Wallace Reid, playing Eric Trent, a young British soldier descended from the soldier who had loved but ultimately failed Joan, pulls his ancestor's sword out of the wall of the trench. Later, falling asleep, he dreams about Joan of Arc and a flashback—the body of the film—follows. After coming to understand his historical complicity in her death, the young man determines to volunteer for a suicide mission over-the-top. He dashes across the battlefield strewn with bodies, and heaves a bomb into the enemy's trench.

> *Ext. German Battlefield—(CLOSE UP—Eric Trent dying)*
> (Searchlight on him). Joan of Arc *FADES IN.* Eric asks her if she forgives him. She nods and says:
> Spoken Title: I FORGIVE.
> Eric dies—Scene *FADES OUT* on Joan's face.[13]

Production

> The labor of preparing for Joan is tremendous.
>
> *Cecil B. DeMille to Jesse Lasky, 17 June 1916*[14]

Preproduction work on *Joan the Woman* coincided with the Democratic convention in June 1916. Nominated for a second term as president, Woodrow Wilson ran, albeit uneasily, on the slogan, "He Kept Us Out of War." Still, the European conflict was not the most salient feature guiding DeMille and Lasky as they planned this expensive war film. Its timeliness was, in fact, superseded by the element of "spectacle."

In the spring of 1916, as Macpherson and DeMille were working on the scenario for *Joan*, "big" movies were making a splash. On 29 May 1916, Lasky wrote DeMille, his most reliable director, about his meeting with Arthur Friend, the Lasky Company treasurer, and Adolph Zukor, president of Famous Players. Even though their two companies had not formally combined at this time, these leaders were collaborating in the planning of productions. "We decided we were making a mistake in doing two pictures of Farrar and so finally wired you to do just the one subject 'Joanne D'Arc' in about 10 reels. It is o.k. for you to spend about $150,000."[15] Lasky and Zukor wanted DeMille to produce a "spectacle;" they would distribute it as a "special."

Specials were differentiated from the "program feature" by ticket price, length, and budget, but Lasky also pointed out another characteristic then fashionable.

> As I wired you the other day, you ought to make every effort to make this feature important from the point of spectacle. I know you are trying to get a good heart story, etc., but the public seems to expect *spectacle* as well, when they pay $1. or more to see a special feature. They are getting $2. in the orchestra for *The Fall of a Nation* and $1. at the Criterion.[16]

Spectacle was accomplished through the mise-en-scene. DeMille reported that "many tremendous and elaborate sets—both interiors and exteriors" were planned, and that the town of Domremy had been built at the old Universal ranch. Hundreds of actors would be deployed in the film's battle scenes. The storming of LaTourelle alone would include "one hundred knights in armor and seven hundred fighting men, bowmen, spearmen, pikemen, etc., and eight pieces of old artillery throwing round-stone balls." These eight hundred comprised only the French. On the opposing side were two hundred English. DeMille warned the producers, "I am taking every precaution possible but, of course, a scene like this, will have its toll of injured, so if you happen to hear of my sending a good many men to the Hospital, don't become unduly alarmed." DeMille had ordered twelve hundred costumes, excluding armor, "so you see the production will not be a baby after all."[17]

The merger of Famous Players with the Lasky Feature Play Company continued to affect the shooting of *Joan the Woman* in the summer of 1916. This business consolidation was in its final, but still fraught, stages in May and June. Early in June, Lasky wrote DeMille: "It is definitely understood that the contemplated merger between Famous Players and Lasky is off. It is also definitely understood that we will keep the Geraldine Farrar production for the Lasky Company alone."[18] By 27 June, there had been a change of direction. "Before this reaches you the merger will have been made public." The sticking point, according to Lasky, was corporate control. For him, the success of the merger hinged on both companies starting from "an even 50-50 basis," and Zukor was angling for a more favorable balance of power. He capitulated, said Lasky, because Famous Players needed product. "They finally realized that they were in a hole regarding scenarios, stories and productions and could not keep up the pace."[19]

In the new company, Lasky would supervise productions at the East and West Coast studios. "The politics, distributing and finances and business end are to be divided between Zukor, Sam [Goldfish], and Arthur [Friend]." He also explained the status of Zukor's attempted take-over of Paramount, though there were "some knotty details still to be adjusted." "Nevertheless," he reported, "through the new directors and new President we are in control." While Zukor may have been short on stories and scenarios, his company brought vital human assets to the merger. Chief among the stars in Zukor's domain was Mary Pickford, whose economic significance made her the subject of agonizing negotiations between Zukor and Lasky. In what would become a motif in the letters mentioning Pickford, Lasky alerted DeMille that the "Mary Pickford enterprise is another one of our big problems." The "problem" was money. "She is already under salary of $10,000 a week." Later, he broke her salary down even further and complained that Pickford was "costing . . . $1666.66 for each week day."[20] DeMille was to direct Pickford after he completed *Joan the Woman*, and Lasky wanted to ensure that efficiency was a component of the preproduction process. In the next chapter I will show how these contractual and financial obligations, coupled with a much more imminent threat of war, combined to affect *The Little American* (1917), starring Mary Pickford and directed by DeMille.

Lasky closed the above letter by making common cause with DeMille and referring to *Joan*. "While you no doubt have your own problems with your big production, the brief outline I had of it in your recent letter proved very interesting." He concluded,

> Just now all that I need is three directors, eight continuity writers and a couple of able men to head some continuity scenario departments. This force and 20 good stories would make my task comparitively [sic] easy. As you know the scarcity of all the above articles you can figure just about the date that things will be easy. I imagine some wars now waging and others pending will have been started and peace will be hovering over the whole globe by the time these problems are solved. With a grip of the hand.[21]

U.S. entry into the war was pending—ten months away—but Lasky was making a joke in this letter of 27 June. Neither war nor peace were foremost in his mind—the deal was. DeMille, making a movie that began and ended on the Western Front, reassured his friend by describing his own rigorous work schedule. On 12 July DeMille, now filming, reiterated that *Joan* required a "terrific amount of labor."[22]

> For instance, I had three weeks of preparation, two of which were practically entirely consumed in reading, which left me but one week to get out my rough synopsis of the scenario. . . .
> My daily schedule is to photograph from ten in the morning to about seven at night; then for about an hour, attend to the business of the day; dine at eight and then work on the scenario from nine to one o'clock. . . . All departments are keyed up to the highest pitch.[23]

In recounting this torturous routine, DeMille may have felt the need to justify the time and money he was costing Lasky. He was also tacitly acknowledging the communication difficulties inherent in working for a company where the corporate directors were separated from (at least some of) their film directors by several thousand miles. Telegrams could cross the country in one day, but they were used for urgent situations requiring brief messages. Letters, which took much longer to travel from the East to the

West Coast, were the usual method of relaying information. For DeMille, they were also preferable, as Jesse Lasky was his friend as well as business partner. "Please write to me as often as you [Lasky] find time. It is a great pleasure for me to hear from you and communicating only by telegraph, is rather a cold proposition. With a handshake."[24]

One month later, Lasky was still worried—but he had a new motto.

> I have learned a great deal since the Famous Players became part of our business. Their negatives all the way through have cost less than ours and their profits have been greater. Now while we must maintain the standard of Lasky pictures up to the high Lasky standard, the productions from both studios will somehow have to be produced within a given cast [*sic*] and a given time or the dividends we expect to pay will not be forthcoming and we will have a big reputation but not be a financial success. While you may not agree with me, my slogan is "Dividends first and art second." Or, rather a blending of the two.[25]

As shooting continued on *Joan the Woman* in the summer of 1916, the newly merged Famous Players-Lasky experienced growing pains. Problems Lasky had found with the quality and quantity of stories and scenarios continued, and new problems with communications between the scenario department on the East Coast and the production studio on the West Coast conspired to reduce him to sentence fragments and punctuation lapses: "This business has got me at last, inasmuch as I am tied down for the summer with no chance for a vacation and one long endless chain of problems staring me in the face and problems that must be solved if my end of the game is to go on successfully"[26] He was too distracted, too discouraged, or perhaps too realistic to end the sentence with a period.

DeMille had his own problems. Now that the task of reconciling a good heart story with the spectacular aspects of costume and setting was accomplished, he began to fret about his star. Farrar had initially agreed to a delay in the start of shooting but then demanded payment of ten thousand dollars for her time. DeMille paid up. "This was somewhat in the nature of a 'hold-up,' but I had absolutely no choice."[27] DeMille had artistic qualms to match his financial concerns.

> She seems to have lost a little something of the great spark of genius that animated her last year. Although she is tremendously enthused over the story and says it is the greatest work of her life, at the same time, that

little spark seems missing. She may get it as we go on in the work, also, she has gotten pretty plump.[28]

DeMille makes no further complaints about Farrar's verve in the correspondence extant in the collection of his papers at the Brigham Young University Library, but reviewers of the finished film, as we shall see, also made mention of her weight. The reviewer for the *Boston Evening Transcript* noted simply: "She is large."[29]

Promotion

We have also laid out a local advertising campaign that, together with the publicity already arranged for and now coming out pretty nearly every day, will make the exploitation of your first big picture the most lavish and impressive exploitation ever given to anything offered to the theatres in this country.

Arthur Friend to Cecil B. DeMille, 27 November 1916[30]

The promotion of *Joan the Woman* got off to a rocky start and coincided with a major shake-up in Famous Players-Lasky. On 14 September 1916, Sam Goldfish—he would change his name to Goldwyn—one of the principal officers in the Lasky Feature Play Company, and Jesse Lasky's brother-in-law, was forced to resign. "Mr. Zukor informed me of the stand he was about to take regarding Sam. . . . Our company was left no alternative as Zukor insisted we must choose between Sam and himself."[31] On that same day, Lasky had written to apologize or to placate DeMille about the "stupid, outrageous blunder" which threatened the cloak of secrecy surrounding the production of *Joan*—the unauthorized release of a production photograph from the film to the *New York Dramatic Mirror*.[32] For DeMille, this was an emergency. Secrecy had surrounded the production of *Joan the Woman*, first to prevent another studio from preempting DeMille's epic and later to create an aura of mystery to pique interest in the film. He wired Lasky immediately on learning of the picture's publication. Lasky, perhaps more concerned with Goldfish's ouster, replied by letter.

I agree with you that it was a stupid, outrageous blunder and regret that in spite of the most rigid investigation we cannot place the responsibility.

In order to avoid a repetition of this,—as fast as the Farrar stills are received they are now being labeled and put aside so that there is no possibility of such a mistake occurring again.[33]

The next day Lasky wrote DeMille to explain his behavior in the "situation" with Goldfish, without making any mention of the publicity snafu. Although Lasky had originally supported Goldfish, time spent working closely with Zukor changed his mind.

> The result of my constant study [of Zukor] was more than satisfactory. It was gratifying. First he is an all around better businessman—he has better foresight—is a better financier and has a broader and bigger grasp of the picture business, than Sam. These facts, combined with the fact that I found he is considered the biggest man in the motion picture industry and incidentally that his reputation for honesty and integrity is remarkable—impressed me.
> . . . To sum it all up I feel that we couldn't have a better man than Zukor as President of our new corporation. Incidentally Arthur and I work 100% more efficiently with Zukor. I feel like a different human being for I have a full chance to express my views, carry out my ideas and instead of being hindered I find Zukor is helpful. You know the pleasure of working without argument and for the first time in the history of our company I feel that there are no inside politics. Not one of us, including yourself, have more personal ambitions than we are entitled to have, and if you will take my judgment in the matter, we can look forward to a more prosperous and brilliant future under the new regime than under the old.[34]

As he had done in an earlier letter to DeMille, Lasky closed with a reference to *Joan the Woman*. "I will try to run out and even bring Blanche with me so that you will have the benefit of some fresh minds when it comes to the final cutting of the big production."[35] Lasky, however, remained enmeshed in business on the East Coast. In October, DeMille reported, "The picture is cutting very well and I believe we will have a very good thing."[36]

In the fall, the East Coast offices of Famous Players-Lasky worked to place *Joan the Woman* in the most strategically advantageous theaters. In Chicago, they booked the Colonial Theater, part of the Jones, Linick, and Schaeffer chain. "We have taken the theater over for a year so you can count on a wonderful showing in Chicago—big orchestra—beautiful theater and all that sort of thing. The Globe Theater deal in New York is off and we are now trying to get the Astor."[37] Ultimately, the decision was made to open *Joan* in the 44th Street Theater in New York. The choice of a theater and the date of the film's opening were very important. The states rights distribution method was the one implemented for *Joan the Woman*.

This strategy involved selling the individual film, rather than a complete program or block of films, and to do this by geographical area. The price negotiated with buyers for "territories" depended on the perception, not necessarily the reality, that the film had played well in New York and Chicago.[38]

DeMille had different concerns about exhibition in the autumn prior to the film's release that continued to reveal the dynamic tension between artistic and business concerns. He wanted the company's own projectionist to travel with the film, at least to its big-city openings. DeMille had been warned that a rival company sometimes bribed the projectionist on a "big picture" to sabotage its exhibition. More practically, he worried that since *Joan* needed to run at different speeds as it played, "it is advisable to have an operator who has grown up with the film and who is conversant with these various speeds."[39] DeMille envisioned this master projectionist traveling with the film's composer, William Furst. These men could rehearse both "operator" and orchestra thus ensuring an exhibition to match the picture's epic qualities.

No public records show that the "operator" traveled with the film, but Furst was present when *Joan the Woman* joined *Twenty Thousand Leagues under the Sea*, *The Americano*, starring Douglas Fairbanks, and *Snow White*, featuring Marguerite Clark, as the big holiday movies in New York City that December.

While timeliness and topicality—in *Joan*'s case linking the film to the war in Europe—were conventional weapons in the promotional arsenal, they were not chosen to introduce *Joan* to the American public. John C. Flinn, Famous Players-Lasky's director of publicity and advertising, based in New York, officially launched *Joan the Woman* in the fall of 1916. No further photographs seem to have leaked to the press, and publicity on the film in the motion picture trade journals like *Exhibitors Herald* and *Moving Picture World* and in local newspapers around the country began in the third week of October. Instead of highlighting the contemporaneous war, the publicity department's selling points included Farrar's star power, her image as a fiery operatic heroine, and her personal good humor in the face of difficult production circumstances. DeMille was cited, the historical Joan was invoked, and the spectacular aspects of the film were emphasized.[40]

Louella Parsons, in a column syndicated in the *Columbus Dispatch* in mid-December 1916, echoed Flinn's campaign points and furthered his cause by embedding *Joan the Woman* in a narrative of suspense.

"Jeanne D'Arc" or "Joan of Arc," Lasky's first spectacular cinematic
production, is being guarded with utmost secrecy. Only scant bits of
publicity have been given out from the studio and only the barest
information can be gleaned. . . . The title, "Joan of Arc," leaked out,
and the world knew that Farrar's entire summer had been spent making
this one picture. She herself was wildly enthusiastic and very
mysterious about her celluloid maid of Orleans.

"I did everything that an opera singer is supposed not to do. I
waded in water up to my waist, shouted with enthusiasm as I led the
French troops to victory, and became for the summer the incarnation of
the spirit of the immortal Joan. I love this character and I put my
whole heart and soul into making her the Joan that France loved but
willingly sacrificed when her visions no longer helped win the
battle."[41]

In addition, there were photographic layouts in a number of the trade
papers and newspapers. These images featured the spectacular aspects of
Joan the Woman: crowd scenes, Joan's burning at the stake, and the variety of costumes and settings used in the film. The name of the film had
been secret, and upon its revelation it became grist for the publicity mill.
Moving Picture World carried an article with the headline "Geraldine Farrar as Joan of Arc, Photodrama on the Life of the Maid of Orleans Soon to
be Shown in Forty-Fourth Street Theater—DeMille Selects Title 'Joan the
Woman.' "[42] The article itself included the following:

Considerable favorable comment was caused by Mr. DeMille's
announcement on his arrival in the East that he had named the
photoplay "Joan the Woman" instead of "Joan of Arc." "The title 'Joan
the Woman' far better expresses the thought of the photoplay," said Mr.
DeMille. . . . [What] we were particularly eager to convey was the
humanness [*sic*] of this remarkable woman, who at nineteen was
commander-in-chief of the armies of France and who single-handed
awoke a nation from an unpatriotic sleep into such activity and valor
that France for all time has continued a free nation.[43]

This article added another element to the narrative of suspense created by
Joan's publicity: "The presentation will be made by Jesse Lasky and the
engagement will continue indefinitely at that theater. Future exhibitions in
other cities continue a matter of mystery."[44]

Local advertising for the all-important New York run began one week

44TH St.

THEATRE

BROADWAY
& 44TH ST.

COMMENCING

XMAS NIGHT

JESSE L. LASKY

Presents

GERALDINE

FARRAR

IN

CECIL B. DE MILLE'S

CINEMA MASTERPIECE

"JOAN THE WOMAN"

FOUNDED ON THE
LIFE OF JOAN OF ARC

DAILY TALK No. 7—The Seat Sale

The box-office will open tomorrow morning at 9 o'clock for the distribution to the public of seats for the engagement of "Joan the Woman." The first performance will take place next Monday, Christmas night. Beginning next Tuesday and indefinitely there will be two performances daily. To accommodate thousands in outlying sections, special attention will be given to telephone reservations. Call Bryant 7292. Tickets 25c to $2

TOMORROW No. 8—For Women
DAILY TALK and Children Only

Fig. 1.1. Advertisement for *Joan the Woman* in the *New York Times*, 20 December 1916. The advertising campaign for *Joan the Woman* featured "Daily Talks."

15

prior to *Joan the Woman*'s opening with a series of advertisements on the theater page of the *New York Times*. Prominent in these ads were the names of the 44th Street Theater, Geraldine Farrar, and the title *Joan the Woman*. Included within the ads' frame was a small image of Joan garbed in a robe or dressed in armor. More significantly, each ad incorporated a "Daily Talk" within its layout.

These "Daily Talks"—short descriptive paragraphs—reiterated the selling points for this film already in the public domain. On Thursday, 14 December, Daily Talk no. 1 introduced the historical Joan.

> An authority says: "Joan of Arc, a mere child in years, ignorant, unlettered, a poor village girl, unknown and without influence, found a great nation lying in chains, helpless and hopeless under an alien domination, and, she laid her hand upon this nation, this corpse, and it rose and followed her."[45]

The 15 December Daily Talk focussed on "The Star." Other topics included: "The Director," "The Exhibition," "The Cast," "The Seat Sale," "For Women and Children Only," and "To Men and Boys."[46]

The Daily Talk entitled "Medieval and Modern France," which ran 19 December 1916, featured the most overt link the film's promoters made to the war in Europe.

> In the dark ages when the fate of France hung by a mere thread a girl rose from the people and saved a nation from obliteration. Soldiers in the trenches today, fighting on French soil, to preserve for themselves and the future what Joan of Arc gave them, declare her figure hovers over them on the field of battle; her spirit leads them to greatness.[47]

Still, while tying the film to the Great War and selling its topicality and timeliness, *Joan*'s publicists also stressed the timelessness and the universality of their subject. Women and children were admonished to heed the "marvelous lesson of self-sacrifice, valor, courage and unselfishness."[48] Men and boys were also addressed in more general terms:

> You into whose hands are given the care and protection of the lives of women of today cannot afford to miss the portrayal of the life of the most wonderful woman who ever lived. You who are old will find

sweetness and comfort in her company; you who are young will be ennobled by her association. [49]

"Joan of Arc is the Woman Christ of all ages," said Geraldine Farrar on the movie page of the *New York Times.*

In her autobiography published in 1938, Farrar would remember that, "The influence of War times suggested a modern prologue and epilogue to introduce an historical and costume play that the producers felt might otherwise lack incentive for popular appeal."[50] Yet acknowledgment of the war in the DeMille and Lasky correspondence during the film's planning and production stages was oblique at best. In fact, the most overt references to the war were in the *Joan the Woman* script. Here DeMille (or Macpherson) included notes showing he wanted verisimilitude in the film's contemporary setting. The description of the trench where Trent lived included the following suggestion for appropriate props.

> This trench should suggest the pitiable attempts of two young English officers—one of them Eric Trent—to make it homelike. A battered Christmas card against the wall reads "Merry Christmas" in mocking satire; and near the bunk of Eric's brother officer is a photograph of a little boy and girl—his children. A couple of cigar boxes are shown— sardine boxes, and a large candy box on the shelf—pipes in a rack against the wall—and a few pictures of officers in groups—cut out of the "London Graphic" and tacked to the wall. A couple of lanterns hang on the wall and several holsters filled with cartridges and revolvers—*anything that would likely be in a modern trench should show.* (emphasis added)[51]

The script even dictated the way the boards should be placed against the wall of the trench: "NOTE: This is the correct procedure to keep the earth from sifting down."[52] These "real bits," then, were located in the most private of places. It is not clear from the correspondence that Lasky read *Joan the Woman*, only that he had seen a plot summary. Neither was contemporary verisimilitude a part of the promotion of the film. The spectacular aspects of *Joan*'s mise-en-scene were confined to its medieval story. The European War had not been pivotal in influencing decisions during the preproduction or production stages of this film and, at least in the opening month of 1917, the war was not crucial to *Joan*'s promotion. Much

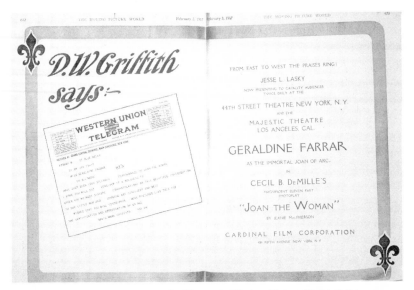

Fig. 1.2. Advertisement for *Joan the Woman* in *Moving Picture World*, 3 February 1917. This advertisement and those on the following pages were set on facing pages and highlighted endorsements, timeliness, and good box office returns.

more frequent and more salient in shaping *Joan the Woman* were concerns about business, budgets, and stars.

Topicality, thus, was not deployed in any comprehensive or systematic way in the advertising campaign to sell *Joan the Woman* to the movie-goers of New York City in December of 1916 and by extension to movie-goers across the country in the territories served by states rights buyers. The history that was offered as salient was French history, but of the Middle Ages and the French Revolution. Identification with Joan was encouraged but only to the extent that she exemplified true womanhood—youth, purity, self-sacrifice, beauty. This is not surprising. Lasky and Zukor, in their concern for success, keyed promotion to what they perceived as most important to the prospective ticket-buyer. The European War was still an issue without a consensus. President Wilson had been re-elected in 1916 on a platform which included the claim that he had kept the United States out of war, but his margin of victory had been narrow.[53]

The "neutrality" of *Joan*'s advertising campaign would end, very soon, in a tactical change corresponding with events on the national and international diplomatic fronts. On 1 February 1917, Germany announced that it

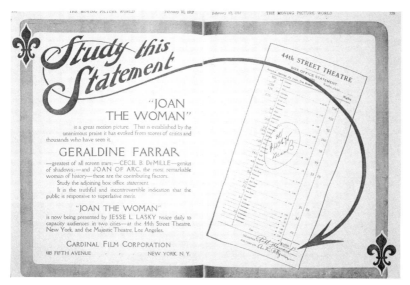

Fig. 1.3. Advertisement for *Joan the Woman* in *Moving Picture World*, 10 February 1917.

Fig. 1.4. Advertisement for *Joan the Woman* in *Moving Picture World*, 24 February 1917.

Fig. 1.5. Advertisement for *Joan the Woman* in *Moving Picture World*, 3 March 1917.

would resume submarine warfare against belligerent and neutral countries alike. President Wilson immediately broke diplomatic relations, but he still hesitated to embroil the United States in a war which had already cost five million lives. Instead, he called for "armed neutrality" when he spoke to a joint session of Congress on 26 February. Preempting a possible congressional vote against the arming of merchant ships, Wilson released the "Zimmermann Telegram" to the press on 28 February. Arthur Zimmermann, the German foreign minister, had wired the German ambassador in Mexico, suggesting that Mexico align itself with the Central Powers, and that, in the event that the United States entered the war, Mexico could reclaim its "lost territories" in Texas, Arizona, and New Mexico. For American citizens, only recently engaged in military incursions into Mexico, the European war was suddenly both immediate and nearby. On 1 March, the House passed Wilson's bill 403–14. However, an amendment to the bill that would have prohibited merchant ships from carrying munitions was defeated 293–125. There was still no consensus for going to war.

   The 24 February issue of *Moving Picture World* carried a two-page ad for *Joan*, one of a series designed to motivate states rights buyers. Previous weeks had presented facsimiles: of D. W. Griffith's telegram praising the

film, and of the balance sheet from the 44th Street Theater. In the 24
February issue, however, distributors were alerted to "The Momentous
Timeliness of 'Joan the Woman.' " The facsimile, set at a dynamic angle in
the layout, was an advertisement which had run in *The New York Evening
Telegram*. Its copy read: "She is leading France and England into battle;
will her spirit hover over Americans?" Beside this facsimile, John Flinn's
publicity department announced, in capital letters, "THIS HALF-PAGE AD-
VERTISEMENT APPEARED IN THE NEW YORK EVENING TELEGRAM ON FEB. 4.
1917. ONE DAY AFTER RELATIONS WERE BROKEN WITH GERMANY."[54]

The ad did not signal a total shift to timeliness as the main selling point
for *Joan*, however. The series of two-page ads continued in the 3 March
issue, heralding, "The $5.00 MOTION PICTURE IS HERE."[55] A hand thrust-
ing through the page held an invitation to a benefit showing of *Joan*, ticket
price five dollars. By mid-March the *Housatonic*, the *City of Memphis*, the
Illinois, and the *Vigilancia*—all American ships—had been torpedoed.
On 25 March, the advertisement for *Joan the Woman* in the *New York
Times* promised "Special preference in the location of seats will be given
to Members of the American Red Cross, National Guard, and Men in
Uniforms of the United States Army and Navy."[56] On 6 April the House
and Senate voted to affirm Wilson's declaration of war. Only fifty represen-
tatives and six senators voted in opposition to United States entry into
World War I.

The advertisement for *Joan the Woman*, which ran in the *Chicago Tri-
bune* on 8 April and noted "She Led her Country to Victory," asked "What
Are You Doing for your Country?"[57] Around the same time, *Motion Picture
News* congratulated the "Live Wire Exhibitors" of Chicago's Jones,
Linick, and Schaefer theater chain:

> Combining recruiting activities in Chicago with the showing of *Joan the
> Woman* at the Colonial, enabled Jones, Linick, and Schaefer publicity
> plan [sic] to work a stunt last week that attracted comment throughout
> the entire city. In cooperation with Captain F. R. Kennedy, chief
> recruiting officer for the United States Army, four girls were dressed in
> Joan of Arc costume and armor. Thus attired they toured the Loop
> section in automobiles, accompanied by army officers, and stopping on
> every corner aided in the enlistment activities.[58]

On 8 April, *Joan the Woman* was beginning its last week at the 44th Street
Theater. Its advertisement simply noted that fact.

Critical Reception

> "Joan the Woman" is above all a director's picture.
>> *George Blaisdell*, Moving Picture World, 1 *January 1917*[59]

> The new "Joan of Arc" spectacle made a deep impression and Miss
> Farrar's screen appearance evoked continuous applause. Producer,
> director and author were congratulated on the high art of the spectacle.

> Diplomats See Farrar in Film, First Showing of New Lasky Motion
> Picture 'Joan the Woman' given in Washington, Star Wires Regrets.
>> New York Telegram, *22 December 1916*[60]

The timeliness of *Joan the Woman* was one element among several that
figured in the critical responses to the film. When reviewers discussed
Joan's prologue and epilogue, however, what they noted was the way this
framing device conformed to classical Hollywood convention. Their eval-
uations were based on narrative effectiveness, not on the verisimilitude of
the trench or the accuracy of detail in the soldier's uniforms or weapons. In
fact, one review noted that, "In a prologue and epilogue an attempt is made
to link the story of the peasant maid to the present and while this typical
movie touch is superfluous, it is so well carried out that it does not detract
from the whole."[61] *Motography*'s reviewer, whose response was generally
laudatory, disagreed.

> There is one thing which might stand criticism in the picture, and this
> not because it seriously effects [*sic*] the quality of the offering, but
> because it is so commonplace in modern "movie" construction. This is
> the fact that the whole story is a visualization of a modern French [*sic*]
> soldier's reflections.[62]

Wid's objected neither to the conventionality of *Joan's* timeliness nor to the
conventionality of the flashback device. Instead, its reviewer objected to
the muddying of the "tragedy" of Joan with the "melodrama" of what was
then typically referred to as "the European war."

> This use of modern incidents is so plainly for that purpose that, to my
> mind it fails utterly to accomplish its aim and, surely, it lessens the
> power of the historical spectacle. If we had been able to see Joan dying
> at the stake on the finish, with the flames that rose about her as the
> last thing on the screen, we could have gone out of the theater
> tremendously impressed. When this scene dissolved back into the
> modern situation we were brought back to the realization that this

modern soldier had been dreaming all this. The effect created by the
big tragedy was lost in the following scenes of modern melodrama.[63]

As will be seen in more detail in later chapters, the inclusion of the modern, war-related prologue and epilogue were adaptations of existing film
narrative practice—a "typical movie touch." World War I, which was
mired in trenches along the Somme and the Marne, had not captured the
imagination of the New York-Hollywood film industry—at least not to the
extent that the special, the spectacle, or the star had. Instead, *Joan the
Woman* was primarily promoted as a costume drama and a star vehicle for
Farrar. The letterhead on the stationery used in correspondence about this
film read, "Cecil B. DeMille's Production, Geraldine Farrar as Joan of
Arc, The Cinema's Greatest Historical Masterpiece."[64] The 31 December
ad in the *New York Times* promised a film "As Thrilling as the Mar-
seillaise," and the 31 January advertisement announced, "FREE beautiful
medieval mural and armorial Art Exhibition in the lobby."[65]

Most of the critical response to *Joan the Woman* focussed on, and
praised, the film's mise-en-scene—its spectacular aspects. Lasky, Zukor,
and Friend had guided DeMille shrewdly when they advised him to make a
"big" picture, and DeMille, heeding their judgment, had succeeded on an
impressive scale. There was consensus among the trade paper reviews—
so important for motivating lucrative states rights contracts—that the sub-
titles, which had been set in a style that mimicked bas relief, were "highly
artistic."[66] Reviewers waxed lyrical over the numbers of soldiers, horses,
costumes, and weapons. George Blaisdell's assessment reached the all-
important exhibitors who subscribed to *Moving Picture World:*

> Mr. DeMille has splendidly staged his subject. He has constructed
> villages and high walls and towers, moats and bridges. And let us not
> forget the cathedral interior. He shows us the shock of battle, the crash
> of contending forces, in big fields and in close-up. There is a thrill in
> these scenes that makes adequate description difficult. His pageantry
> is superb. Hundreds of steel clad men, a-horse and a-foot armed cap-
> a-pie, stir us with their soldierly evolutions.[67]

Critics were ambivalent in their appraisal of Farrar. DeMille's observation
that she was plump translated into an aesthetic concern with the fit between her body size and the popular perception of Joan of Arc. Alexander
Wollcott writing in the *New York Times* missed the "valiant frailty" traditionally associated with Joan of Arc.[68] Other reviewers, while noting her

deviation from the normal portrayal of Joan's youthfulness and wispiness, found a solid realism in Farrar. "Is she physically the Maid of Orleans? Undoubtedly Joan was of medium height and stocky build—a peasant girl in all physical semblance. Then Miss Farrar is Joan to the life."[69] The reviewer for *Moving Picture World* employed a similar rhetorical ploy to avoid an ungallant assessment of Farrar's weight and age. "We may feel that Geraldine Farrar . . . portrays a woman of regal dominating presence rather than the simple child of God and of France to whom religion and patriotism were the same."[70]

Motion Picture News and *Wid's* both worried about unfavorable reaction by the Catholic Church to *Joan the Woman.*

> The author and producer have bucked up against another proposition which may mean serious opposition in certain sections, and that is a possible controversy with the Catholic Church. . . . I fear that the detail given to the part played by the archbishop and the monks in the persecution of Joan may cause some agitation against this picture by the Catholic Church. That thought should at least be given some consideration when you are planning to handle this production.[71]

The home office in New York must have also feared a Roman Catholic reaction because they sought to head it off by quoting from the *Encyclopaedia Britannica*'s description of Cauchon, the priest who sentenced Joan to the stake—"he was excommunicated posthumously by the Pope, his body exhumed and thrown in the sewer"—in the program for the New York run of the film.[72] In later years DeMille would remember only that a member of the New York censor board objected to Joan's expression of despair as she faced death.

> "There is one thing that has to come out."
> I said to her, "What is that, Madame?"
> "That line where Joan of Arc says, 'Oh Lord, my God, why has Thou forsaken me?' "
> "Do you know where that line came from originally?"
> "I don't care where it came from. It means that God would forsake someone and it has to come out."
> The minister said to her, "I don't think you realize, Madame, it was said by Jesus on the Cross."[73]

The line remained in the film. It apparently was not heretical that Joan of Arc was being paralleled with Jesus Christ.

Fig. 1.6. Geraldine Farrar as Joan of Arc. Images of large, strong women were common in World War I posters. Still from *Joan the Woman*, courtesy of the Museum of Modern Art.

Fig. 1.7. Joan of Arc as portrayed in the posters of the War Savings Stamps campaign. Courtesy of Walton Rawls, *Wake Up America*.

Regardless of the critical appraisal of her performance, both Joan of Arc and Farrar's interpretation of Joan resonated throughout the months of United States involvement in World War I. In March 1917, just before the American declaration of war, the *New York Times* reported that a young girl living in France claimed to hear voices as Joan did. In 1918, New York dedicated Joan of Arc Park on Riverside Drive.[74] The historian David M. Kennedy has noted that the wartime curriculum devised for school children and endorsed by the government stressed themes of patriotism, heroism, and sacrifice. Chief among the role models offered to young Americans was Joan of Arc. "Nowhere, however, was it mentioned that the enemies then were English—an awkward instance of the untidiness of history, knowledge of which might have sullied the bright cause of Allied unity."[75] DeMille and Macpherson had also finessed this "problem" of the "untidiness of history" by having Joan fall in love with the ancestor of the contemporary British soldier, Trent. A poster issued in 1918 by the Treasury Department to encourage the sale of War Savings Stamps was illustrated by an image of Joan of Arc in armor, looking remarkably like Geraldine Farrar and sounding remarkably like the advertising copy from *Chicago Tribune* for *Joan the Woman* cited earlier: "Joan of Arc Saved France. Women of America Save Your Country. Buy War Savings Stamps." Farrar herself would take part in the Treasury Department's Liberty Loan Drives.[76] Whatever some of *Joan*'s critics thought about the appropriateness of Farrar's size and shape and age in rendering the Maid of Orleans, propagandists for the war effort approved. The posters designed during World War I to recruit soldiers, to urge savings of money and food, to sell Liberty Bonds and War Savings Stamps, and to arouse the nation to Wilson's call to arms, consistently featured a strong, large female figure. With arms bared, astride a horse with an American flag as background, sometimes envisioned as Columbia, sometimes as Joan of Arc, these figures reiterated DeMille's vision.

Distribution

> We have the larger part of the United Kingdom still open. I have found great antipathy to this picture there and in France, which of course was quite a disappointment.
>
> *Emil E. Shauer, assistant treasurer, Famous Players-Lasky, to Cecil*
> *B. DeMille, 1 May 1919*[77]

The strategy of states rights distribution necessitated a successful run on Broadway to reassure exhibitors around the country that the risk of booking the film was minimal. In January 1917 Lasky wrote DeMille, "On account of the negotiations with 'state[s] rights' buyers it has been necessary for us to keep the house full so it has been well papered every matinee and evening performance, but the general impression abroad is that we are doing a big business and that the picture is a big hit."[78] On 31 March 1917, the only territories remaining in the United States were Pennsylvania and West Virginia, and rural states in the Midwest.[79] By 31 March 1919, *Joan* had earned $385,229.60 in the United States despite apparently well- disguised losses in New York during its 44th Street Theater run and losses in Philadelphia and Pittsburgh.[80] DeMille had spent twice the $150,000 Lasky had authorized in 1915, but it was still his highest grossing film until *Male and Female* in 1919.[81]

Selling *Joan* abroad, however, had raised problems. Emil Shauer, assistant treasurer of Famous Players-Lasky, wrote DeMille in May 1919 that the picture was not selling well in Great Britain or in France. In fact, "I have found great antipathy to this picture. . . . "[82] DeMille replied, "I can appreciate the difficulties with this picture in England and France, and under the unfortunate circumstances, think the showing for the world outside the United States of a hundred and twenty-nine thousand dollars is excellent."[83] *Joan the Woman* may be indicative of problems then facing the international distribution of war films more generally, especially after the Armistice in November 1918. Both allies and enemies could find sufficient fault with the way they were portrayed to preclude buying distribution rights. Still, Shauer was persistent; he did make some sales to countries in the Triple Alliance.

> I have succeeded in selling "Joan the Woman" for the remaining
> Foreign territory as follows:
> Italy   L1,500
> Greece   8,200 frcs
> Turkey
> Bulgaria
> Hungary
> Germany
> Austria
> This now practically disposes of this picture for the world.[84]

Practical Patriotism

> I am taking the position that I am very willing and anxious to go out and
> fight in any rank or place the Government may be able to use me, but if
> they desire me to do motion picture work—that is a very different
> matter. . . .
>
> *Cecil B. DeMille to Jesse Lasky, 16 October 1918*[85]

The production, distribution, and exhibition of *Joan the Woman* illustrates
the workings of "practical patriotism." So does the war-time career of
Cecil B. DeMille. On 21 April, only two weeks after the United States'
declaration of war, *Moving Picture World* reported that DeMille had offered
to help organize a citizen's militia in Los Angeles. He would equip a troop,
seventy-five strong, with rifles, ammunition, and a machine gun, in case
war threatened the city.[86] The following week's issue of *Motion Picture
News* noted that the Lasky studio, where DeMille served as director-
general, was a "sub-recruiting station" for a regiment of the home guard.[87]
In June the motion picture trade papers published the story that DeMille
had bought $50,000.00 worth of Liberty Bonds and had committed his
company to support the dependents of its employees "called to the colors."[88] These reports of DeMille's exemplary citizenship helped to burnish
the image of Famous Players-Lasky for a major component of their
clientele—the film exhibitors.

In August 1917, after *Joan* had been in distribution for seven months,
and after two more DeMille features, *Romance of the Redwoods* and *The
Little American*, had been released, DeMille attempted to take an even
more activist role in the war. He wrote Lasky asking permission to take
projectors and films "over there" to raise the morale of troops in the
trenches: "Will you kindly lay the following before Mr. Zukor and advise
me jointly whether you deem the action that I contemplate taking would be
as consistent with good business and the wellfare [*sic*] of this firm as I
believe it to be patriotic?"[89] DeMille described a plan to combine his
vacation time with the government's business.

> I have received recently a letter from Secretary of War Baker,
> relative—as you probably know—to acting upon the War Cooperation
> Committee of the Motion Picture Industry, and asking for suggestions.
>   From my talks with Captain Ian Hay Beith, Browne, Pouyet and
> Dupont, all of whom have recently returned wounded from France, and
> from other reports, including much that I have read from official and

> unofficial sources, I have come to the conclusion that one of the great
> elements in the winning of the war is going to be the fight against the
> boredom of the men.

DeMille proposed a solution to this problem. He had developed a "portable dynamo" which could generate electricity sufficient to power a film
projector. DeMille would take his machine and prints supplied by Famous
Players-Lasky to the second-line trenches to entertain the men "resting
and awaiting their turn to serve in the first line." DeMille justified his plan
by invoking the precepts of practical patriotism: "It would serve three
great purposes: Primarily the great good to the men; secondly, the great
good to this firm; and thirdly, the great good to me."[90]

Lasky telegraphed his reply. The company, he wrote, was only one year
into its consolidation with Famous Players, and was still expanding. They
had just signed Vitagraph star Clara Kimball Young and, even more significantly, had acquired a half-interest in their competitor Louis Selznick's
production and distribution businesses. Given this set of changing circumstances, Zukor would not be amenable to any plan, however well-
intentioned, which would interfere with the release schedule of DeMille's
films. "The company is depending a great deal on your four special productions and plan to release them at regular intervals before July thirty-first
next year."[91] DeMille, unable to conform the scope of this project to the six
weeks of his vacation, remained on the homefront.

Beginning in March 1918, DeMille collaborated with army intelligence to track industry personnel and others, mainly in the Los Angeles
area, suspected of pro-German sympathies.[92] This extracurricular activity
did not interfere with his directorial duties, and, in fact, may have enhanced his supervisory function within the studio. DeMille came to spy
work via his membership in the American Protective League, a citizens
group formed in Chicago in the spring of 1917 which operated in cooperation with the United States Justice Department. Adopting a hierarchical
military structure, the League tapped business leaders throughout the
country. These leaders recruited "lieutenants" and operatives within the
ranks of their workers to keep eyes and ears open for suspicious "unpatriotic" behavior.[93] United States Attorney General T. W. Gregory praised
the role the APL played in the interest of national security.

> The American Protective League has become by far the largest and
> best organized of these bodies [organizations of volunteer citizens] and
> has constituted a most valuable auxiliary to the Bureau of

Investigation. Its membership appears to have been carefully safeguarded, and includes many of the leading citizens of our country. The assistance and information furnished by it in connection with the registration and violations of the draft law have alone fully justified its existence. [94]

DeMille lived up to his designation of director-general as he provided a variety of services to the Intelligence Office in the Los Angeles district. To help him in these intelligence endeavors, DeMille drafted Fred Kley, referred to as "FK," production manager of the Famous Players-Lasky studio, as well as "S.A." and "F.L.C.," who were actresses on the lot, and "G.S." Unfortunately, only contextual clues within their reports hint at the identities of these informers. In the case of G.S., neither pronouns nor job-related indicators exist. Secrecy was fundamental to the pyramid of authority both in DeMille's "unit" and in the APL generally. While DeMille and Fred Kley knew the identities of their "agents" in the field, the agents did not know each other, and snafus occurred as agents turned each other in. [95] From the spring through the summer of 1918, DeMille and his cohorts within Famous Players-Lasky and within Fox and Universal split their time between movie-making and spying.

DeMille sent Lieutenant Thaddeus Knight a list of the cities in which Famous Players-Lasky had film exchanges. [96] Later, T. R. Moss, Captain in the Infantry, asked DeMille for a list of all the towns in which there were theaters that played Famous Player-Lasky films. [97] This desire for information about sites of film exchanges and movie theaters indicates that the Army's Intelligence Office, Los Angeles District, Western Department, at least considered the possibility of tapping into Famous Players-Lasky's nation-wide distribution network in order to spy on those it deemed suspicious. Further, a certain understanding and appreciation of the nature of the movie audience is implicit in these requests. Although the APL was officially concerned with routing out and reporting pro-Germans, its system of plant surveillance came to be used by employers to monitor labor union activism in the work place. [98]

In addition to information about film exchanges and the location of movie theaters, Lieutenant Knight also asked DeMille for a different sort of help. This letter is representative of several requests made of DeMille to check up on those who spoke against American war aims.

> It has been brought to the attention of this office that one Von
> HARDIN who has been employed at various Motion Picture Companies,

late of the Peralto Motion Picture Company and now believed to be working for the Griffith Studios on Sunset Blvd., is very pro-German and should be investigated. Information can be secured from a man named Pennell at the Peralto Motion Picture Company.

Kindly look this man up and advise us of the results.[99]

A different case, the suspicious behavior of one Paul Weigel, reveals the lengths to which DeMille went to meet the military's needs.

Replying to your two letters of May 9th, regarding the case of Paul Weigel, I have instructed our Engagement Department to place him at work in the Lasky studio on Monday. I will then be in a position to get closer to him. . . . Woods, whose first name is Walter, at Universal City, and Ben Harris, at the Fox plant will receive an immediate investigation by the operatives in those studios.[100]

DeMille's "operative," G.S., who "had known Weigel for a number of years," reported they had dinner together. "He did remark that Germans in this country had to be very carefuly [*sic*] about expressing their views but at no time did he say anything which would lead me to believe he had any enmity whatever toward the United States."[101] DeMille sent the report along to Lieutenant Lewis. "Acknowledge receipt of report on Mr. Paul Weigler [*sic*], for which I thank you."[102] Woods was also screened. "I have to report that I have carefully investigated Walter Woods, through Mr. McRae at Universal City, who reports Woods to be enthusiastically American, although strongly anti-Wilson at the last election, voting the Republican ticket."[103]

DeMille also reported on actor Bryant Washburn, who had gained fame after his role in *Skinner's Dress Suit*. Washburn, who worked for Essanay, was suspected of being a "slacker," for allegedly dodging the draft. After investigating, however, DeMille's operatives found that Washburn had been the victim of "the man with the grudge." An assistant director at Essanay was apparently jealous of Washburn and enamored of Mrs. Washburn.[104] In a text reading like the scenario for a feature film, DeMille's agent reported that Eubanks planted the tip about Washburn's draft evasion with his former workmates at the *Chicago Tribune*. The story got even more entangled in film studio politics when Zukor offered Washburn a job and George K. Spoor, head of Essanay, countered with the offer of a higher salary. The account filed by DeMille's agent reported the following:

The Threat: Victor Eubank then went to Mr. Spoor and said "Don't worry about losing Washburn—when I get through with him no company in the world will want him—and he'll be glad to work for you for anything he can get."

The story ended happily, for Bryant Washburn anyway. The Secret Service investigated and gave him a "complete 'bill of health.' . . . Washburn was then called to the office of the head of this department [the Secret Service] in Chicago and [the department] made an official apology for the inconvenience he had been caused in the matter." *Tribune* reporters who had broken the story named Eubanks as their source, and "further went on to say that George Spoor (of Essanay) himself had offered them a big bribe to make it impossible for Washburn to work for Paramount."[105] The report, unlike the classical Hollywood narrative, did not wrap up its loose end: Eubanks's fate remains unknown.

In October 1918 DeMille again talked of going to the front.[106] This time he would head a documentary unit. "This would take me to France about Jan. first but probably for no longer than three months."[107] Lasky responded in early November. Armistice was in the air, but the company had other reasons for hoping DeMille would stay in California.

> Frankly we are all delighted at the outcome of affairs as the bookings on your subjects are very good, indeed, and the DeMille specials would have been sadly missed on the Artcraft Program.
> . . . Of course, the epidemic and the closing of theaters throughout the country have put an enormous crimp in our bankroll.[108]

DeMille was still needed. The influenza epidemic in the fall of 1918 had closed theaters and studios for several weeks and had disrupted Famous Players-Lasky's production and distribution schedules. Revenue on his films would help to refill the corporate coffers.

Conclusion

The sudden ending of the war has focussed all our minds on the European and foreign markets.
Jesse Lasky to Cecil B. DeMille, 14 November 1918[109]

Between December 1916, when *Joan the Woman* was released, and December 1918, Cecil B. DeMille directed an additional eight movies. Only

Joan, *The Little American*, and *Till I Come Back to You* had war-related elements within their narratives. Given DeMille's obvious hawkishness, it is significant that only three films from this period tell war stories. Current fashion in film genre—in the epic, in the case of *Joan the Woman*—combined with the exigencies of expanding business (the merger of Famous Players and the Lasky Feature Play Company), to override both DeMille's personal aesthetic preferences and his private ambitions to go to war. Three days after the Armistice, on 14 November, Lasky wrote to DeMille. As he had in all of his correspondence during the period from 1914 to 1918, Lasky linked war, and now peace, with business.

> However, the worst [of the influenza epidemic] is over and we expect our income will reach a normal basis in about 2 or 3 more weeks. Nevertheless, this epidemic, entirely unprecedented in the history of American business, has cost our company over $1,000,000. However, the war is over and this is some compensation as we are bound to greatly increase our foreign business and we look for wonderful results in this country as soon as it is wide open again. [110]

In the quotation that serves as the epigraph for this chapter, *Moving Picture World*'s editorial writer noted that good might accrue to the U.S. film industry as a result of the European War. The "overimportation" of "cheap features" would no longer threaten its reputation for quality products or compete for market share with American-made films. Now, four years later, Lasky's comment was a measure of the advantage the U.S. industry had gained. American companies would export *their* films to countries they had previously vied with. Further, organizations like Famous Players-Lasky had used the years from 1916 to 1918 to expand, absorbing smaller production studios as well as Paramount's distribution system, and they would soon begin to purchase movie theaters. For now, control of human assets—the movie stars—guaranteed film producers widespread distribution and exhibition for their movies. World War I afforded stars, as it did the companies which employed them, the opportunity to increase their prestige with the American public and their contractual leverage with their studio bosses. The wartime career of Mary Pickford, the focus of the following chapter, is exemplary in this regard.

2

The Films of World War I
1917–1918

Discussion has been rife as to whether the public wants the war theme
in its moving pictures. . . . To the ordinary observer it would seem that
the public does want the war note so long as it is sincere. It wants a
picture that tells the truths about the daily lives of the brave boys who
are fighting our battles at the front.

Milwaukee Journal, *9 June 1918*[1]

THE GREAT WAR PERVADED civilian life after April 1917. Citizens
were urged to forgo meat and wheat so soldiers would have more; they were
urged to buy Liberty Bonds and Thrift Stamps. The war also affected businesses, as companies lost male personnel to military service, as they worried about being designated "nonessential," and as they coped with operating stores and factories on "Heatless Mondays." After the United States
entered the conflict, Geraldine Farrar, with other popular stars, enlisted in
fund-raising efforts on the homefront, speaking in the Treasury Department's Liberty Loan campaigns. When audiences went to see *Joan the
Woman*, the war-relatedness of its plot and its promotion was augmented
by the aura of patriotism emanating from its star. On the face of it, the most
salient historical context for the films produced in the period from 1917
through 1918 would seem to have been the war, but this was not the case.

There is a dearth of historical and critical writing linking World War I
and the movies. What little exists suffers from a problem this study seeks
to remedy. Articles with titles like "Hollywood and World War I" and
books like Michael Isenberg's *War on Film: The American Cinema and
World War I* catalog only the war-related films that the industry offered for
distribution.[2] These works provide no production history for the films they
list. Moreover, they leave the reader with the mistaken sense that only war-
related narratives were produced, and that these films appeared fast on the
heels of United States entry into the conflict. Generalizing from such incor-

35

rect historical premises, authors like Isenberg make statements such as, "In Hollywood films of the World War I years, much can be discovered about the American popular mind, its common beliefs and prejudices, and its way of accepting war as a necessary evil."[3] In reality, the Hollywood films of World War I resulted from a complex decision-making process in which East Coast industry personnel evaluated the commercial strengths of their stars and directors and responded to the concerns of their exhibitors, who in turn interpreted the likes and dislikes of *their* clientele. Star persona, narrative convention, and the demands of a regularized release schedule, among other factors, mitigated the impact of timeliness and topicality on the production process.

In fact, the films of World War I were a mixed lot. Movies with war-related narratives included Hate-the-Hun propaganda, exemplified by titles like *The Kaiser, the Beast of Berlin,* and *The Prussian Cur.* In these films mustachioed German officers, already identified with Erich von Stroheim, tossed babies out of windows, raped young women, and murdered innocent civilians. Not all war stories were so virulent. In *The Little American,* discussed later in this chapter, Mary Pickford plays Angela, an American born on the Fourth of July. She is in love with her German neighbor. After an ill-fated voyage to Belgium, and many plot twists, she liberates her love from a prisoner-of-war camp, brings him back to the United States, and presumably marries him. While there were war films in release over the nineteen months during which the United States was engaged in World War I, the preponderance of movies playing in picture palaces and neighborhood theaters across the land did not tell stories about the war. Comedy and drama, literary adaptation and original scenario, scripts with war-related narratives and, more frequent, scripts with no narrative relation to the war—all were offered by film producers to the exhibitors, and by the film exhibitors to their local clientele.

In general, film producers and distributors reacted to the war tactically. Benjamin Hampton described a three-to-six month production process as the norm for feature-length films, and the preproduction and production phases for *Joan the Woman* and Pickford's films fell within this range.[4] Studios could, if they chose, respond in timely fashion to the pressing issues of their day. Short-term production of war-related narratives did increase, and some of them received special treatment in distribution. Such tactical adaptations, however, did not alter producers' long-term strategies. The quality standards for the feature film did not change, nor was the variety of narrative content limited.

Fig. 2.1. Virulent anti-German films appeared late in World War I. Here is a series of three images from *To Hell with the Kaiser* that ran in *Exhibitor's Trade Review*, 8 June 1918.

Film Production 1917–1918: "The Exhibitors Tell What They Want"

More pictures like "A Poor Little Rich Girl" and "Rebecca of Sunnybrook Farm."

. . . More big pictures. Society plays with pretty gowns, beautiful women, clean themes and plenty of love moments.

. . . Comedies. Every day occurrences with a humorous vein. Human stories of contemporary times, with correct settings, beautiful outdoor scenery and Good Titles. More quaint and loveable characters.

Motography, *9 March 1918*[5]

The film industry did not alter its production schedule immediately, and it did not change its production tactics to exploit the commercial potential of the war. In April, May, and June of 1917 there were relatively few war-related narrative films in distribution. This trend continued even after September 1917, the first new movie season after American entry into the war. Production decisions were based, as in the case of *Joan the Woman*, on existing trends.[6] In rectifying some of the misconceptions in the conventional wisdom regarding the films of World War I, it will be helpful to take a detailed look at the actual number of war films produced over the course of 1917 and 1918, and at exactly when those films were released.

In proportion to the number of films in release while the United States was involved in World War I, the number of films bearing any relation to the events of the war was small. In April 1917, film exhibitors looking to see what was available to screen in their theaters would have consulted, among other sources, the trade journal *Moving Picture World*. Five hundred and sixty-eight titles were included in its "List of Current Film Release Dates."[7] Four newsreels accounted for 41 entries, while 8 topical documentary films and 9 war-related short subjects that were part of split reels—usually combining cartoons, editorials, and scenics—provided another 15 choices. The episodes of 2 serials, *Patria* and *The Perils of the Secret Service*, comprised 8 entries. *War Prides*, a parody of the Alla Nazimova drama *War Brides*, and a pair of two-part dramas, *True To Their Colors* and *Captain Marjorie's Adventure* were also listed. Finally, 8 feature-length dramas were also available for release. These included *The Spirit of '76*, *The Birth of Patriotism*, *The Dark Road*, *Joan the Woman*, *Womanhood Glory of the Nation*, *Darkest Russia*, *The Honor System*, and *The Submarine Eye*.

Thus, about 14 percent of the 568 available films were war-related, and half of these were newsreels or documentaries, the types of films traditionally suited to picturing current events. It is also significant that four of the documentaries and two of the dramas were distributed as states rights features. This category generally contained films handled individually (instead of as part of a block or package) and films that were not produced by an established film studio like Universal or Fox. In all cases but one, in April 1917 the states rights films were the sole offerings of their distributors. These distributors were themselves marginal within the film industry.[8]

The mainstream film producers, in other words—whether they distributed many films, as did Pathe, Universal, Mutual, Metro, Paramount, and Triangle, or relatively fewer films, as did Essanay, Kalem, Selig, Bluebird, or World—were not, at this date, exploiting the war, neutrality, or preparedness in their feature films to any great extent. War-related feature films would not become a significant factor in the "List of Current Film Release Dates," until September 1918, two months before the signing of the Armistice ending the war.

The intervening seventeen months between April 1917 and September 1918 saw a slow yet steady increase in the production and distribution of war-related narrative films. September and October were the opening months for the film industry's "show year."[9] Conventional wisdom within

Fig. 2.2. Patriotic Fox advertisement in *Moving Picture World*, 13 October 1917, on two facing pages. Fox's patriotic rhetoric heralds a variety of films, only two of which are war-related.

the industry had it that business during the summer months was slow, and thus the coming of fall was marked, not only by cooler weather, but also by producers' enthusiastic announcements of their autumn line-up. Paramount, heralding the release of *The Ghost House, Arms and the Girl, The Trouble Buster, The Call of the East, The World for Sale, Babs Burglar, The Son of His Father, The Price Mark,* and *The Antics of Ann,* proclaimed, "It is the logical beginning of the fall season in motion pictures and a more auspicious opening could hardly be desired.[10] Only *Arms and the Girl* had a war-related narrative. A Fox advertisement in the 13 October issue of *Moving Picture World* reminded exhibitors, in timely language and images, that *The Honor System, Jack and the Beanstalk, The Spy, The Conqueror, Camille, When a Man Sees Red,* and *Aladdin and His Wonderful Lamp* were "At the front with Fox. Here are seven valiant soldiers who 'went over the top' with Fox—Safely crossed no man's land and are now firmly entrenched miles in advance."[11] In fact, however, only two of these seven, *The Honor System* (previously distributed by Facts Film Company) and *The Spy,* corresponded to the military rhetoric of this advertisement.

The 1917 season, occurring six months after U.S. entry into the war, would have offered the industry sufficient time to put war-related pictures into production. It was reasonable, from a business standpoint, to expect the movies opening the major studio's release schedule to reflect industry thinking on the most commercially feasible tone it might set for at least the first half of the coming year. In September 1917, a theater manager consulting *Moving Picture World* could find 563 items available for distribution. Only 80 of these films had either a narrative or documentary relation to the war, and 6 different newsreels accounted for 40 of these titles. There were 11 war-related documentaries, 6 comic or educational shorts which were parts of split reels, and 1 episode of the serial *The Perils of the Secret Service* listed. Additionally, there were 4 short comedies or cartoons and 18 feature-length dramas offered by film distributors. States rights distribution accounted for 9 documentaries, 2 of the comedies, and 4 of the dramas.

While there was a net gain of only three war-related items over April 1917, a trend had begun in the production and distribution of war-related material. The data for September and early October reveal that the larger, more important distributors had begun carrying war-related films as part of their total product line. Pathe listed Thanhouser's *War and the Woman* and *Under False Colors*, Metro included *Miss Robinson Crusoe*, *The Slacker*, and *The Silence Sellers*, and Mutual offered the Mutual Star Production *Her Country's Call*. Universal, Goldwyn, and Greater Vitagraph also offered war-related feature films for release. The Paramount and Fox release schedules, however, show that war-related narratives made up only a minor portion of a studio's total film offering. Production strategy remained consistent, yet allowed room for topical adaptation.

One year later, the films headlining the new season continued to follow the trend of including timely, war-related narrative films, but never to the exclusion of other genres. The 5 October 1918 "List of Current Film Release Dates" offered 496 titles.[12] This total, down 44 from September 1917, represented a decrease in the number of films being produced in 1918, a shift that was noted by both *Variety* and Cranston Brenton, chairman of the National Board of Review.[13] Seven newsreels accounted for 34 entries. There were 11 topical documentaries, including 2 films produced by the federal government's Committee on Public Information, *Our Bridge of Ships* and *Pershings Crusaders*. Thirteen short and feature-length comedies, 5 Mutt and Jeff cartoons, 1 short animated drama (Windsor McCay's *The Sinking of the Lusitania*), *Bill Stringer's Poems* (a series of one-reel patriotic comedy-dramas issued semi-monthly), and 54 feature-length dramas with war-related narratives were in distribution. There was an increase in the numbers of war-related movies, particularly feature films with war-related narratives. This number was higher than in any preceding month (April comes closest with 36 feature films), yet the total number of titles for films with a narrative or documentary link to the war still accounted for only 23 percent of all film titles listed by the *Moving Picture World* service.

The Debate over War Films

Start right now with comedies. When people go to the theater they seek relaxation.

Epes Winthrop Sargent, Moving Picture World, *9 June 1917*[14]

All this talk that people want to forget the war is all bunk, pure and simple. Give me a war picture carrying a good story dealing with the happenings in France and I'll play it every time in preference to some wishywashy artistic thing that means nothing.

Moving Picture World, *27 April 1918*[15]

With the United States committed "over there," both the trade press and the popular press debated the kinds of films that should be produced and exhibited in wartime. Implicit in the arguments raised by film producers, editors, columnists for *Moving Picture World*, stars, distributors, local film reviewers, and film exhibitors were their positions on the appropriate function of popular culture, especially during a period of national crisis. The discussion revealed two opposing points of view that did not change significantly over the course of the war. One position held that movies should provide light-hearted escape, while the other argued that films ought to show contemporary reality. The debate manifested the film industry's attempt to gauge public opinion and preference.

In the 9 June 1917 issue of *Moving Picture World*, Essanay announced it was eliminating "depressing stories." "Practically all future Essanay features," it stated, "will be of the straight comedy or comedy-drama type. To make people laugh and forget their troubles will be the chief aim of these pictures."[16] This idea was repeated by Epes Winthrop Sargent, author of the column "Advertising for Exhibitors" that ran in *Moving Picture World*. He cited the English as an example for the American film producers to follow. "When people go to the theater they seek relaxation. . . . Give them comedies and light plays and get your military stuff from the news weeklies and the English and French war pictures."[17] The emulation of England and championing comedy as the proper film genre in wartime were often repeated points in this debate, and these attitudes carried over into 1918. As late as June 1918, the *New York Times* published Jesse Lasky's description of what type of films to expect from Paramount and Artcraft.

> [He] and his associates consider it the duty of moving picture manufacturers to "inculcate" the spirit of cheerfulness during the war, and that corporation will therefore eliminate morbid, tragic and depressing elements from its output.
>
> In addition, we have become convinced that photoplays dealing with religious subjects, fairy tales, allegories, costume plays and the like are neither desired nor accepted today by exhibitors or public. This conviction is a result of a thorough canvass of the situation, a campaign of extensive character in which showmen in all parts of the country have been interrogated as to their experience with motion pictures.[18]

Within the context of these remarks, the relatively small percentages of war-related films on the market would seem to indicate that film producers in Hollywood, Chicago, New York, and New Jersey were acting in accord with this theory of obligatory cinematic cheerfulness. Another side to this public discussion however, complicates such a tidy appraisal.

In April 1917, Bluebird Photoplays, promoting two war-related films, *Treason* and *The Eagles Wing*, cited the timeliness of their product as a selling point to exhibitors.[19] The editorial policy of *Moving Picture World* was unabashedly in favor of the patriotic film. A 9 March 1918 editorial stated, "Pictures will be the greatest force in thus working us all up to the proper fighting spirit and that will be the best picture which drives us farther into the fight."[20]

The movie writer for the *Milwaukee Journal* summarized the terms of the debate and perhaps most accurately described the situation as of June 1918.

> Men there are who rise up and proclaim that during war the public wants to think not of wounds and horrors but of mirth and joy and therefore comedy and the frothiest of drama are the offering.
>
> However, ranged on the other side are the heavy cinema producers.

> Either they are convinced that the public wants the war note sounded
> in the theater as it sounded in daily life or they are taking long
> chances with their money which has been freely invested in
> tremendously expensive films.[21]

Although they were being produced and distributed in ever-increasing numbers over the months of U.S. involvement in World War I, war-related narrative and documentary films never dominated other films. My research does not corroborate film historian Kevin Brownlow's conclusion that Hate-the-Hun films "poured into the theaters like poison gas" at any time during American involvement.[22] Nor was it the case, as Charles Reed Mitchell stated, that, "Once the decision in favor of war had been announced by President Wilson, torrents of war romances burst forth from the industry."[23] Instead, there was a slow yet steady increase in the numbers of war-related feature films advertised in *Moving Picture World:* 8 dramatic features listed in May 1917, 18 in October 1917, 28 in March 1918, 32 in August 1918, and 54 in October 1918. This cautious consistency indicated that the production of war-related feature films was the result of decisions to respond tactically to the war through the timely adaptation of film narratives, and, further, that this decision was based at least in part on the testing of this type of film in the marketplace. There had been vociferous opposition to U.S. entry into the war, and it may have been the case that film producers were waiting to see what the popular consensus would be before committing themselves and their products to any single point of view. Further, it is simply not true that, as one film historian has suggested,

> Once America showed signs of entering the war, the commercial film
> producers . . . quickly jumped on the commercial bandwagon of
> patriotism. In a very short time they produced such stirring anti-
> German dramas as *A Daughter of France, War and Women, The Kaiser*
> and *Beast of Berlin* while even Charlie Chaplin's *Shoulder Arms* heaped
> ridicule on the German military.[24]

In fact, *Daughter of France* and *The Kaiser, The Beast of Berlin* were not released until March 1918. *Shoulder Arms*, which I will discuss in Chapter Five, opened its first run at the Strand in New York City, on 20 October 1918, only weeks before the war ended. The other particularly strident anti-German films also appeared late in the war: *My Four Years in Germany*

(March 1918), *To Hell with the Kaiser* (June 1918), and *The Prussian Cur* and *Kulture* (both in September 1918).

Distribution: The Special and the War Film

Just as every good retail merchant will occasionally hold a special sale
to attract new customers and retain old ones, so does the showman offer
a special inducement in the way of an extraordinary entertainment.

Motography, *28 July 1917*[25]

Still, numbers do not tell the whole story. All films in release were not equal: brighter stars, bigger promotional efforts, and more elaborate exhibition differentiated film from film, creating a hierarchy ranging from (top to bottom) the special film to the program picture. While films with war-related content were always the minority of all films in release, the conclusion does not follow that war-related films were insignificant. Certain of these films stood out. They received more press attention, and their audiences knew they were prestigious.

Distributors identified and offered a "top-of-the-line" product. Famous Players-Lasky distributed its "standard" features under the heading "Paramount Feature," while its more expensive feature films, starring Mary Pickford, Douglas Fairbanks, and William Hart, among others, were handled through Artcraft. Other distributors distinguished among their pictures on the basis of quality and production and distribution costs. The term "special" was used with some consistency by other distributors to identify those films being described here as prestigious. As Fox had its Fox Special Features, so Universal had its Universal Special Productions, Goldwyn its Goldwyn Specials, and Metro its Metro Specials. In a brief filed with the Federal Trade Commission investigating the practice of block booking in the 1920s, the Famous Players-Lasky Corporation characterized the special.

Theaters cannot exist and prosper on a succession of super special
pictures, each widely exploited and each advertised as the greatest
picture made. The rentals which distributors of such pictures are
forced to ask require exhibitors to operate their theaters at capacity
and at prices too great to be consistently maintained. The backbone
of the exhibition business is the ordinary program picture, few of
super special quality, none bad, but all of consistently average
quality.[26]

Fox, in an advertisement in the August 11, 1917, issue of *Moving Picture World*, described its "Fox Special Features" thus: "Length 5 and 6 reels. Each picture based on a successful novel or stage play."[27] Thus, higher rental, more elaborate exploitation, and a high-toned source for the film, as well as its length, served as selling points to distinguish these films from the standard product.

Another characteristic of the "special" may be inferred from a comment made in a 1919 publication entitled *The Story of the Famous Players-Lasky Corporation*. While describing the feature films to be produced in 1920, it noted: "Announcement has also been made that several specials will be made for release by this company by Mayflower Productions, under the direction of George Loane Tucker. Maurice Tourneur will also give some pictures."[28] "Specials" status was also given to films contracted for distribution outside of the studio's own product. Just as war-related feature and documentary films were the minority of all films in distribution during the nineteen months of American involvement in World War I, so war-related narrative and documentary specials were the minority of all specials listed in the Program and Feature Release sections of the "List of Current Film Release Dates." Of the 130 "specials" appearing between April 1917 and December 1918, 37 (about one-quarter) were war-related. This included serials and features, narrative and documentary films. In fact, such a variety of films fell under this rubric that, for the purpose of determining prestige, it becomes necessary to determine the *most* special of the special. Fox, Universal, Mutual, Goldwyn, and Metro all use the category; however, the release dates listed alongside these films show that for the most part they were being released weekly. The regularity of release dates suggests that while these films may have enjoyed top-of-the-line status in the list of Fox productions, they were not conceived of as extraordinary, or treated unusually during distribution.

While some films were listed under the heading "special," certain other films were designated "special" parenthetically. For instance, in the "List of Current Film Release Dates" for 7 April 1917, Universal offered Powers' films for distribution.[29] Eight films, mainly split reels consisting of a comedy and an educational or scenic short, were contained under this heading. Listed for release on 22 March 1917, however, was *The Strangest Army in the World*, followed by the parenthetical description "War Special." In the same issue of the *Moving Picture World*, Fox Films included *The Honor System* among nine films with release dates from 26 February to 1 April. This title was also followed by the description "Special release-drama." *The Birth of Patriotism, War on Three Fronts, Jack and the Bean-stalk, American Methods, Mother O' Mine, The Manx Man, For the Freedom of the World, Inner Voice,* and *Over There* were also parenthetically identi-fied as specials during the months of United States involvement in World War I. Significantly, six of these films were war-related, suggesting that they were produced by or contracted from independent producers outside of the established production or distribution schedule for the year. In other words, it was probable that these films did represent efforts by the industry to respond to the predominant topic of the day, the war.

Paramount-Artcraft also distributed Paramount-Artcraft Specials. They came late in the war and included *The Hun Within*, released 8 September 1918, and *Private Peat*, released 18 October 1918. Both of these films were war-related. An advertisement in the *New York Times* for *The Hun Within* noted that "This is the first of a magnificent special series of nine Paramount-Artcraft Specials for the season 1918–1919."[30] These two films reflected a "higher" top-of-the-line as well as Para-mount's increasing use of the war as a topic for the films it produced and distributed.

There was one other method of distribution accounting for a very small number of the most prestigious of films, the roadshow. The distribution and promotion of roadshown movies were handled by the producer of the film rather than through a film exchange. As a rule, these played in legiti-mate theaters rather than movie theaters, with large or augmented orches-tras, and garnered higher ticket prices than films screened in movie theaters. Advertising for roadshows was often carried on the theater page rather than the movie page in newspapers, and these films, because of their less institutionalized mode of distribution, could be more flexible in the length of their run. They typically played longer than the standard run, and they were able to remain longer if demand warranted. They were a special attraction.[31]

Greater Vitagraph adapted Sergeant Arthur Guy Empey's war memoir *Over the Top* and distributed the film as a roadshow. It opened at the Lyric Theater, New York City, on 31 March 1918. Ticket prices ranged from twenty-five cents to one dollar in the evenings, and the advertisement in the *New York Times* noted that "Sergt. Empey will appear personally to-night and at every performance for the first week."[32] *Exhibitor's Trade Review* carried an advertisement for "The Great Two-Step 'Over the Top Boys,' The Official Empey March Theme especially composed and pre-sented with the Marvelous Photoplay of Empey's world famous Book and in

Fig. 2.3. Advertisement for *Over the Top* in *Exhibitor's Trade Review*, 20 July 1918. The film, based on the memoirs of Sergeant Guy Empey, was distributed as a roadshow.

which Sergt Arthur Guy Empey (himself) personally appears."[33] *Over the Top* played four weeks at the Lyric.

    D. W. Griffith's *Hearts of the World*, also a roadshow, was the longest-running and arguably the most prestigious film produced and released during the entire period of U.S. participation in the war. This romance between the children of American neighbors living on the Rue de la Paix in a French village was a good example of the way in which the war could be incorporated as a plot device in an otherwise conventional, melodramatic love story. An early intertitle introduced it as, "an old fashioned play with a new fashioned theme." Griffith also stated the theme in another intertitle: "God help the nation that begins another war of conquest or meddling! Brass bands and clanging sabers make very fine music, but let us remember there is another side of war."[34] *Hearts of the World* showed the other side of the Great War. The marriage plans of Lillian Gish and Robert Harron, the "Girl" and the "Boy," were interrupted by war. The Germans advanced on their village, the Boy's mother died, the Girl was mistreated at the hands of the enemy, and in a wonderfully eerie mad scene the Girl, clutching her wedding dress, roamed across a desolate battlefield searching for the Boy. The film's climax came as the Boy fought a German (played by Erich von Stroheim), nearly lost, and was saved by the arrival of French and American troops. The film concluded in "Happy Times." "America— returning home after freeing the world from Autocracy and the horrors of war forever and ever." Viewers saw shots of American flags, followed by ships at sea, and a flag-draped portrait of President Wilson. *Hearts of the World* ended with a shot of the Boy and Girl waving flags against a backdrop of bright light. Audiences loved it.

Hearts of the World played at the 44th Street Theater in New York City from 4 April 1918 to 5 October 1918, and it reopened at the Knickerbocker Theater in New York, on 6 October. The *New York Times* quoted "the statistical expert in Mr. Griffith's office [to the effect that] more than 742,000 persons will have attended the 370 exhibitions of the film at regular Broadway theater prices."[35] Although it may be argued that film exhibition in New York City was the exception and not the rule for moviegoers in the United States, a survey of the run that *Hearts of the World* enjoyed in Milwaukee, Wisconsin, which will be discussed in the following chapter, reinforced the notion that this film was a major event.

While a minority of all films in distribution in 1917 and 1918 were war-related, about half of the most prestigious and expensive movies— "specials" and roadshows—were war-related. Further, it was significant that the "biggest" movie produced and exhibited during the war was D. W. Griffith's *Hearts of the World*. So, in answer to the question, What were the films of World War I? I propose the following answer. People regularly attending such movie theaters as the Alhambra in Milwaukee, Wisconsin, the Ziegfeld in Chicago, or the Rialto in New York City saw a variety of films. They saw more feature-length narratives than documentaries; they saw more nonwar-related stories played on the screen than war-related stories. Yet, when on special occasions spectators went to such theaters as the Davidson in Milwaukee, the Olympic in Chicago, or the Lyric in New York City to see a movie instead of a stage play, about half the time they paid "Broadway prices" to see some facet of the war enacted.

Thus war-related movies occupied an alternative and elevated position within the film industry's production and exhibition schedules. The major producers like Famous Players-Lasky included war-related pictures among their standard releases in increasing numbers over the months of American involvement, but never to the exclusion of other types of entertainment. Whether this was due to a philosophy of obligatory cheerfulness in films or to a principle of pragmatic business management which found it more efficient to continue making the sorts of films that had previously been made, or whether the situation reflects a mixing of these two positions is difficult to determine without greater access to studio documents. Howard Thompson Lewis, approaching the film industry from his position as professor of marketing in the Graduate School of Business at Harvard in the early 1920s, suggested that financial gain was at the heart of industry decision-making. "Its [film industry's] builders had ideals, but if there had not been times when the business yielded a profit those ideals would have remained forever in the realm of the imagination."[36] Still, the business "promoters" did not make their decisions in a vacuum. The case of *Joan the Woman* illustrated the role of timeliness in the film production and exhibition process.

The 1917–1918 filmography of Mary Pickford further illustrates the range of influences affecting the businessmen on the East Coast and the creative personnel in Los Angeles. Not least among these considerations was the public persona of the star. Pickford's first war film, *The Little American* was released in July 1917. In discussing the character Pickford played—a young woman born on the Fourth of July who lived in Washington, D.C.—the movie writer for the Kokomo, Indiana, *Dispatch* set Pickford within the paradigm of her previous roles.

> For the first time [*sic*] since her appearance in Artcraft pictures, "America's Sweetheart," Mary Pickford, will be seen at the Isis Theater commencing Monday as a modern American girl in modern gowns, in *The Little American*, a gripping patriotic photodrama by Cecil B. DeMille and Jeanie Macpherson. In *Less than the Dust* the famous star was seen as an East Indian, in the *Pride of the Clan*, as a Scottish lassie, in *A Poor Little Rich Girl*, as a child and in *A Romance of the Redwoods* as a New England girl of the days of '49, but in *The Little American* she blossoms forth as a wealthy young American girl in beautiful gowns and modern costumes by Lucile and Madame Frances.[37]

Production, distribution, and exhibition, here represented by Pickford's most recent films; her distribution company, Artcraft; and her current image as a modern, well-dressed, versatile actress combined to sell *The Little American* to the movie-going citizens of Kokomo. This amalgamation of a young adult Pickford, the war, and fashion did not spring full-blown from the heads of Lasky, Zukor, the officers in Famous Players-Lasky, DeMille, or Macpherson. Instead, debate and discussion about a suitable vehicle for Famous Players-Lasky's most expensive star ensued through the early months of 1917.

The Films of Mary Pickford

> We have talked it over here and believe that at this particular time, when other companies are striving to catch the national spirit, by producing timely pictures with semi-patriotic titles—Mary Pickford in a production called "The American Girl" would create a good deal of advance interest.
>
> *Jesse Lasky to Cecil B. DeMille, 5 March 1917*[38]

Mary Pickford's World War I filmography showed the diversity of products available to theater managers and their audiences. On 6 May 1917, a writer for the *New York Times* reported to readers on the films they could look forward to seeing from one of their favorite stars.

> Mary Pickford is one of the first movie stars to grab the patriotic bull by the horns. Word was brought by Jesse Lasky from California last week that Miss Pickford's next picture would be *The Little American*. She has just completed a film called *Romance of the Redwoods* and after the patriotic one will pose for *Rebecca of Sunnybrook Farm*.[39]

The quotation confirms one of the trends evident in the films produced, distributed, and exhibited during the nineteen months of United States engagement in World War I. Like most stars in the years 1917 and 1918, Pickford worked in films with a variety of subject matters, only some of which were war-related. *Rebecca of Sunnybrook Farm* was released in September 1917, *The Little Princess* in November 1917, *Stella Maris* in May 1918, and *How Could You, Jean?* in June 1918; it wasn't until the release of *Johanna Enlists* in September of 1918 that a feature-length Mary Pickford film again presented a war-related story. Thus, only two of Pickford's eight films released while the United States was engaged in World War I had war-related narratives, the same percentage cited earlier for all feature films produced during World War I. Although neither was an Artcraft Special, which was the very top of the Famous Players line, the Artcraft designation signified that *The Little American* and *Johanna Enlists* were distributed differently from the standard program pictures. In fact, one of the contractual points of contention among Pickford, her mother, and

Fig. 2.4. Advertisement for *Johanna Enlists* in *Motion Picture News*, 14 September 1918. The film was one of two war-related movies starring Mary Pickford.

Adolph Zukor was the way in which her films were used to "force" exhibitors to rent the entire block of Paramount product.[40] The prominently advertised high salary paid to Pickford (which was also a topic of discussion in the business correspondence of Lasky and DeMille) also guaranteed a special care and handling of Pickford's work. In addition to these institutional markers of prestige, the audiences arriving at the theater bought their tickets with expectations of quality based on an eight-year acquaintance with "Little Mary" at the movies.

Cecil B. DeMille and Jesse Lasky took account of Pickford's star persona as they fashioned a suitable film for her early in 1917, and *The Little American* was the result. *Joan the Woman* had been running for nearly a month in New York City when Lasky wrote DeMille in January 1917. He and Zukor were not sure that a topical, war-related story was the right vehicle for Pickford or for Famous Players.

> We have just been considering your wire of January 18 in which you
> ask us to decide between a western story for Pickford and a modern
> story placed somewhere in Belgium. We are sure that the western story
> is preferable at this time. Even though your other story would not have
> shown actual war, it is best for us to keep away from anything bearing
> on the conditions-past, present or future in connection with the
> European conflict. This is particularly true with Pickford as the star.[41]

The resulting western story, *A Romance of the Redwoods*, went into production on 17 February 1917, only three days after Pickford arrived in California from the East Coast, and was completed 23 March. This film, however, did challenge the Pickford stereotype—deliberately. As they discussed starring Pickford in a western, Lasky cautioned DeMille,

> The Pickford situation is really critical. . . . She has insisted on doing
> typical Pickford stuff until the public have become tired of it. She
> needs a director with force and you need not be afraid to do a DeMille
> type of piece rather than the Pickford type. The public will surely be
> pleased to see her in something radically different from what she has
> done before.[42]

In *Romance of the Redwoods*, Pickford played Jenny Lawrence, a teenaged orphan from the East who traveled West to live with an uncle she had never met. However, unknown to her, the uncle had been killed by Indians and his papers stolen by a bandit, Black Brown, on the run from the law. Jenny eventually discovered her "uncle's" true identity, yet still saved Brown from a vigilante party out to lynch him. She accomplished her rescue by convincing the vigilantes that she was pregnant. Instead of hanging this "bad man" who had reformed and who did love Jenny, the justice of the peace married the couple. Vachel Lindsay wrote a glowing review entitled "Queen of My People." He argued that DeMille and Macpherson had written a script that allowed Pickford's character greater breadth than she had displayed in earlier films. "In the Romance of the Redwoods it begins to appear that the higher the imagination of Mary Pickford's scenario writer and director, the more sensitive her response." Lindsay watched the movie six times, and he concluded his essay by crowning Pickford queen of popular culture, high culture and, in fact, national culture, and noted: "I was glad Mary was beginning to emerge. I have found her portrait among Botticelli's muses in the Chicago Art Institute. . . . To repudiate this girl in haste is high treason to the national heart."[43] Despite Lindsay's encomiums, *Romance of the Redwoods* did not please the "typical" Pickford fan. Manager Harvey C. Horater of the Citizen's Alhambra Theater Company in Toledo, Ohio, complained to Artcraft. "We just finished a week's run on 'A Romance of the Redwoods' to poor business . . . this too in the face of the fact, that, the Alhambra has been known as a Pickford house for three or four years." Horater's assessment of the problem with the film was that Pickford played against type. "We did NOT cater to, or rather we did not GET the Kiddies . . . the writer is of the opinion that Pickford should not appear in any picture that is not suitable for children, and the last one certainly was not. . . . "[44] Horater was not alone. Harry D. G. Robinson, president of the New Jersey Theatres Company, wrote his film supplier, Arthur G. Whyte, manager of the New York Exchange. "Before closing, I only hope Miss Pickford's next picture will make up for the awful picture, entitled, 'A Romance of the Redwoods,' that she has just appeared in."[45] Al Lichtman, general sales manager for Paramount Pictures Corporation, interpreted theater-manager displeasure in a letter to Lasky in late May 1917.

> "A Romance of the Redwoods," while considered an excellent picture from a technical viewpoint, is not especially pleasing to motion picture patrons. Most Pickford fans are disappointed in this type of film because it is so different from the usual type of play in which Miss Pickford appears.
> Judging from the letters we have received from various exhibitors it

> would be well to bear in mind the fact that Miss Pickford should have
> charming girlish roles giving full play to her smile and curls, and
> comedy should dominate her stories.[46]

Lasky and Zukor, fortuitously, would not learn of audience resistance to
this more mature, less conventional portrayal until May, *after* production
of *The Little American* was completed. Unable to adjust the film's narrative
to audience taste at this late date, the East Coast publicity people countered potential displeasure through the promotional campaign designed
for the film. This in combination with the entrance of the United States into
the war in April served to mitigate some, but not all of the complaints of
inappropriateness by the movie-going public. *The Little American* and
Pickford's subsequent war-related activities in support of the homefront
had a lasting effect on her public image.

In addition to issues of timeliness and star persona, Lasky and Zukor
were also concerned about cost as they negotiated with DeMille.

> In asking you to do at least two Pickford pictures, our first thought,
> was not so much the feeling that we would get a much better grade of
> picture for her than we are getting at present—although better pictures
> of Pickford are absolutely essential—but the big thought that prompted
> us to send Pickford west and have you direct her was the hope that we
> would get a good picture at minimum cost.[47]

Although Pickford's previous three films—*Less Than the Dust, Pride of the
Clan,* and *A Poor Little Rich Girl*—had garnered good returns at the box
office, the costs of each production had cut into the company's profits. "As
it is we are a couple of hundred thousand dollars in the hole,—not because
the Pickford pictures do not bring in plenty of money but because they
have been too expensively produced."[48] Lasky also warned DeMille that
upon completion of her second picture with him Pickford might want to
return to the East. "I am absolutely certain that if she comes back here
after you are through with her—that her pictures will cost, if produced
here, 50% more than if produced by Melford [the director scheduled to
take over after DeMille] on the coast."[49]

By 5 March 1917, as the production of *Romance of the Redwoods* was
wrapping up, before its unfavorable reviews came in, Lasky and Zukor
changed their minds about the efficacy and the appropriateness of doing a
war film with Pickford.

> I wonder if you and Jeanie couldn't write something typically
> American and something that would portray a girl in the sort of role
> that the feminists in the country are now interested in—the kind of
> girl who jumps in and does a man's work when men are at the front.
> At any rate, some character and plot that would catch the national
> spirit that is rampant throughout the country at the present time.
> I am really waxing quite enthusiastic about the idea.[50]

Their change of heart represented the workings of practical patriotism. In January it did not make good business sense for the New York office to risk putting Mary Pickford into a film with a war-related narrative. By March Pickford's image had not changed—*Romance* would not be released until May—but market conditions had. Germany had announced resumption of submarine warfare against both belligerent and neutral countries in early February, and Wilson had released the Zimmermann Telegram, with its promise that Germany would return "lost territories"—including parts of Texas, New Mexico, and Arizona—to Mexico in the event that country joined its alliance. By late February the advertisements for *Joan the Woman* began to bear the impress of timeliness. In his 8 March letter to DeMille, Lasky expressed concern about the heating up of hostilities. "This War scare is most unfortunate as it may affect our business. I pray to heaven it will blow over."[51] DeMille, however, had not hesitated to use the European War as plot material in *Joan the Woman*, nor was he neutral. He closed his replies to Lasky in late February with the lines, "Trusting you are not bitten by a German Zeppelin," and "If you can catch one, send me a tame German for my curio box."[52]

By mid-March Lasky and Zukor were so confident of success with *The Little American* that Lasky wrote DeMille they would like to release this timely film before *Romance of the Redwoods*. "You should do everything possible to get on with "The American Girl" and we will release it the moment it is finished. The idea is so good that I wouldn't talk about it around the studio as someone else might beat us to it."[53] This deadline was not met, however, and *The Little American* was released in July 1917.

Competition with other companies, a volatile international situation, and the potential of crafting a role that would both stretch and remain faithful to the principal elements of the Pickford persona helped Lasky and Zukor to "wax enthusiastic" where they had previously hesitated. DeMille and Macpherson wrote an original story for Mary Pickford about an American girl who was loyal to the United States and her country's French allies, but who, while despising the Prussian System, was in love with an individual German. *The Little American* went into production on 13 April, only days after the United States entered the Great War. The picture was completed 22 May 1917.

Timeliness, Narrative Convention, and "Little Mary"

WILL SALE [*sic*] ON "VERITANIA" SATURDAY.

BEST LOVE,

ANGELA[54]

The narrative conventions of the classical Hollywood cinema and the characteristics of the star system had become standardized by 1917.[55] The timeliness desired by Lasky and Zukor, which was touted as realism, was shaped by the requirements of the Pickford persona and the need for a unified narrative structure, in addition to the actual events of the war. It is also important to note that the "real" events like the sinking of the *Lusitania* and "accurate" representations of French, British, German, and American characters that appear in this film bear the marks of the propaganda of the war period. In other words, stereotyped images of friend and foe in the conflict had also become conventionalized by 1917. DeMille and Macpherson drew upon the physical and behavioral traits ascribed to these "types" as they told their tale.

The studio synopsis of *The Little American* declared that:

> The birthday of Angela Moore is the same as that of her country—the fourth day of July. She is a typical American girl living in Washington. She is courted by Count Jules de Destin of the French embassy, but her affections are centered in Karl Von Austreim, a young German-American, who although he lives in Washington, has been educated in Germany.
>
> Karl has proposed to Angela and has just been accepted when he is secretly called to join his reserve in Germany and vanishes from sight before war is declared. Jules goes to join his French regiment. Angela receives no word from Karl, and when her aunt, living in a French chateau, requests that she join her, Angela gladly accepts and writes Karl that she is sailing.[56]

The Little American opened by introducing the film's three main characters. It is useful to cite the description of these scenes from the film script to let the parallel between intentionality and propagandistic national stereotyping show. Jules de Destin, of the "Fighting Destins," helped by his Japanese valet, is trying to dress. "The top of the chiffonnier holds the Count's various bottles of toilet water—silver brushes and somewhat effeminate trappings."[57] At this moment all that Destin was fighting was his wardrobe—he couldn't find an appropriate tie in the welter of clothing surrounding him.

Next, Karl von Austreim, "WHO PLEASES A GERMAN FATHER BY ATTENDING SCHOOL ABROAD—AND AN AMERICAN MOTHER BY SUMMERING IN THE "CAPITAL." Soon after first appearing, he will stand before a portrait of his paternal grandfather, at which point the script specifies that: "He must look obviously a German with sweeping moustachios." Karl's father was described as an "irascible, crabbid German of 60, with a grizzled imperial and shrewd dark eyes under bushy brows."[58]

Pickford was first presented in a way which highlighted her trademark features—her smile, her curls, and her gaiety. Karl, her next-door neighbor, aims his binoculars in her direction and "ANGELA MORE'S FACE FADES IN FRAMED BY SUGGESTION OF BINOCULAR HOLES. SHE SMILES MERRILY." Karl looks again and this time, "BACK OF ANGELA'S HEAD FADES IN. SHE SHAKES HER CURLS MERRILY UNTIL THEY ARE ALL DANCING, BUT DOES NOT TURN AROUND."[59] As star of this film Pickford was introduced a second time, and this time the theme of the story was presented.

Subtitle: MARY PICKFORD
                        AS
                        ANGELA MORE

SCENE 3.

(*FADE IN*) *Int. Against Black Velvet.*
American flag FADES IN, ripples back and forth in the breeze—finally unfurls openly as if blown by steady breeze. Portrait of Angela FADES IN onto flag. (FADE OUT)[60]

Thus far, *The Little American* played like a love story—two young men in love with the same girl. But in Scene 4 the fourth important character appeared. An intertitle announced "THE SHADOW OF COMING EVENTS." A "Royal" person, was seated in a "throne-like" chair decorated with a "double German Eagle." His face is not revealed, instead the shot framed "part of his rich white uniform. His arm in its white braided sleeve rests along arm of chair." The next intertitle registered the speech of this personage.

"WE SHALL NOT LET A MERE 'SCRAP OF PAPER' INTERFERE WITH THE VIGOR-
OUS ADVANCEMENT OF PRUSSIANISM." The paper referred to here was an
1839 treaty in which England, among other European countries, had
agreed to defend the neutrality of Belgium. The German chancellor,
Bethmann Hollweg, is quoted as saying "just for 'a scrap of paper' Great
Britain is going to make war."[61] The first "timely" Prussian atrocity the
film documented was the sinking of the ship Angela sailed in on her voyage
to France.

Angela booked passage on the *Veritania*—an allusion, of course, to
the *Lusitania*, which a German submarine had sunk on 7 May 1915. All
told, 1,198 people died in this attack, including 128 American citizens.
(One of the survivors, actress Rita Jolivet, would later tour movie theaters
telling her story. As he prepared his autobiography in 1957, DeMille made
a note that Jolivet had also provided him with her first-person account of
the sinking.[62]) Angela survived the torpedo attack, clutching a small
American flag which Karl had given her as a birthday present, and she
arrived in France in time to meet Jules, who had lost an arm to the war, and
to witness the German advance upon her (now dead) aunt's chateau.

Karl was part of the contingent attacking Angela's chateau, which she
had converted into a field hospital. Von Austreim, believing that Angela
died in the U-boat attack on the *Veritania*, had become increasingly embit-
tered and had fallen entirely under the sway of Prussianism. No longer an
individual, he followed orders and seemed devoid of the charm and culture
he possessed when he lived in Washington.

Scene 149

Int. Wine Cellar-Near Stairs. NIGHT

Karl and one of the other officers have been drinking heavily. Karl
throws down one empty bottle—picks up another—smashes its head
off and starts to drink with his companion as the third officer comes up
with his arms full of bottles—and this is Fritz. The 2nd officer says to
him with a leering smile:

Spoken Title: "WHERE ARE THE PRETTY GIRLS, FRITZ?"

Karl not only drank and looked slovenly, he succumbed to Prussian
"bestiality" by nearly raping Angela: "The awful thing he had intended
fairly engulfs him for a moment. . . . " Unable to help Angela save the
women working for her, he speaks the propagandist's line, "You don't

understand—Angela! I'm powerless to stop those men—I'm only a part of the System." Angela answered, "SOMEWHERE IN THIS HOUSE [*sic*] WHO IS SOMETHING MORE THAN A SPLENDIDLY DRILLED BEAST!"[63]

Finally Angela was humiliated beyond Karl's endurance when his commanding officer told her to pull off his muddy boots. He realized the errors of his ways and later defended her when she was caught transmitting information about German artillery positions to Jules. Angela and Karl were about to be shot by a firing squad when the French guns aimed true, routed the enemy, and left Angela and Karl, in each other's arms, at the base of a crucifix in the rubble of a church.[64] Although Karl became a prisoner of war, Angela persuaded Jules to arrange his release, and she brought him back to America. The last image in the film is the Statue of Liberty.

Although we have seen Germans torpedoing the ship of a neutral country and killing its American women and children passengers, raping French civilians, and shooting old men, mothers, and young children, and although we have even seen Karl nearly rape Angela, she still loves him, brings him home, and, we presume, marries him in the shadow of Lady Liberty.

This film portrayed the full range of enemy stereotypes that would become obligatory in succeeding World War I war films—an officer replete with monocle and little mustache and German soldiers drinking wine from broken-necked bottles, wantonly destroying paintings, leering and lunging at civilian women, and murdering children and old people. Yet the successful resolution of the romantic conflict established at the beginning of the narrative included Karl; the war had delayed but not changed its conventional course.

As in *Romance of the Redwoods*, the character Pickford played forgave and loved a man who had, for a time, been "bad." In both films she not only forgave and loved the man, she also saved his life. The spunk and cheerfulness her audiences had come to expect of "Little Mary" manifested itself again in these two "DeMille type" films where she played a young adult. Still, the criticisms of *A Romance of the Redwoods* did affect future choices of Pickford vehicles. While there had been no time to alter the narrative of *The Little American* and damage control was handled in its promotion, it is significant that this film was followed by *Rebecca of Sunnybrook Farm* and *A Little Princess*. In both films, both based on classic children's literature, Pickford played a child. *Stella Maris*, the third film to follow *The Little American*, was a drama. Here, Lasky and Zukor hedged their bets. Pickford played two roles: the lovely, rich, young woman Stella Maris and the homely, impoverished, abused, and murdered girl, Unity Blake.

Promotion and Exhibition

> Naturally you will boost the name of Mary Pickford for all you are
> worth. . . . It should be an easy matter to place window cards or the half
> sheet posters (the herald) in window of stores, at soda fountains (where a
> Mary Pickford sundae could be sold) and at counters where women's
> goods are sold.
>
> *Promotional suggestions offered in* Exhibitor's Trade Review,
> *14 July 1917*

By 26 May 1917, Lasky had received both the complaints about the character Pickford portrayed in *A Romance of the Redwoods* and still photographs from the newly completed *The Little American*. He was enthusiastic about the film. "It looks to me," he wrote DeMille, "like you are going to have a marvelously interesting picture."[65] It seems likely that the publicity department in New York realized the challenge it faced selling a film where Mary again portrayed a young woman, and, also as in *Redwoods*, one

Fig. 2.5. Promotional materials from *The Little American*. Patriotism was one of the film's main selling points.

who was attacked. Attempted rape would not play well with the "Kiddies." The selling points for *The Little American* needed careful consideration.

When the film was released in July, *Exhibitor's Trade Review* carried Artcraft's exploitation suggestions:

> Play up the patriotic elements of the story and mention that it is based on the present war. . . . For cards, throw-aways, etc., follow this wording: "Mary Pickford in 'The Little American.' "[66]

It would be more difficult to fault the young adult Pickford when she was nursing French soldiers and helping to defeat the Hun, while, at the same time, the film would be able to target a more specialized audience—young adult women. It would also be more difficult to fault a character wearing dresses designed by Lucile, Lady Duff Gordon, then a well-known British couturiere who had opened up shop in New York and Chicago and who had begun to design clothes for the Sears Roebuck catalog.[67]

It was with the release of *The Little American* that Famous Players began seriously to promote the tag line "America's Sweetheart."[68] Artcraft's exploitation suggestions end by offering possible headlines: "See America's Sweetheart in *The Little American*," "American Girl Helps France," "She is Helping to Defeat Germany," "Little Mary's Latest," "Plucky Girl Helps in War."[69] Artcraft's suggestions for promoting *The Little American* by linking Mary with patriotic action and women's goods marked a change in Pickford's persona. She was no longer only "Little Mary," her previous appellation; she was "Our Mary," representing an ideal of modern American youth and femininity, and linked inexorably with consumer culture. Part of her audience still resisted such nuancing. Exhibitors voiced a range of opinion about Mary's success in the role of Angela Moore. Some responses registered uncertainty about the appropriateness of the role for the actress at the same time they praised the film.

> Third run to turn away business. Not a good Pickford part, however. Drew good business. A patriotic picture with unnecessary brutal detail. Without this the picture would have been much better. Star misplaced in the production.[70]

Still, most of the reviews in newspapers around the country were positive, and Pickford brought down the house when she appeared at Clune's Auditorium in Los Angeles.

Fig. 2.6. Advertisement for *The Little American* in *Motion Picture News*, 7 July 1917. Timeliness was another selling point used in the film's promotional campaign.

It was announced in the newspapers that "America's Sweetheart" would greet the audience on opening night. . . . All the seats in the theater had been filled, the lobby was stuffed with people, and for a block east and west of the building traffic was well nigh impeded.

When the little Artcraft star stepped out upon the stage, there was an ovation such as a victorious general might expect to receive from a frenzied populace. For ten minutes the house shook with a storm of applause.

At last "Our Mary" was able to make herself heard and she made a very brief address that brought forth another tumult. In it she told the audience that no greater joy could come to her than to know that "The Little American" was stirring the hearts of the nation's picture patrons to a higher realization of their duty, and a stronger sense of patriotism. [71]

One departure from the generally favorable reception enjoyed by *The Little American* nearly marred its success. Major Funkhouser, the movie censor in Chicago, found much to decry in the film.

Chicago

I cannot pass this picture BECAUSE it would offend the Germans here, who did not start this war.
Major Funkhouser, Chicago film censor quoted in Chicago Tribune,
3 July 1917[72]

Der Major Woof
headline in a Chicago daily paper quoted in Variety,
20 July 1917[73]

On 3 July 1917, Mae Tinee, the movie writer for the *Chicago Tribune*, alerted readers of her daily column that Major Funkhouser, the chief of the censor board of Chicago, had banned *The Little American* because it might offend the city's German residents. Tinee blasted his decision. "Let us hope that the Major will rub the sleepy seeds from his eyes in the near, near future, discover that the United States is at war with Germany, and that the picture in question is not only anti-German but is pro-American. . . . "[74] The photograph opposite Tinee's column was a still from the film showing Mary Pickford as Angela Moore talking with the German officer. Its caption read "Mary Pickford Pleading with the German Colonel in 'The Little American.' " On the next day, the Fourth of July, Tinee took her crusade off the movie page and into the news section of the paper. The headline threw down the gauntlet. "Let Funkhouser Cast Filmy Eye on This Array! 'Little American' in Other Cities Passed by Censors." The article's lead asked, not so rhetorically, "Why do the movie fans rage?" and Tinee mustered her evidence that Funkhouser had made a serious mistake in refusing to allow *The Little American* to be shown in Chicago. She quoted from a favorable review in the *New York Tribune;* she reported on the answers she had received to her queries of other cities where the film was scheduled to play. Washington, D.C., Boston, Pittsburgh, Philadelphia, a number of cities in Ohio, Detroit, Worcester, Massachusetts, Newark, New Jersey, and Buffalo, New York, all found the film acceptable for their citizens.[75] Making the most of a windfall, The Evanston Strand, a theater in suburban Chicago, booked the film, advertising "COME TO EVANSTON, You Cannot See This Picture in Chicago. Every True American Should See This Great Masterpiece."[76] Tinee continued her barrage on 6 July, reporting that Artcraft was suing to force Funkhouser to rescind his ban. Artcraft not only sued. In a tactic we shall see employed by George Kleine in promoting *The Unbeliever*, the distributor arranged for a private showing of *The Little American*. Guests were invited to view the film and render their verdict. As the *Chicago Tribune* reported, "The owners of Mary Pickford's newest film play, 'The Little American,' have arranged for a private showing of the film and Maj. Funkhouser, the critical second deputy, wasn't invited." Among the invited guests were an array of Chicago's opinion makers: the president of the University of Chicago, prominent church leaders, a representative of the state Attorney General's office, city aldermen, and society women.[77] The day after the special screening the *Chicago Tribune* reported the unanimous results of this select poll. " 'The Little American' should be shown!"[78]

In more official proceedings, a jury was impanelled, and Judge Sabath set to rule on the merits of Artcraft's case by 13 July. The atmosphere in his courtroom was charged. The *Chicago Tribune*'s reporter noted, "When Carl H. Pierce, agent for the film company, stated that there were no longer any Germans in America, it took considerable rapping by bailiffs to restore order."[79] Funkhouser had not only defied the movie-goers, movie writers, and aldermen of the city of Chicago. In refusing to lift his ban voluntarily he also took on George Creel, the man President Wilson had appointed to head the Committee on Public Information, the government's official propaganda agency. *Variety* was also covering that story, with its broader implications for national film distribution.

When asked to review his [Funkhouser's] decision and possibly reverse it, he replied that he would allow the film to show provided it was considered alright by George Creel, the newly appointed government news censor. . . . Creel did view the picture and saw that it was intensely anti-German, it being a severe arraignment of the character of Prussian autocracy which America is fighting against. He then sent a wire to Funkhouser reading: "Have just seen film picture entitled "The Little American." See nothing in it to justify refusal of a permit and feel strongly that the picture should be shown."

When the Major was asked what he would do in the light of the wire, he is reported to have replied "And who in the Hell is George Creel? His wings have been clipped already." Later Funkhouser denied making such a remark.[80]

The case was decided on 15 July. The headline read: "Jurors Say You Can See 'Little American' Film: Only One, Von Moos, Against Forcing Permit."[81] Aaron Jones of Chicago's Jones, Linick and Schaefer theater chain, began to make arrangements for exhibiting the newly legal film, and on 21 July it opened to the public at the Studebaker Theater. "The Chicago Public CAN SEE the Picture It Has Been Waiting for—the One the Censors Said Chicago Should Not See!" read the advertisement in the *Tribune*.[82] The story remained a news item in the motion picture trade papers through the end of July.[83]

The notoriety experienced by *The Little American* in Chicago was unusual, the film did not encounter this degree of opposition anywhere else during its run. Still, the case was significant. It illustrated the centralization and quick deployment possible within national production and distribution companies like Famous Players-Lasky and Artcraft, and it illustrated the importance of big city markets like Chicago to the successful—profitable—distribution of a film. It also illustrated the degree to which movies could excite the public. Funkhouser worried about the detrimental effects on Germans and German-Americans living in Chicago, while Tinee and others who advocated lifting the ban applauded the potential of the film to strengthen resolve on the homefront, encourage enlistment, and spark patriotism.

The controversy surrounding *The Little American* was also significant because it illustrated the rhetoric of "superpatriotism" which, strident enough that July in Chicago, would only increase in volume as the war progressed. This attitude of extreme chauvinism cast suspicion on the loyalty of German-Americans and the ethnic institutions that nourished

Fig. 2.7. Advertisement for *The Little American* in the *Chicago Tribune*, 17 July 1917. The Evanston Strand Theater capitalized on Funkhouser's refusal to allow the film to be shown in Chicago.

Fig. 2.8. Advertisement for *The Little American* in the *Chicago Tribune*, 21 July 1917. The Studebaker Theater also made use of the publicity attending *The Little American* in Chicago.

their culture and language. Calls went out for the abolition of German-language newspapers. The loyalty of Lutheran churchmen and their congregations was questioned. People with Germanic surnames were fair game for patriotic zealots. German-Americans couldn't win for losing. Even when German-Americans participated in the war effort on the home front, superpatriots warned, "Beware of the German-American who wraps the Stars and Stripes around his German body."[84] Superpatriotism would subtend the efforts of the American Protective League in the film studios in Los Angeles, and ultimately this repressive attitude would contribute to the suspicion and fear that led townspeople in Collinsville, Illinois, to lynch Robert Paul Prager, a German-American who had lived in the United States since 1905. The townspeople were convinced Prager was preparing to sabotage a mine in nearby Maryville.[85] A man like Funkhouser, banning a film called *The Little American*—starring "Our Mary"—out of concern for the feelings of German-Americans was fighting an uphill battle.

Ultimately, the court decided the fate of *The Little American* in Chicago. Perhaps because of the brouhaha surrounding its exhibition, it played a long run in the city and met with favorable exhibitor response. After closing at the Studebaker, where it had opened triumphantly, if belatedly, on 21 July, it immediately reopened at the Castle Theater. Manager Weil wrote to the column "What the Picture Did for Me," in the exhibitor's trade paper, *Motography* (published in Chicago), that *The Little American* was "one of Mary Pickford's greatest pictures. The finest production ever played at this theater. Excellent business."[86] He wrote back a second time. "We are holding this over for a second capacity week at the Castle. It is fine and pleases all patrons."[87]

Mary Pickford herself did not enter the fray in Chicago. She remained America's Sweetheart, wearing gowns designed by Lucile. Pickford also began to participate in a publicity strategy of allying herself with causes to aid soldiers overseas and the government at home. As we shall see in the next section, reports of Pickford's war-related work appeared in the press alongside advertisements for her nonwar-related firms, like *Rebecca of Sunnybrook Farm* and *The Little Princess*. In a July 1917 issue of the *Minneapolis Tribune*, Pickford was shown giving an ambulance used in *The Little American* to the American Red Cross. The headlines read: "Mary Pickford Urges All Film Stars to Contribute Ambulances to the Red Cross."[88] In August, the *Milwaukee Journal*, the major newspaper in another city with a large German population, reported that she had purchased a second

Mary Pickford Starts Ambulance

Having presented an ambulance to the local Re Cross, Mary Pickford is now industriously at work at ranging to have a number of the popular photodramati

Mary Pickford presenting her second ambulance for service in France Lieutenant Henry Woodward.

Fig. 2.9. As part of the promotion of *The Little American,* Mary Pickford donated an ambulance to the Red Cross. From *Motography,* 28 July 1917.

ambulance and was "binding herself to maintain both this and another ambulance she had earlier given the same organization." This story, entitled "Little Mary Patriotic," closed by noting, "Miss Pickford recently addressed a mass meeting of 10,000 people in San Francisco to stimulate the purchase of Liberty Bonds."[89] On the same day this piece appeared in the *Milwaukee Journal,* the "Pictorial Weekly" of the *Chicago Tribune* featured her photograph, with a caption that read: " 'The Little American' Mary Pickford, presenting Wallace Reid of the Lasky Home Guard [DeMille's regiment] with the regiment's colors. We predict that Little Mary with her braid and buttons, will be setting the fashion."[90] The actress had fused with her role, and Lucile had designed her "uniform."[91]

Serving the Homefront

> Known throughout the nation as "America's Sweetheart," Mary Pickford
> is readily living up to what might be expected of the owner of title in the
> present great crisis. Since President Wilson's declaration of war, "Our
> Mary" has devoted considerable time and personal effort in furthering
> the cause of her country.
>
> Motography, *7 July 1917*[92]

Partly as a result of playing Angela Moore in *The Little American*, Mary
Pickford came to be seen by her public as a model "little American." The
promotion for the film renamed her "Our Mary," and "America's Sweetheart," and both names stuck. Mary spent the remaining months of World
War I helping to win the war "Over There" by boosting the government's
efforts to rally the homefront. These activities functioned to enhance her
image as *America's* Sweetheart and *Our* Mary. This image, in turn, helped
guide public expectation of the characters she would play in her films, in
addition to garnering Pickford the goodwill of her fans. It also cast the
shadow of the war on all her films, those with no narrative relation to the
war—the majority of her work—as well as *Johanna Enlists*, her second
war-related film.

As early as 7 July 1917, the *New York Mirror* reported the following:
"Mary Pickford is thanked by San Francisco mayor. Liberty Loan Committee Also Expresses Appreciation of her Work."[93] That same month, the
rotogravure section of the *New York Times* showed "Our Mary," dressed in
a military-style suit, delivering a fully equipped ambulance to Lieutenant
Henry Woodward for use by the Red Cross in France.[94] Later in the month
the *Times* reported that she was trying to interest other picture stars in
outfitting an entire ambulance unit.[95] She got press coverage for performing in benefits for the French Emergency Hospital Committee, for giving
toys used in *The Little Princess* to French war orphans, and for "adopting"
the six hundred soldiers of the 143rd California Field Artillery, and 144
aviators of the 14th Aero Squadron.[96] As their "godmother" Mary hosted
parties for the soldiers, kept them supplied with cigarettes, and presented
them with lockets, containing her photograph, when they went overseas.
In return, *Motography* reported that 143rd made Mary an honorary colonel, and that Colonel Fanuef, their commanding officer, presented "Our
Mary," with a silver loving cup from the regiment."[97] The *Toledo Blade*
reported that she started a fund for the Red Cross, that she also led a
recruiting parade in San Francisco, and that she did handiwork. And it

continued: "Studio actors knit with Mary Pickford. Notwithstanding the fact that the famous star is more than 'doing her bit.' She sets Example for Others in Famous Players-Lasky Studio."[98] In addition, she raised money for the United States Treasury Department's Liberty Loan Campaigns by making speeches around the country, and she starred in "100% American" a short narrative film made for the 4th Liberty Loan Campaign by Famous Players-Lasky.

Her character in this film was independent and spunky, like Jenny Lawrence, Angela Moore, and Rebecca of Sunnybrook Farm. A cast of five, including Mary and Monte Blue, enacted the idea that "There are two factors in the great war: One abroad and one at home. Over there: Democracy battling Autocracy. Over here—Will Power battling Temptation." Mary listened to a bond salesman speaking at a carnival and took heed of his pleas to "Be a Bond Spendthrift." She abstained from buying ice cream and walked twenty-seven blocks home instead of paying a nickel to take the street car. Soon Mary saved enough money to buy a bond. After a few twists, the plot concluded on a note of victory. The "boys" came home, and Mary and a soldier friend led the grand march at the 100-percent American ball. The film closed with another, direct pitch for war bonds. The Kaiser, carrying boxes labeled Clown Prince, Autocracy, Brute Force, Kulture, Atrocities, and Militarism, teetered on a tightrope suspended between schematic France and Germany and suspended over the "soup." Mary picked up a softball labeled "Fourth Liberty Loan," threw it, and knocked the Kaiser figure into the "soup." As Mary looked straight at the camera, the title read, "Yours may be the Bond to knock him off his perch." The last image of the film follows with Mary pointing directly at the audience (a stance reminding viewers of "Uncle Sam Wants You" posters that were also in wide circulation).

Pickford accomplished this war work as she continued to meet her contractual demands, releasing a film about every two months over the course of the war. Her public could follow the promotional campaigns for these nonwar-related comedies and dramas, and they could also follow her progress around the country selling war bonds. Her war work was also used to promote her films.

Even though the narrative of *How Could You, Jean?*, released in June 1918, bore absolutely no relation to World War I, its pressbook offered exhibitors feature articles entitled "Mary Pickford Busy Working in Pictures and Aiding Uncle Sam," and "Uncle Sam Stops Filming of Picture: Mary Pickford's Film Work Interrupted by Patriotic Duty Call." In the

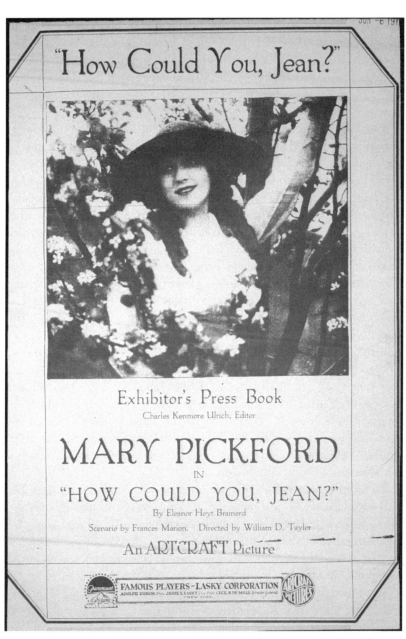

Figs. 2.10–11. Here and on facing page, two images from the press book for *How Could You, Jean?* Although the film had nothing to do with World War I, exhibitors were encouraged to promote Little Mary's patriotism in their advertising.

(Continued from Page 13)

MARY PICKFORD A COOK
IN HER NEW PHOTOPLAY

**Charming Artcraft Star Will Be Seen in
Another Delightful Role**

WANTED—A good cook, not too good looking, but just average.

That isn't the way it was advertised, but it might have been for all the good it did pretty "Jean Mackaye," an impoverished aristocratic girl, when she sought a situation as a cook. The applicants for a cook's position just wouldn't have "Jean" because they were afraid—well, they couldn't "get it" that good looks and good cooks could have anything in common.

Mary Pickford plays "Jean" in her next picture, "How Could You, Jean?" which will be displayed at the .... Theatre next .... and it gives her another opportunity to display her rare versatility, so well shown in "Rebecca," "Stella Maris," "Amarilly of Clothesline Alley," "M'liss," all entirely different characterizations. As "Jean," Miss Pickford essays a role which it is believed, will be a worthy successor to her portrayals of the last year which have made her position at the top of the list of the world's screen artists, more secure than ever.

UNCLE SAM STOPS
FILMING OF PICTURE

**Mary Pickford's Film Work Interrupted by
Patriotic Duty Call**

UNCLE SAM nearly played havoc with Mary Pickford's newest photoplay, "How Could You, Jean?" It was just after the starting of the picture that "Our Mary" was asked by Secretary McAdoo to come to Washington and aid the Third Liberty Loan drive, and Director William D. Taylor almost forgot that he, too, was a patriot when he viewed his schedule daily.

The Liberty Loan drive almost drove the thoughts of the picture out of the minds of both star and director, particularly, when towards the approach of the time to leave California, the weather man unpatriotically took a hand in the proceedings and provided a superabundance of cloudy weather.

As it was, despite the desperate efforts to get through in time, several scenes had to go over until the return of Miss Pickford from her swing around the circle as another of her "bits" to win the war. "How Could You, Jean?" will be shown at the .... Theatre next ...., and Manager ——— predicts that the demand for seats will be enormous.

CAN BEAUTY SOLVE
SERVANT PROBLEM?

**Mary Pickford Supplies Answer in New
Picture, "How Could You, Jean?"**

WHAT chance has a pretty girl in the solution of the servant problem? That's a question that has been discussed ever since persons of means engaged persons less fortunately situated to do their menial work.

Mary Pickford, in her forthcoming photoplay, "How Could You, Jean?", which will be shown at the .... Theatre next .... solved the question by hiding her beauty behind the camouflage of a green Swedish servant, after wife after wife gazed upon her pretty face in the employment office and "passed her up" as a girl who was too good-looking to possibly be any kind of a cook. The assumption of the disguise is just the beginning of one of the most delightful roles ever assumed by the acknowledged queen of the screen. The supporting players in the picture are of the usual high Artcraft standard.

15

Fig. 2.11

73

film, Pickford played an aristocratic but impoverished young woman who adopted a Swedish disguise in order to gain employment as a cook. By the time *How Could You, Jean?* was released, Mary Pickford had spent eleven months performing a variety of well-publicized war work. More subtly this time, the press book suggested exhibitors conduct a mail campaign. The sample letter included the following statement:

> The popularity of "America's Sweetheart," aside from her genius as a motion picture player, will make this presentation at our theater an epochal event. Coupled with these qualifications, "How Could You, Jean," is a photoplay of exceptional human interest, in which "Our Mary" has a role which will both delight her admirers and add new laurels to her wreath of fame as a screen player of the highest attainments.[99]

Thus, Mary's popularity in the months prior to the release of *How Could You, Jean?* could have been measured by the quantity of articles and photographs in the trade and popular press reporting the number of war bonds she sold, the numbers of toys she gave to French orphans, and the numbers of lockets and cigarettes she gave to infantry men and aviators. Whether the audience was coming to see a "Mary Pickford" film, an Artcraft film, or the movie for its own sake, their expectations about what they were buying with their ticket were based on Pickford's public persona. This persona had developed in part from the roles she had played in her films, in part from her off-screen activities which were, at least during the nineteen months the United States was engaged in World War I, overwhelmingly war-related.

World War I did have an impact on film production. Some of the most prestigious and some of the most memorable films made and released during 1917 and 1918 were feature-length films with war-related narratives. Still, the impact of the war on the industry's production of its standard product was not pronounced, as the example of Pickford's war-time output illustrates. Genre, however, is not the sole determinant of war-relatedness. A study of the promotional suggestions and the cultural context for the reception of *How Could You, Jean?* directs our attention to the function of the star (and arguably other publicly known production workers) in our categorization of "the films of World War I."

3

Programming Theaters and Exhibiting
Movies in Wartime

And when the war is over and the country again filled with gladness, it
will be a difficult matter to wean patrons from the theaters that
established a clientele during the dark hour when entertainment was not
merely a pleasure but a necessity.

Adolph Zukor, Moving Picture World, *2 February 1918*[1]

DURING 1917 AND 1918, movie theater managers worked to make
their houses necessary to both their local patrons and the federal government. Like film producers, exhibitors accomplished this mission by adapting standard business practice: using their buildings, as well as the films
and live acts on their bills, to woo customers and aid the war effort. As
early as 1915, Epes Winthrop Sargent, author of *Picture Theater Advertising* (and columnist for *Moving Picture World*), had urged managers to promote their theaters as vigorously as they promoted their entertainment
programs. "Films are but a part of what you have to sell. Advertise all your
features."[2] In choosing films, both feature-length and shorts, and in the
methods adopted to promote such film programs, theater managers reacted
to the war; even while the strategies already in place for running their
businesses remained constant. From Roxy Rothapfel, the trend-setting
manager of the Rivoli Theater in New York City, to C. W. Martin at the
Temple Theater in McCook, Nebraska, exhibitors' ultimate goal was to
make their theaters an integral part of their communities. Participating in
the war on the homefront, film exhibitors were simultaneously creating
goodwill for their houses, and they knew it. Like film producers, they were
operating well within the boundaries of practical patriotism.

On 27 December 1917, the Rivoli opened at Broadway and 49th, New
York City. Described by a writer for *Moving Picture World* as "The Last
Word in Picture Palaces," Roxy Rothapfel's newest theater included an
illumination system capable of flooding the auditorium with colored lights,

a scent dispersal system to fill the auditorium with "suggestive" aromas, and a stage setting entitled "The Conservatory of Jewels," promising "to make even blasé Broadway open its eyes." The film chosen to inaugurate the Rivoli was a Paramount-Artcraft release, *The Modern Musketeer*, starring Douglas Fairbanks, but this feature made up only the second half of the program. It opened with "The Victory for Democracy," a pageant that traced American history from Plymouth Rock until "the United States entered the present war to make the world safe for the principles on which the nation was founded." This was followed by soloists, orchestral numbers, a ballet and "film novelties of every sort."[3]

The United States had been fighting in the World War for eight months when Roxy Rothapfel opened the Rivoli. The events of the war filled newspapers and mass circulation magazines. The Treasury Department had conducted two Liberty Bond Drives, and the United States Food Administration had enrolled 10.5 million people in its Food Conservation Campaign. Representatives from all branches of the motion picture industry had met with a broad spectrum of governmental agencies to plan how its members could best aid the war effort. The war—its homefront preparations and its battlefront news—preoccupied the government, the film industry, and the American people. In opening his 2,500 seat theater, Rothapfel bowed to the topicality of the war, but not in his choice of a feature film.[4] Instead, the war entered the Rivoli through the "Victory for Democracy" pageant and, no doubt, through some of the other live acts, newsreels, and film novelties with which he introduced *The Modern Musketeer*. Almost redundantly a review of the Rivoli's opening concluded: "The entertainment he [Rothapfel] will provide will be entirely institutional in any event, and it will be a case of going to the Rivoli to see a show, not going to see a certain picture at the Rivoli."[5]

Going to the Movies

It is up to every exhibitor in the country to bend every effort toward doing his "bit" whenever and wherever possible. The exhibitor is a potent factor in that all important thing, public opinion. I do not mean by this that he should clutter his program with war films and news pictures of soldiers. . . .

Harold Edel, Moving Picture World, *22 December 1917*[6]

We can gain a more complete understanding of the variety of ways theater managers of the period invoked the timeliness of World War I—while simultaneously working to increase, entertain, and inform their audiences—by reconstructing the typical theater-goer's walk through its lobby and into the auditorium, to focus finally on its screen. Many of the following examples are culled from the pages of exhibitor trade papers, particularly *Moving Picture World* and *Motion Picture News*. Film exhibitors sent items to such columns as "Advertising for Exhibitors" (Sargent's column) and "Live Wire Exhibitors," sharing tactics that had worked and asking for feedback from their colleagues. Thus, specific ploys may have sparked imitation, and, in addition to providing descriptions of what exhibitors were actually doing, these columns are indicative of what was thought to be appropriate and effective business management. While this catalog of exhibition practices is illustrative of theater managers' responses to the specific situation of war, it also illustrates promotional strategies already practiced by exhibitors and espoused by the trade press. In his 1915 book *Picture Theater Advertising*, Sargent had pointed out: "Advertising as it is generally understood, is the art of selling by means of publicity, but advertising is not merely a matter of printing from types, of posting lithographs, of sending out a sandwich man. The real advertising is everything that may attract the trade."[7] The following examples should be considered in this light, as forms of advertising designed to attract trade. While war-related activities taking place in movie theaters informed citizens of governmental needs like food conservation and financial support, they simultaneously promoted the movie theater sponsoring them. It is also important to note that homefront programming was not necessarily part of a coordinated promotional campaign for a war film. Thus, the advertising value of allowing the Marines to set up an enlistment booth in a theater lobby, and in permitting speakers to lecture about the causes of the war during a film's intermission, lay first in attracting customers to a specific theater, and only secondly to the feature film being shown there. In programming and promoting their theaters during American involvement in World War I, theater managers had a great number of options.

Outside the Theater

The theater's facade could be decorated, making it a prominent sight on the block and manifesting a patriotic attitude. In Boston, the front of the Globe Theater was decked with flags and bunting that would remain, said manager Frank Meagher, until "something more definite breaks regarding the war." Not to be outdone, the manager of the Modern Theater, also in

Boston, unfurled the second largest flag to be found in that city, and flew it suspended from steel cables over Washington Street.[8]

Theater managers could invoke the war in the very act of selling tickets. In May of 1917, the Stanley Theater in Philadelphia sold its tickets to customers on provision that they agreed to respect the flag.[9] When Catherine Russell Bleeker took over management duties at the Broadway Theater in New York City, she announced that soldiers and sailors would be admitted free, "all days except Sat. and Sun. and holidays."[10] Free admission was not the only way exhibitors could demonstrate their civic-mindedness at the door. They could, and often did, donate a portion of the ticket receipts to various war fund drives. In Seattle, in the summer of 1917, the manager of the Clemmer Theater announced that the "entire receipts on June 25 as well as the salaries of theater employees for that day would be donated to the Red Cross."[11] The Clemmer drew even more attention to itself by hiring small boys to walk around town costumed as huge red crosses. C. W. Martin of the Temple Theater in McCook, Nebraska, donated his proceeds for a week to the First Liberty Bond Drive.[12] While donating to the Red Cross or Liberty Bond drives was a timely response to the war, the strategy of contributing to worthy causes was already a part of the theater managers' promotional repertoire. Sargent, in the 1915 *Picture Theater Advertising*, advised:

> If there is a movement to collect a fund, let him [the manager] not only be a contributor to the fund. He should aid to influence others. He should let his house be designated as a depository. He should give a benefit matinee. He should make his theater a rallying point.

This belief that the exhibitor should "influence others," was voiced before United States entry into the war. Without the pressure of the national emergency to motivate action, columnist Sargent pointed out the benefits accruing to exhibitors who took his advice: prominence to the house and prestige to the theater manager.[13]

Inside the Lobby

As the advertising value of donating money to civic projects was recognized and advocated as good theater management, so the use of the lobby to attract trade had likewise been recognized. *Picture Theater Advertising* devoted a chapter to "The Lobby as Advertisement," and a 1927 handbook on theater management by Sargent and John Barry more clearly specified the role played by decoration in the lobby: "The theater lobby, like any other show window, sells the institution."[14] During World War I, the theater manager often chose to fill his show window with war-related decoration. Whether the feature film on the bill was war-related or not, the theater's lobby offered the exhibitor further opportunities to do "a little something of special effectiveness . . . bearing on the war."[15]

In its 18 April 1917 issue, *Moving Picture World* apprised its exhibitor subscribers of the availability of a "Beautiful Fac-Simile Painting" with dimensions of thirty by forty inches, presented in a three-inch gold frame and selling for ten dollars: "The President's face is done in water color and oils, and the American Flag is worked up beautifully in artistic reproduction of the proper shade of red and blue, giving in all a permanent display for the lobby."[16] The United States Food Administration also offered a free, six-color poster that they urged exhibitors to have "framed and kept permanently on exhibition in the theaters."[17] Douglas Fairbanks linked the promotion of *Wild and Wooly,* a western in which he starred, with a campaign to raise money for the Red Cross. Exhibitors should

> present an attractive lobby display with placards urging patrons of the theater to contribute to the Red Cross Fund. A coin box will be placed in the lobby of the theater so that patrons may donate their 'bit' on passing in and out of the theater.[18]

Harold Edel, manager of New York's Strand Theater and columnist for *Moving Picture World,* offered exemplary conduct to fellow exhibitors until his death in October 1918. On 18 February 1918, in the lobby of his theater, Edel unveiled a bronze tablet bearing the names of all the Strand employees in the Service.[19] In addition to recognizing service personnel, theater lobbies could also, as already mentioned, be used to advance enlistment efforts. *Motion Picture News* suggested contacting local recruiting officers and offering them access to theaters, both for actual recruitment and for less direct recruitment through posters, arguing that: "It is good policy to do this. Your patrons will know you are doing it for the common good, and it will help the standing of any theater to be always first in such thoughtfulness."[20]

In the Auditorium

By the time patrons had bought or been given their tickets and had passed through the theater lobby on their way to seats in the auditorium, theater managers, or "live wire exhibitors," as *Motion Picture News* called its most innovative readers, had ample opportunity to call attention to their patriotism and to their theaters. Once inside the auditorium, additional strategies were tapped.

Music roused patriotic feelings, in yet another example of adapting existing exhibition practice to a specific situation. Sargent's *Picture Theater Advertising* had also noted that music could serve as an advertisement for the theater. In January 1918, *Moving Picture World* reported that Baltimore had made the playing of the National Anthem obligatory at every "public function, concert or entertainment."[21] The *New York Times* reported that the Rialto Theater had received so many requests for patriotic music that it had hired two additional trumpeters.[22]

The stages of the theaters were available for a number of war-related purposes. In Buffalo, New York, the managers of the Star and Teck Theaters used them as propaganda space, placing large signs there that asked, "Have you bought a second Liberty Bond?"[23] In addition, the government's propaganda bureau, the Committee for Public Information (CPI) sponsored the Four Minute Men, a corps of 75,000 men and women in some 5,200 communities in the United States who were available to make talks of four-minute duration during the reel changes at motion picture theaters. Close study of this organization yields information about the federal government's assessment of the audience for movies. It also highlights the government's belief in the possibility of forging a united polity and the probability that such unification could occur at the movie theater.

The Four Minute Men

On 31 March 1917, Donald M. Ryerson made a speech, most likely on the importance of military preparedness, during intermission at the Strand Theater in Chicago.[24] Ryerson was co-founder with Medill McCormick of the Four Minute Men, whose name was an allusion to the Minute Men of the Revolutionary War and also a direct reference to the amount of time it took to make reel changes in the movie theater. The function of the Four Minute Men was to "provide a national mouthpiece under centralized direction at Washington," one that worked with the patriotic assistance of the motion picture industry, through which the messages of the Government departments to the people [could] be cleared without confusion."[25] Whether the conditions ensuring such a lack of confusion resulted from faith in the clarity of the message, faith in the homogeneity of the audience, or something intrinsic to the movie-going experience was not addressed.

The Four Minute Men had a hierarchical organizational structure. A national director in Washington, D.C., supervised associate directors in various sections of the country. Under these associate directors were state chairmen, local chairmen, and finally the Four Minute Men themselves. The director in Washington assigned speaking topics. With each topic came a "Bulletin of Instructions" for preparing the speech and a "Budget of Material" containing facts deemed necessary to that preparation. Sample outlines and speeches were also provided. Four Minute speakers were encouraged to tailor the material they were provided to suit their individual personalities, but they were not to veer from the assigned topic, and they were not to exclude any of the main points.

The array of topics covered by the Four Minute Men indicates the concerns of the government and highlights those topics on which it needed a public consensus. For instance, from the beginning of the war until January of 1918 movie audiences across the country might have heard speeches about:

> The Liberty Loan, 23 May–15 June
> The Red Cross Hundred Million Dollar Campaign, 18–25
> Food Conservation, 1–14 July
> Why We Are Fighting, 23 July–5 August
> A Nation in Arms, 6–26 August
> What Our Enemy Really Is, 26 August–23 September
> Onward to Victory, 24 September–7 October
> The Second Liberty Loan, 8–28 October
> The Food Pledge Campaign, 29 October–4 November
> Maintaining Morals and Morale, 12–25 November
> Carrying the Message, 27 November–23 December[26]

The goal of the Four Minute Men was to deliver specific, fairly uniform messages across the broad front of the American movie-going public. Writing in 1939, James R. Mock and Cedric Larson, historians of the CPI, made an analogy between the Four Minute Men and radio broadcasting. In their view, these speakers were "America's nation-wide hook-up . . . united under CPI leadership for coordinated and synchronized expression of Wilsonian doctrine."[27] In the summer of 1918, before the advent of commercial radio broadcasting, 35,000 Four Minute Men echoed President Wilson by delivering his Fourth of July speech in theaters across the country.[28]

To whom did this "mighty chorus" speak? University of Chicago professor Bertram Nelson, who established a school for Four Minute Men in Chicago, characterized the Four Minute Men's constituency: it was not only the illiterate, it was also the apathetic. "Every night eight to ten million people of all classes, all degrees of intelligence, black and white, young and old, rich and poor, meet in the moving picture houses of this country, and among them are many of these silent ones who do not read or attend meetings. . . . "[29] In a speech addressed to the "15,000 Four Minute Men of the United States," President Wilson also voiced the prevailing ideas about the role of the organization and the makeup of its audience.

> Men and nations are at their worst or their best in any great struggle. The spoken word may light fires of passion and unreason or it may inspire to highest action and noblest sacrifice a nation of freemen. Upon you Four Minute Men, who are charged with a command of your audience, will rest in a considerable degree, the task of arousing and informing the great body of our people so that when the record of these days is complete we shall read page for page with the deeds of army and navy the story of the unity, the spirit of sacrifice, the unceasing labor, the high courage of the men and women at home who held unbroken the inner lines.[30]

The Committee for Public Information estimated that over the course of the war the Four Minute Men made 755,190 speeches to a total of 314,454,514 people. While not all of these speeches were given in movie theaters, a significant proportion were.[31] Primary source material expressing exhibitors' points of view about allowing Four Minute Men into their places of business is scarce, as the issue seems not to have been covered by the trade papers. This in itself may indicate a lack of resistance on the part of theater managers. J. Seymour Curry, in his history of the Four Minute Men in Illinois, noted that William Brady and Adolph Zukor in New York, and Ascher and Schaefer, heads of a Chicago area theater chain, were "quick to see the great patriotic service they might do the nation" by lending the Four Minute Men their support.[32] They were also quick to see the benefits of such service.

Curry reported that the actual arrangements between the Four Minute

Men and the theater managers in Illinois were worked out between representatives of the Four Minute Men and Joseph Hopp, chairman of the Executive Committee of the Motion Picture Exhibitors League of America. At a national level, the Four Minute Men obtained the sanction of the National Association of the Motion Picture Industry (NAMPI), which named that speaking group as the sole official representative of the government in the movie theaters of the United States. Curry pointed out that this guarantee of exclusive access was in the film exhibitors' best interest as it insulated them from "scores of unreasonable demands which might be made upon them from a multiplicity of so-called 'patriotic' organizations or individuals of good, bad and indifferent character."[33] This gate-keeping function helped to protect the national message from individuals speaking words not scripted in Washington, individuals potentially fragmenting rather than consolidating public opinion about war-related issues.

Government officials were careful not to transgress the theater-owner's goodwill. Reminders occurred with some frequency even as late as 24 December 1918 that Four Minute Men must not speak longer than four minutes.[34] The final bulletin stated, "Let us not yield to the sentiment that this is our last appearance . . . and permit ourselves to exceed our distinguishing time limit."[35] Care was taken in the selection, assignment, and training of speakers. For instance, in Cincinnati a board composed of a teacher of speech, a movie theater manager, and a Four Minute Man screened all aspiring Four Minute Men to "see that they are up to a minimum standard of effectiveness, classifying them according to their relative abilities, so that the very best men may be sent to the more important theaters."[36] Chicago had the school for Four Minute Men established by Bertram Nelson, the University of Chicago professor. The federal government officially recognized the contribution of theater owners and managers in the fall of 1918 by issuing a certificate "in recognition of the patriotic service of granting to the Four Minute Men the exclusive privilege of speaking to the audience."[37]

Although the Four Minute Men were organized to speak only in movie theaters, by August 1917 they had branched out and were addressing church groups and civic organizations. A Women's Auxiliary, a university branch, and a Junior Four Minute Man program in the grade schools were developed. By October 1918, Four Minute Singing had been innovated, although it was stressed that "singing and speaking should be kept distinct, except that the singing will be introduced with a few explanatory and inspirational words." Again the sanctity of the time

Figs. 3.1–2. "Smiles" films provided a time-honored way to attract an audience into a theater to see themselves pictured on the screen. Above and on facing page, two images from the *Milwaukee Journal*, 10 and 11 October 1918.

limit was reiterated. "In neither case must the stage be held for more than four minutes. Four Minute singing, like four minute speaking means FOUR MINUTES."[38]

The Screen inside the Auditorium

Once the houselights dimmed and the movie-goers' attention was directed to the screen, the theater manager had a final opportunity to promote his

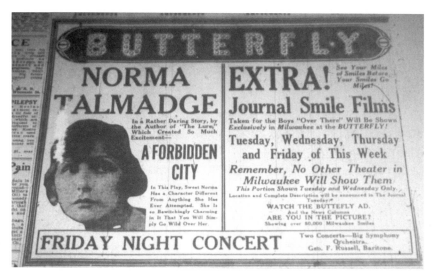

Fig. 3.2

theater by striking the patriotic chord. An advertisement in *Motion Picture News* read: "Attention Patriots Do Your Bit. Open or close every show with the Stars and Stripes. 60 feet or longer at only 10 cents a foot."[39] This patriotism by-the-foot was offered for sale by the American Bioscope Company. Slides were another option. The Excelsior Illustrating Company of New York sold "a few of the other beautifully handcolored patriotic slides, 25 cents."[40] Or exhibitors could make their own slides. Joseph Yeager, owner of a chain of theaters in Raton, New Mexico, showed slides of local men who had enlisted. "They [the slides] are making a hit now and he has a full set for later use should they be killed or perform some unusual service."[41] Exhibitors also made use of newsreels showing hometown boys at boot camp. Later in the war "smiles" films provided another way for exhibitors to connect their theaters to their community, their nation, and to the war in Europe. People were invited to stand on a particular street to be photographed by a cameraman, often employed by a local newspaper. The resulting film was to be sent to Europe and shown to the soldiers. These films were first screened in the local movie house, however, providing the exhibitor another time-honored way to attract the trade.

Finally, as was illustrated in the preceding chapter, in addition to these gimmicks, the exhibitor also had access to a variety of cartoons and short documentaries picturing the war and war-related activities with which he could surround his feature film.

Clearly, it was difficult for the theater-goer in New York, McCook, Nebraska, or Milwaukee, Wisconsin, to escape the war by going to the movies. Even if the featured film starred Douglas Fairbanks as *The Modern Musketeer* (1917) or Theda Bara as *Cleopatra* (1917), chances were good that the screening would begin with a rendition of the "Star Spangled Banner" and that slides would be shown advising patrons to substitute corn for wheat and fish for meat. Even cartoons like "O U-Boat" would serve to remind those in attendance of the world outside the theater.

Exhibitors' Rationale

Create in the minds of the local public [the belief] that your house is as necessary to the enjoyment of the films as are the films themselves. Then make it so.

Epes Winthrop Sargent, Moving Picture World,
29 December 1917[42]

Like Harold Edel and Roxy Rothapfel in New York, theater managers in cities like New Orleans, Seattle, and Buffalo, and in smaller towns like Raton, New Mexico, and Perry, Missouri, used the topicality and timeliness of the World War as one of the factors helping to determine how they would program and merchandise their theaters. At this point in the economic development of the film industry, the production and distribution branches were becoming vertically integrated, but the exhibition branch was still a separate entity. Although some theater chains were forming in Chicago and Philadelphia, among other cities, and although these independent theaters and chains of theaters depended upon film producers and distributors for their film product, theater managers cast themselves as competitors with the film producer for the public's loyalty.

Moving Picture World, a leading exhibitor trade paper encouraged an independent attitude in its readers: "Make people come to the theater because your house is the trademark of good shows. Don't ride on the popularity of a brand. Do just what the brand has done."[43] In so programming their entertainment and promoting their theater, film exhibitors were not acting alone, nor was public service their sole impetus. In adapting their business practices to the exigencies of the times, exhibitors were behaving like the businesses which surrounded their theaters. David M. Kennedy, a historian of the homefront, has pointed out that American businessmen had profited from the European preoccupation with the war during the neutrality period: the United States' economy came out of its 1913–1914 recession, and factories were operating at full capacity. "When neutrality ended in April 1917 businessmen moved to preserve and extend the enviable position they had enjoyed for more than two years."[44] Speaking even as the guns of August sounded overseas in 1914, Lewis J. Selznick declared, "So far as this company is concerned, the turmoil in Europe could not be all for the worse."[45] Exhibitors continued to promote timeliness after the Armistice in November 1918. Epes Winthrop Sargent's column "Advertising for Exhibitors" encouraged managers to "Watch for the returning soldiers. Make your house [theater] the place where they receive their official welcome. Don't try to make money out of it at the moment. Let it simply work for future business."[46]

During the World War I period, businesses advertising in newspapers around the country urged consumers not only to buy house dresses and pots and pans but also to buy War Savings Stamps. The Feagins Company in Los Angeles decorated its front window with models of missiles in a patriotic display, and the ranks of the Four Minute Men were filled with doctors, lawyers, and community businessmen. And film exhibitors were proving themselves fit members of any chamber of commerce: they developed long-range business strategies to make their theaters permanent and influential institutions within their communities, thus ensuring their longevity.

As well as responding to peer pressure from business colleagues, theater managers were also responding to the trade practices of the more nationally oriented film producers and distributors. In 1917–1918, major producer-distributors such as Famous Players-Lasky spent large sums on national advertising campaigns promoting their product; Paramount also sent "exploiteers" into the field to work with theater managers in the advertising and promotion of films at their theaters.[47] Pressbooks, like the one for *How Could You, Jean?* cited in Chapter Two, were full of tips to exhibitors and samples of posters and other promotional materials that local exhibitors could purchase from their film distributors. Thus newspaper advertisements in the *New York Times* and the *Chicago Tribune* for *The Little American* all made use of the same images of Mary Pickford— images originating in the pressbook for the film. Smaller distributors like

George Kleine also kept in close touch with theater managers via regional exchange agents, providing more channels for national influence on local practice.

In addition, conventional wisdom within the exhibition sector of the industry held that the theater manager had a civic duty to perform, and an image to build and maintain. In September of 1917, Sargent's "Advertising for Exhibitors" column published an "Exhibitor's Catechism": a list of questions that served the theater manager as an examination of his showman's conscience, pointing him to a variety of areas which needed attention if he wanted to attain fiscal salvation. Among those questions which addressed management issues, like cleanliness, admission price, and projection, were some that assumed the existence of a relationship between the theater manager and his community:

> What have I done to make my theater one of the community's social centers?
> Am I a member of the local merchant's organization?
> Have I ever attempted to get local merchants to cooperate with me for mutual benefit?[48]

Implicit in those questions was the belief that the theater should be a civic forum as well as a venue for entertainment, and that the theater manager should be a leading citizen as well as an entertainer. The point was made more explicitly in a short cautionary tale published in an April 1917 issue of *Motion Picture News*. Under the title "Be A Town Figure," was the story of an "old timer" and a "bright young fellow":

> The old timer ran a picture show in the "opera house." He charged an unvarying price of admission. His program was liked as he was liked— because both could be depended upon.
>
> Along came a bright young fellow with new-fangled notions who built himself a dazzling theater, installed sensational pictures and charged ten cents against the old timer's fifteen.[49]

In the face of this business competition, or "opposition," as it was called, the old timer did not change his business practices. He continued to be active in town affairs, unlike the bright young fellow who pinned his success solely on flashy gimmickry.

> The old timer changed his attitude—not a hair's breadth! . . . When
> Main Street was to be repaved, his voice carried its usual weight.
> When the question of a new wing for the high school came up, his
> opinion was taken as seriously as the town banker's.

This fable culminated in a moral lesson for the exhibitor. "At the end of the third year, the newcomer sprinted out of town on a trail of debts. Is the old timer still doing business? The last we heard of him he had been elected to the town board of trustees."[50]

Cooperation with other businesses and participation in community activities were ways of building goodwill for the movie theater. The assumption was that the more goodwill that accrued to one's house, the firmer was the foundation on which that institution rested. Barry and Sargent, expanding upon Sargent's 1915 how-to book for exhibitors, stressed the importance of goodwill but redirected attention to its real beneficiary: "One of the assets of any business institution is good will. Though intangible, it is very real. . . . It sells tickets when special production and outstanding bargain programs are not offered."[51]

Thus, theater managers allied themselves with the war effort in visible ways designed to attract trade and to build the base of their regular clientele. Flags were displayed, as were photographs of Wilson; exploitation stunts like costuming children as red crosses and sending them into the streets were tried; advertisements in newspapers offered free tickets to soldiers and families of soldiers. Newsreels of local boys in uniform or of local folk were screened to attract patrons. Advertisements for movies urged consumers to buy Liberty Bonds and also to come to the theater. Film exhibitors identified themselves with other businessmen in collecting for war funds, promoting recruitment, and providing their theaters to serve as forums for civic events. In the short term, these tactics helped exhibitors to fill the seats in their theaters; the long-term hope was that they would function strategically and help to institutionalize the theater within the community. A closer and more comprehensive look at exhibition in one American city, Milwaukee, Wisconsin, helps to bring the opportunities and the challenges faced by these business people during World War I into sharper focus. For while the federal government joined film producers and distributors in needing a mass audience, in Milwaukee, local tensions threatened to detour national efforts to communicate propaganda or entertainment.

Milwaukee, Wisconsin

> Our nation is involved in the greatest war of all history. . . . Since our
> participation in that struggle, the citizens of Milwaukee have worked
> with an admirable spirit to meet every need of the government and the
> community growing out of the war. They have done this without regard
> to their opinion of war or their views as to peace.
>
> *Inaugural Speech of Daniel Hoan, socialist mayor of Milwaukee,*
> *November 1918*[52]

The citizens of Milwaukee professed a full range of reasons for opposing
participation in World War I. First, being situated in the Midwest, it joined
neighboring farm states in its isolationist attitude to any involvement in the
conflict so far away.[53] Second, while Milwaukee was an urban rather than a
rural center, as of the 1910 census its population was 53.5 percent ethnic
German. The city boasted a vibrant Germanic culture including a
German-language newspaper, social clubs, and a brewing industry. Third
was the significant role of socialists, who traditionally opposed participation in war, in city politics. Socialists were elected to the Milwaukee city
council, the mayor's office, and the House of Representatives in 1916 and
1918, and Milwaukee supported a socialist newspaper, the *Milwaukee
Leader*. Finally, Wisconsin was represented in the Senate by the Progres-
sive Robert LaFollette, Sr., one of only six senators voting against Wilson's
declaration of war in April 1917. In the House of Representatives, nine of
the fifty members voting against the war were from Wisconsin. This combination of geographical, ethnic, and political characteristics dealt Wisconsin's and especially Milwaukee's public image a severe blow when it was
brought to national attention by the journalist Samuel Hopkins Adams in a
series of articles he wrote in 1918 for *Everybody's Magazine*. "To appreciate properly the Wisconsin situation, it is necessary to bear in mind the
extent and power of the alienizing influences." Hopkins closed his analy-
sis of the "Wisconsin situation" with the rather patronizing suggestion of a
potential good to be derived from American participation in the war: "Here
and now is Uncle Sam's opportunity to make this nephew state truly one of
the family."[54]

Wisconsin's officials, its business people, and its citizens replied by
pointing out that their state was the first to organize a State Council of
Defense on 12 April 1917. The Council aimed to educate Wisconsin citizens about the causes of the war and to protect the state from subversive
influences. County and local branches helped to carry out the Council's

goals. It published *Forward,* a weekly newspaper that informed citizens of the latest needs of the Food Administration, the Treasury Department, and the Red Cross.[55] Wisconsin also had a higher rate of enlistment than other midwestern states, and a lower percentage of men of military age who failed to respond to the draft. By January 1918, *Forward* boasted that one out of fifteen soldiers in France was from Wisconsin. The state had oversubscribed the first and second Liberty Loans as of January 1918 and had contributed one million dollars to the first Red Cross War fund.[56]

Milwaukee, like Wisconsin, did its civic duty. Once the United States entered the war, most socialists in the city worked for the war effort.[57] Mayor Daniel Hoan helped organize the Milwaukee County Council of Defense on 30 April 1917, serving as its chairman until the end of 1918. A. M. Simons, a journalist for the *Milwaukee Leader,* supported the government so actively that he needed to resign his position on the paper and was expelled from the party. He took a salaried position with the Wisconsin Defense League and directed the Speaker's Bureau that supervised the activities of the Four Minute Men. Socialists like Simons were not alone in putting government needs first; many ethnic Germans in Milwaukee demonstrated their allegiance in public ways. The Germania Building was renamed the Brumder Building and the statue of Germania standing in front was removed. Two banks—the Germania Bank and the German-American Bank—became the National Bank of Commerce and the American National Bank, respectively. The Deutscher Club suddenly became the Wisconsin Club and several hundred Milwaukeeans with German surnames had them "Americanized."[58] Milwaukee's theater managers, at once part of a national industry and a local constituency, participated in this civic public relations campaign for their state.

Going to the Movies—in Milwaukee

> Every Milwaukeean should see [*Hearts of the World*], partly because it is
> great Art, but even more because its plot is such as will uncover a
> deeper vein of patriotism in every man, woman and child with eyes to
> see and a heart to feel.
>
> *editorial*, Milwaukee Journal, *1 August 1918*[59]

Theater managers in Milwaukee enlisted with their colleagues around the country to win the war on the homefront. Even though Milwaukee's unique demographic profile provided an opportunity for exhibitors to act idiosyncratically as they programmed and promoted their houses, they fell in line

Fig. 3.3. Advertisement for *Our Allies in Action* in the *Milwaukee Journal*, 5 May 1917. Milwaukeeans were invited to find friends and relatives among the prisoners of war in this rare admission of the city's ethnic identity.

with practices standardized and disseminated through trade journals like *Moving Picture World* and *Motion Picture News*. In fact, I can document only one instance of theater programming or film promotion alluding to the ethnicity of 53 percent of Milwaukee's population, and this occurred soon after American entrance into the war. On 5 May 1917, the Paradise Theater showed *Our Allies in Action* and advertised: "See for yourself the battlefields where the stars and stripes will soon be planted. . . . [See] German prisoners of war. Some may be friends or acquaintances."[60]

Theater managers operated under their industry's mandate to fit their theater into the local community. In Milwaukee, this meant following the lead of business and civic leaders to try to foster a public image of 100-percent Americanism.[61] Movies, commerce, and American vitality achieved a perfect union in April 1918, when Gimbels department store hosted a Liberty Bond rally with Douglas Fairbanks as the government's salesman. In addition to lending financial support to the war effort through the purchase of Liberty Bonds, Milwaukeeans also contributed when they paid a war tax levied on movie tickets.

The *Milwaukee Journal*'s film writer calculated her city's share of the $3,988,860 that the government earned from its war tax on theater admissions: "The average per month for the district since the tax became effective has been 50,000 of which the city of Milwaukee had paid approximately 3/5 or 30,000. Of this it is figured that considerably over half is attributable to motion pictures."[62] Her statistics suggest that at least 750,000 tickets were sold in Milwaukee each month. The population of Milwaukee in 1920 was 459,147. Clearly, movie-going was a popular pastime. The same Hate-the-Hun movies, like *The Claws of the Hun, To Hell with the Kaiser*, and *The Kaiser, Beast of Berlin*, played in Milwaukee, over the course of the war, as in other cities and towns in the United States. Elmer Axel Beck, a junior high school student during World War I, went to see *To Hell with the Kaiser*. His memories clearly indicate the importance of exploitation tactics in influencing public opinion:

> One Sunday afternoon I went to the Greenfield Theater, a neighborhood movie house and saw on the silver screen *To Hell with the Kaiser*. I don't remember anything from the film except that it portrayed the enemy. But I do remember two things. One was that the title started up the circulation of this advice on word usage: "Don't say 'the hell with the Kaiser,' that means you don't care what happens to him. Say 'to hell with the Kaiser,' because that's where we want him to go." My second thing I remembered is that everyone who attended was handed a leaflet with a picture of "Kaiser Bill." His face, mustache with upturned ends, spiked helmet, was the bulls-eye of a target, concentric circles around it. Directions on the leaflet were to tack the target on your backyard fence and shoot "Kaiser Bill." If you didn't have a gun or even a BB rifle, you were expected to throw stones at him.[63]

Beck also remembered winning the Junior Four Minute Man speech contest at his school: his topic was "Why Liberty Bonds Are a Good Investment." His family made "trench candles" by rolling up the daily newspaper, either the *Journal* or the socialist *Milwaukee Leader*, dipping the cylinder in wax and taking it to school for shipment overseas. For Beck, going to the movies was part of life on the homefront, of a piece with tilling a victory garden, eating Liberty sandwiches (hamburgers), buying Thrift Stamps, and throwing rocks at Kaiser Bill's image.

The manager of the Greenfield Theater was not alone as he promoted his theater by "present[ing] a little something of special effectiveness . . . bearing on the war." In July 1918, *Variety* reported that "a Milwaukee

Figs. 3.4–9. Milwaukee exhibitors copied their colleagues around the country by invoking the war in programming their theaters and promoting feature films. In figure 3.4, an advertisement for the Butterfly Theater in the *Milwaukee Journal*, 28 October 1917, features *The Price Mark* and local folk.

theater is admitting free any patron who presents a letter from a soldier who is overseas."[64] Milwaukee also instituted the practice of singing patriotic songs, as well as other contemporary songs, before feature-film screenings. An advertisement for the Alhambra Theater boasted, "We started Community Singing as an experiment. Now it's an assured success. We yield to the public demand and will continue it one more week with Frederick Carberry directing."[65]

Timeliness was invoked through the choice of a feature film and a speaker when the Strand Theater commemorated the sinking of the *Lusitania*, with *Lusitania* Week in May 1918. *Lest We Forget*, a movie about the sinking of that ship starring Rita Jolivet, one of its survivors, was

Fig. 3.5. Advertisement in the *Milwaukee Journal*, 12 May 1918, for the Strand Theater features Rita Jolivet in *Lest We Forget*.

shown, and Jolivet made a personal appearance at the theater.[66] In July, a different speaker appeared on the stage of the Alhambra. An advertisement in the 21 July 1918 issue of the *Milwaukee Journal* advised readers that they could come to the Alhambra Theater to see William S. Hart as "Shark Monroe, the savage master of a sealing schooner," and also to hear Lieutenant John Hewitt, who had just spent thirty-one months at the Front.[67] Milwaukee theater managers also offered newsreels of interest to their clientele. On 28 October 1917, the Butterfly Theater offered "Local Boys at Camp McArthur" in a program with *The Pricemark*.[68]

Milwaukee—like other big cities across the United States—hosted the roadshow *Hearts of the World*. Fannie Gordon, the movie reviewer for the *Milwaukee Journal*, described the superlative qualities of D. W. Griffith's film, which included its very arrival in the city.

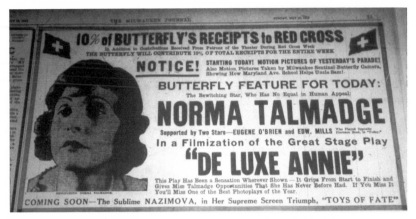

Fig. 3.6. Advertisement in the *Milwaukee Journal*, 19 May 1918, highlighting contributions made to the Red Cross from the run of *DeLuxe Annie*.

Who of us who, in "autrefois," endured the flickerings of the "nickel show" in the cause of cinema art, dreamed in that period only a dozen or so years gone by, that the day would come when a motion picture production would come to Milwaukee in a sixty-foot baggage car? Who, even the king of optimists himself, would have dreamed then of a motion picture accompanied by its own thirty-piece symphony orchestra . . . ?[69]

Hearts of the World ran an unprecedented six weeks at the Davidson, a legitimate theater, opening 29 July 1918 and closing 7 September. It played only twice daily, with ticket prices ranging from twenty-five cents to a dollar and fifty cents in the evenings, and from twenty-five cents to a dollar for matinees. Its longevity at the Davidson was the result of popular demand. An advertisement in the *Milwaukee Journal* noted,

The *Hearts of the World* has set a record for a waiting line of ticket buyers at the Davidson Theater. Tuesday night the line extended from the box office for ½ block down 3rd Street and in many places it was doubled or tripled by the ones who were accompanying the actual buyer of the ticket.[70]

This same advertisement explained that seats were available two weeks in advance. An editorial in the *Journal* also urged readers to see the film.

Fig. 3.7. Advertisement in the *Milwaukee Journal*, 9 June 1918, for the Alhambra
Theater announces community singing.

The Journal commends the play first of all to those loyal Americans
whose love of democracy and fair play has kept them on the path of
right from the very beginning of the world war. Such will find the film
a confirmation and an inspiration. The Journal's appeal does not stop
with them. It would urge to see the play all those who grumble about
the petty difficulties which the war has brought.[71]

Such ballyhoo was justified, for the presentation of *Hearts of the World* was
spectacular. As Gordon noted of the light and sound effects that accompanied the film: an "electric storm" was created with "lightning flashes,
thunder and wailing winds. . . . Hundreds of gallons of water are forced
against a concave surface under high pressure and add to the realism of the
scene."[72]

Hearts of the World was not the first war movie to be presented in such
grand style. *The Unbeliever,* the last film produced by the Edison Company, played Milwaukee in late May and early June of 1918. Its advertisement in the 2 June *Milwaukee Journal* noted:

Eighth Tremendous Day of the picture that has broken all Strand
records. The greatest war story the war has produced. . . .
    Notice to the Public. Almost 30,000 people have seen "The
Unbeliever" at this theater during the past week. We are firmly of the
opinion that fully that many more loyal Milwaukeeans wish to view this
thrillingly appealing patriotic spectacle. It carries the message direct to

Fig. 3.8. Advertisement for *Hearts of the World* in the *Milwaukee Journal*, 1 September 1918.

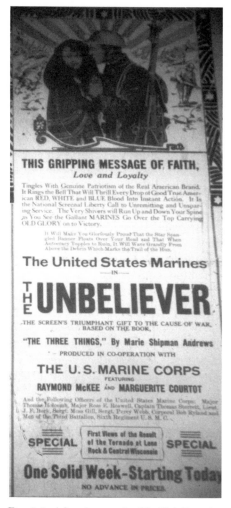

Fig. 3.9. Advertisement for *The Unbeliever* in
the *Milwaukee Journal*, 2 June 1918. Both
The Unbeliever and *Hearts of the World* enjoyed successful runs in Milwaukee.

every American heart that the world must be made safe for democracy
mainly through the efforts of this nation.

"The Unbeliever" was made in cooperation with the United States
Marines and officially sanctioned by attachés of the government. We
are in receipt of countless letters from representative citizens endorsing
it as the most timely drama of the present war. Therefore we are

holding "The Unbeliever" for the coming week so that all who wish may see. Charles C. Perry [manager] Special: Journal-Pathe Pictures of Milwaukee's own regiment—the Boys from Camp Custer—and the Memorial Day Parade.[73]

The rhetoric of this advertisement reveals the tensions and the pressures forming the context for reception of movies in Milwaukee in 1917 and 1918. German cultural heritage, ethnicity, and socialism to the contrary, Milwaukeeans—in large numbers—were "loyal" and possessed of "American" hearts. No wayward nephew, Milwaukee was, rather, integral to the national family making the world safe for democracy. Charles Perry was providing service to his community by allowing the film to be held over for an additional week so more people could publicly affirm their patriotism by attending his theater. By programming the nationally distributed feature with newsreels of local folks—soldiers and civilians—he helped Milwaukee join step with the patriotic effort that was taking place along the national homefront and the battlefront overseas. Footage of the Memorial Day Parade allowed the audience to participate in an event, a commemoration of the Civil War, in which they had been, unequivocally, on the "right" side. In this way, Perry was doing his best to advance the patriotic cause. He also presumably would continue the record-breaking business he had enjoyed in the preceding eight days *The Unbeliever* had played The Strand.

Since Perry's advertisement was prominently displayed on the movie page of the most widely read local newspaper, Milwaukeeans had access to the identity it offered them whether they attended movies or not. The pressure of the times, exercised socially and politically, encouraged its adoption.

Government Regulation

The tax on admission to this theater helps to keep the firing line intact.
manager of the Elmwood Theater, Buffalo, New York,
22 December 1917[74]

At the same time that World War I offered exhibitors in Milwaukee and elsewhere the opportunity to increase their trade and more firmly establish their theaters within their communities, it also presented them with a specific set of challenges in the form of the war tax, the imposition of ten weeks of Fuelless Tuesdays, and other more localized restrictions on exhibition.

A three-pronged tax was levied on the motion picture industry beginning in October 1917. Both raw film and the positive print were taxed, and starting 1 November 1917, a 10-percent tax on theater admissions over a nickel was instituted. The film producers, responsible for the tax on film footage, passed their costs on to the exhibitor in the form of a uniform fee of fifteen cents per reel per day. Within the exhibition branch of the industry this provoked much anger. Film producers argued that all taxes should be paid by the ultimate consumer of their product, the movie-goer, and it was up to the exhibitor to collect these taxes. Film exhibitors countered that the increase in their cost of doing business caused by such a surcharge would drive them out of business. This often vitriolic exchange between producer and exhibitor, however, took place in the trade press and in their business correspondence; it did not attract attention in the popular press. Instead, the public heard about the tax on theater tickets, a tax that exhibitors were less loathe to pass on to the consumer. Sargent devoted an installment of his column "Advertising for Exhibitors" to suggestions from his readers for countering patron displeasure with this tax: "This tax was so generally commented on in the newspapers that the public was ready for it, but there is a difference between a tax in the newspaper and a tax in the box office." Sargent related how exhibitors in Cleveland formed a committee to educate the public about the amount and method of payment for the tax, but of special concern was the need to reassure consumers that, "Uncle Sam gets it—we don't." In practice the tax on theater admission gave the exhibitor yet another advertising point. A Minneapolis theater-owner sought to convince potential customers that buying a ticket to his theater and paying the 10-percent tax would help "to swell this great Liberty-for-the-World-Fund."[75]

The film exhibitor was also able to turn the Fuel Administration's business-closing order to his advantage. In January 1918 the Fuel Administration ruled that for the ten Mondays from 21 January through 25 March no fuel could be used to heat such places as theaters, business offices, or stores east of the Mississippi River. The film industry acted quickly and in concert, and on 20 January the *New York Times* reported that Harry A. Garfield, head of the Fuel Administration, had amended the order.

> Theaters, moving picture houses and other places of amusement where alcoholic drinks are not sold are to be permitted to remain open on the ten Mondays beginning January 21, so that the vast army of workers in the territory east of the Mississippi who must remain idle . . . may

have some place to go. The theaters and amusement places, however, must remain closed on ten Tuesdays instead.

The article reported that Garfield had reached this decision after being contacted by President Wilson, who "expressed sympathy with the plea of the theatrical managers. The President received a delegation of the managers at the White House on Thursday."[76] On 8 February 1918, *Variety* reported "Picture Business Satisfied with Garfield's Holidays." The article noted that neither producers, distributors, nor exhibitors were adversely affected by the closing order.

> Despite pessimistic predictions, the heatless and workless Mondays have not caused the picture industry any material losses. . . . One exchangeman said to a *Variety* representative "I doubt if any manufacturer suffered a material loss under the unusual conditions. Exhibitors themselves have been doing such phenomenal business Mondays that few complaints have come from that quarter. Exhibitors have virtually been having a series of three holidays with Saturday, Sunday and the new Monday holiday bunched. I place my loss at a minimum.[77]

Moving Picture World ran the following headline: "Blue Tuesday Means Good Mondays, Telegrams to Goldwyn Tell of Big Business Sunday, Monday and Wednesday."[78] And the *Chicago Tribune*'s movie column "Right Off the Reel," quoted one local exhibitor as saying:

> When we were told that we had to close on Mondays my heart was like lead. That meant decided loss. But when the order was changed and Tuesday named as closing day, things looked bright. . . . Monday being closing day for stores and offices gives us enough business to make up for dark Tuesday.[79]

Conclusion

The industry is the same in 1918 that it was in 1917. It is the world that is different. . . .

Exhibitor's Trade Review, *20 July 1918*[80]

World War I presented film exhibitors with a set of challenges to their business, and they responded by attempting to turn those challenges into opportunities. Through advertising movie-goers were encouraged to see the theater as a necessary, inexpensive, and entertaining relief from the worries and inconveniences of the war, and, conversely, they were encouraged to consider attendance at the theater as a way of participating in the war effort in that the theater tax and contributions to war fund drives advanced the national cause. In still another advertising angle, exhibitors promoted the educational value of newsreels and other documentary programming. In general, film exhibitors were successful. *Moving Picture World* sent reporters to various parts of the United States in January 1918 to report on business conditions and found that, while some exhibitors pointed to the war tax as a problem, most pointed to nonwar-related factors such as weather—excessive cold and snow in the Midwest, and drought in Texas and around San Francisco—as the major obstacles to their business.[81]

Exhibitors in Milwaukee joined their colleagues around the country and enlisted in the war effort on the homefront. Their behavior illustrated the degree to which exhibition was standardized across the United States. Despite trade press advice to blend the theater into its local venue, exhibitors used ideas derived from nationally circulated motion picture press books and columns in national trade newspapers as they sold their entertainment to Milwaukeeans. Within the city limits, exhibitors, like their colleagues in the chamber of commerce, worked to foster a patriotic public image for Milwaukee.

4

The Film Industry and Government Propaganda on the Homefront

Following up on the splendid work it has been doing for Uncle Sam in
connection with the Liberty Loan, the National Association of the Motion
Picture Industry is planning to continue in cooperation with the Federal
Government throughout the period of the war.
Exhibitor's Trade Review, *23 June 1917*[1]

FILM PRODUCERS, DISTRIBUTORS, exhibitors, and such allied
trades as suppliers of theater fittings and publishers of theater programs
enlisted in the U.S. government's war effort on the homefront. Combining
the desire to help their country with the realization that such help could
further their own business goals, these various members of the film industry were willing to cooperate with government agencies. Only a structure
was needed, and this was provided by the newly formed trade group the
National Association of the Motion Picture Industry (NAMPI). NAMPI's
cooperation with the government gave its members—the film companies,
their leaders, their stars, and theater owners—the opportunity to integrate
more fully with the many other industries mobilizing the homefront, and so
to join the existing industrial and popular culture of the country.

The events described in this chapter reflect a belief in the need for a
national consensus and the faith that such a consensus was achievable at
the movies. After providing a brief survey of NAMPI, I will consider two
instances of government-film industry interaction orchestrated by NAMPI
that are of particular interest here. These two cases—the cooperation of
the film industry in the food conservation efforts of the U.S. Food Administration and its cooperation in the war bond drives of the U.S. Treasury
Department—are paradigmatic of the reciprocal relationship of the film
industry and the U.S. government.

On 11 October 1917, Crockett Brown, manager of the Unique Theater
in Nashwauk, Minnesota, replied to a request from the U.S. Food Administration. In a mass mailing, exhibitors had been asked to screen a film

series entitled *Food Will Win the War* and to lend, "hearty support to the government in placing on the screen and in the lobby of your theater pictures, slides and posters to be distributed in the near future."[2] Brown's response read as follows: "Through the medium of his screen he [the film exhibitor] can spread the gospel of patriotism, he can encourage enlistment, and he can assist our government officials in presenting accurate information, necessary instructions and valuable advice. . . . "[3] This favorable reply was typical of many responses the Food Administration received from film exhibitors to their appeal, and it serves to illustrate the varied forms that cooperation took.

Citizens of Nashwauk attending the Unique Theater on a Saturday night in October to see Madge Kennedy in *Baby Mine*, might, on entering the theater, have passed a framed certificate, emblazoned with an eagle, proclaiming that "Food Will Win the War" and certifying that the Unique Theater, "is a member of the U.S. Food Administration."[4] They might also have passed a table stacked with food conservation pledge cards ready for signing. Before the feature film started, they might have watched a slide that projected in red, white and blue the following announcement: "The Food Campaign is on. Every woman in America must be enlisted before Oct. 28. Are *you* doing *your* bit?"[5] In the space of time between reel changes, a Four Minute Man—the local school superintendent or banker—might have further exhorted the audience to join the campaign to conserve. NAMPI provided the personnel and the infrastructure to accomplish these federally initiated directives, and thus provided Crockett Brown and his colleagues with a way of developing an aura of respectability and a niche in the cultural life of their ever-expanding clientele.

NAMPI

To promote a more enlarged and friendly intercourse between those
engaged in the industry and to do and perform all such acts as may tend
to promote the welfare of the industry at large.
Moving Picture World, *22 July 1916*[6]

The National Association of the Motion Picture Industry was organized in July of 1916 when the existing trade association for producers and distributors, the Motion Picture Board of Trade, proved unable to mediate a dispute between its members and the Motion Picture Exhibitor's League of America.[7] NAMPI took as its mission to enroll representatives from all sectors of the motion picture industry. Its five classes of membership in-

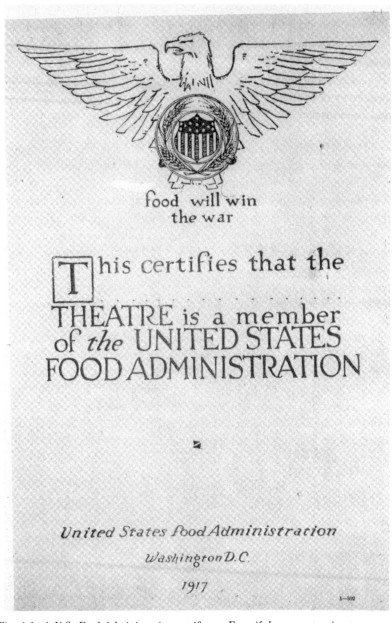

food will win
the war

This certifies that the

THEATRE is a member
of *the* UNITED STATES
FOOD ADMINISTRATION

United States Food Administration

Washington D.C.

1917

Fig. 4.1. A U.S. Food Administration certificate. Even if they were coming to see a comedy having no narrative relation to the conflict, theater patrons were reminded that there was a war on, and that the theater and its management were active fighters on the homefront.

cluded producers, distributors, exhibitors, supply and equipment companies, and a general division comprising trade papers, actors, insurance
companies, and advertising agents. The make-up of its board of directors
reflected the numerical weight of these classes as well as the exhibitors'
vocal dissatisfaction with the organization of the defunct Board of Trade.
After elections in July 1917, the exhibitors' class had fourteen members,
the other classes, seven each. Membership on the board of NAMPI ranged
across the film industry, including such companies as Universal, Goldwyn, Bell and Howell, Pathe, Vitagraph, and *Moving Picture World*, and
such individuals as Adolph Zukor, Lee A. Ochs (president of the New
York Motion Picture Exhibitors of America), N. C. Cotabish (National
Carbon Company), William A. Johnson (editor, *Motion Picture News*), and
D. W. Griffith. William Brady, of the production firm World Films, was
elected president. It is significant that the board contained men who were
gaining power and prestige within the industry by conducting their businesses in a particular way; they were expanding, in part, through the
acquisition of other companies. While NAMPI wanted a broad industry
representation and a large membership, the make-up of its board of directors also reflected a desire to exercise control over that membership.
Above all else "practical" business tactics were to be implemented by
industry leaders.

Regardless of ulterior motives, the stated goals of NAMPI represented
the industry's main concerns: to facilitate discussion among all facets of
the industry, to monitor government regulation of their business, to mediate disputes among members, and to serve a public relations function
between the industry and the public.[8] NAMPI's more specific goals and
worries were manifested in its standing committees, which were focussed
on membership, finance, publicity, hostile legislation, censorship, taxation, fire-prevention regulations and insurance, foreign trade, copyrights
and trademarks, standards and labor issues, among others. When the
United States entered World War I, NAMPI added support for governmental initiatives to the list of its functions.

After April 1917, President Wilson was faced with two immediate
problems—mobilizing troops to fight the war in Europe and mobilizing the
American citizenry to support the war on the homefront. To win the domestic cooperation vital to the war effort, Wilson issued Executive Order 2594
on 13 April 1917, establishing the Committee on Public Information and
naming George Creel, a newspaperman from Colorado who was an avid
Wilson supporter, as chairman. Creel aimed to muster public opinion to
the government's cause. His challenge was "to devise machinery with

which to make the fight for loyalty and unity at home and for the friendship and understanding of neutral nations of the world."[9]

Creel identified his job as a "plain publicity proposition, a vast enterprise in salesmanship, the world's greatest adventure in advertising." Although censorship was a function of the Committee, he preferred to view the CPI's mission as one of education. According to Stephen Vaughn, an historian of the CPI, "The Committee on Public Information was established out of a desire to avoid repression, out of hope that the story of American ideals was sufficient to win the support of the people both inside and outside the United States."[10] That motion pictures were made-to-order for such salesmanship was not lost on Creel or others in Wilson's administration.

Cooperation between the government and the film industry, represented by NAMPI, began as early as 23 May 1917, when its president, William Brady, acting in response to a request from Secretary of the Treasury McAdoo, called a meeting of representatives from the motion picture industry to discuss ways in which the film community could aid the First Liberty Loan Campaign.[11] One month later *Exhibitor's Trade Review* reported that a War Cooperation Committee had been created "to handle all matters in which the motion picture can be used to further the interests of the American Government in the world war."[12] The government had contacted the industry through the one trade association comprising representatives from all its branches; NAMPI had responded to a specific request for help with the First Liberty Loan and had in the process willingly expanded its role.

One of NAMPI's accomplishments in these initial dealings with the government was to provide a facade of industry unity. The summer of 1917 saw a bitter fight within the Motion Picture Exhibitors' League of America over the election of its president. Brady attempted to mediate but was unsuccessful, and the discontented minority bolted to form the American Exhibitors Association. *Moving Picture World* speculated that the consequence of such internal dissension was a weakened bargaining position for exhibitors in their dealings with film producers and distributors. "Not only this but organizations representing other branches of the industry have been so far unable to consult with any real representative organization of exhibitors."[13]

NAMPI offered precisely what less cohesive industry groups such as the Exhibitors League and less broadly representative groups such as the Society for Motion Picture Engineers, the Motion Picture Directors Association, and the Associated Motion Picture Advertisers could not—one organization representing all facets of the industry. Thus NAMPI could more easily influence the industry's public image as well as its business practices. Furthermore, the men assuming leadership positions in NAMPI were also becoming leaders in the industry. Their aims could be furthered by their trade association. By July 1917, NAMPI claimed to include 75 percent of producing companies, and by March of 1918 it included "82 producing companies, thus representing 90% of film manufacturers in the country." In addition, it claimed to be equally representative of the other branches of the industry.[14] Effective cooperation in the war effort became one of NAMPI's primary selling points as it recruited new members. A letter sent to those companies not yet affiliated with NAMPI argued that "only through coordinated effort could the best results be obtained for the Government in the prosecution of the war."[15]

NAMPI's membership increased over the course of the war, and it successfully presented the public image of a united front. *Moving Picture World* credited William Brady with the achievement: "Another thing: he has held the N.A.M.P.I. together longer than any similar body in the motion picture trade has been able to exist—and that's a lot for one man to do."[16] Brady's diplomatic skills served the interests of both the government and of NAMPI.

As a further index of his prestige and his political abilities, Brady received a letter from President Wilson on 28 June 1917. This letter is significant as an early indication of the government's desire, expressed through its chief executive, to use the propaganda channels the film industry could provide. It also states a contemporary point of view on the image of the film industry.

> My Dear Mr. Brady:
>   It is in my mind not only to bring the motion picture into fullest and most effective contact with the nation's needs, but to give some measure of official recognition to an increasingly important factor in the development of our national life. The film has come to rank as a very high medium for the dissemination of public intelligence and since it speaks a universal language it lends itself importantly to the presentation of America's plans and purposes.
>   May I ask you, as chairman by my appointment to organize the motion picture industry in such a manner as to establish direct and authoritative cooperation with the Committee on Public Information of which Mr. George Creel is chairman? It is much to ask but my knowledge of the patriotic service already rendered by you and your associates makes me count upon your generous acceptance.[17]

President Wilson's letter functioned to confirm an embryonic industry-government plan of cooperation. By this date Brady had already contacted other governmental agencies offering the assistance of the film industry. On 11 July, NAMPI's War Cooperation Committee went to Washington to meet with George Creel and to tour the departments to which they were assigned. The delegation was well received. *Exhibitor's Trade Review* reported that "the secretaries and heads of departments outdid one another in their enthusiasm over the power, influence and patriotism of the motion picture screen."[18]

Once appointed and introduced to Washington, the War Cooperation Committee went to work. Arthur Friend of Famous Players-Lasky was assigned to the Food Administration, where one of his first official acts was to send a memo "To All Manufacturers and Distributors of Pictures" announcing that he was in Washington and that he would be glad to consult and advise with anyone in the trade in regard to its [USFA's] future activities." He also pledged to keep exhibitors and others in the industry informed of future plans by publicizing the Food Administration's programs in motion picture trade papers "at the earliest possible moment."[19] By 7 September 1917 the first Food Administration-film industry joint effort was underway. Cooperation with the Treasury Department was manifested in both money and motion pictures. In June 1917, Lasky employees donated $75,000 to the First Liberty Loan, and in September the *New York Times* reported, "A film production designed to help sell the next Liberty Loan was exhibited yesterday morning at the Strand Theater."[20]

Within a month and a half of United States entry into World War I, NAMPI had succeeded in identifying itself as the sole representative of the entire motion picture industry, thus enhancing its credibility within the industry, and placing itself in a stronger position to attract new members. As far as the government was concerned, the most efficient access to the resources the film industry could offer came through NAMPI and its War Cooperation Committee. NAMPI had also succeeded in filling its War Cooperation Committee with men in positions of authority throughout the industry, thus lending prestige, credibility and influence to the enterprise. NAMPI was especially skillful at rallying exhibitors—who made up the largest segment of the film industry and was the group whose cooperation was most crucial for success in bringing the government's various messages to the public. Brady and the NAMPI board were shrewd in their organization of this diverse and often fractious group.

In order to avoid antagonism between NAMPI and exhibitors national organizations—the Motion Picture Exhibitors League of America and the American Exhibitors Association—Brady developed an alternate structure with a chairman and delegations in each state, one including many exhibitors who belonged to neither trade association. Wisconsin provides an example of the way in which state chairmen could further delegate duties and create an efficient distribution system for government propaganda.

J. E. Sherwood, manager of the Grand Theater in Madison, Wisconsin, was named Wisconsin state chairman. He appointed a postmaster in each town containing a movie theater to head a subcommittee in that city or town. *Forward*, a journal of the Wisconsin State Council of Defense, reported that five hundred appointments were made, and that "the letters of acceptance [were] invariably surcharged with a spirit of patriotism and a desire to be of the highest service in any way possible."[21] Slides, posters, and other material were sent to Mr. Sherwood, who forwarded them to the delegated postmasters, who in turn distributed them to the local theaters.

Members of the War Cooperation Committee also wooed exhibitors through the trade press. A memo sent in May 1918 from the director of publicity for the War Loan Organization reported that "Mr. Zukor's committee [assigned to the U.S. Treasury Department] further enlisted the vigorous cooperation of the trade papers of the motion picture industry in urging theater owners throughout the country to cooperate." In addition, Zukor's committee provided a mailing list of all motion picture theaters in the United States. The War Cooperation Committee praised the exhibitors' participation, writing, "Their co-operation has been uniformly efficient, prompt, and enthusiastic."[22]

NAMPI and the United States Food Administration

I am interested in the program that you outlined as per your
memorandum of August 8, and hope that you will make motion pictures
a valuable adjunct to our campaign of education throughout the country
for the elimination of waste, substitution of perishable food stuffs for the
non-perishables and such other educational features as may be
warranted from time to time in order to help win the war.

Herbert Hoover to Arthur Friend, August 1917[23]

On 9 August 1917, future president Herbert Hoover, then chairman of the United States Food Administration (USFA), issued a formal invitation to Arthur Friend, treasurer of Famous Players-Lasky and a member of the

War Cooperation Committee of NAMPI to "take entire charge of the Motion Picture Department of the Food Administration, in cooperation with Mr. Allen and other members of our Publicity Organization."[24] The Motion Picture Division became a part of the USFA's Educational Division, headed by Ben Allen. Hoover himself would exercise final approval of film projects. "You will understand that before any reels are released or any scenarios arranged, they must be submitted to me for final approval. This is in line with the general policy of the whole organization."[25]

According to Hoover, the task of the Food Administrator was two-fold: one, to promote food conservation at home "so as to supply the allies with food stuffs during the war and all Europe after the Armistice;" and two, to limit harmful speculation in food.[26] The motion picture industry represented by Arthur Friend joined the press, the advertising industry, and door-to-door canvassers in a vast campaign to promote voluntary food conservation. Historians of the Food Administration agree that the press was the most important channel for information and solicitation; they also agree with William Mullendore's assessment, however, that, "[t]his advertising campaign also included the valuable cooperation of the motion picture theater."[27] A catalog of the Food Administration's motion picture activities serves as a template for cooperation of the film industry with the federal government and illustrates the active involvement of all sectors of the motion picture industry in the government's mission.

The aid the film industry rendered took a variety of forms. Film producer Thomas Ince suggested that film and theatrical producers should refrain from using real food in their productions as a conservation measure, and film stars were supportive. "It will be my pleasure to cooperate in the use of substitutes for food values in my photoplays," responded Mary Pickford.[28] More important, the industry arranged for the distribution of Food Administration short-subject films through Universal, Pathe, and Mutual newsreel distributors. This was accomplished despite Pathe's annoyance that all three companies would receive the same footage.[29] Cost was kept to a minimum in this distribution scheme. Friend reported to Ben Allen, head of the Educational Division which housed the Motion Picture Unit, that the news film of Wilson signing the Food Bill and of Hoover leaving the White House after his appointment as Food Administration head would be distributed gratis, and that he "planned to repeat this process and issue pictures of similar length, i.e. within 200 feet, in the same manner every week or two."[30]

Arthur Friend enlisted film exhibitors to participate in the Food Administration's extensive Second Food Pledge Card Drive which took place 21–28 October 1917. The Pledge Drive was a multi-media event, with slides sent out free to exhibitors. Series A was to run the week of 14 October and included five slides containing slogans like the following:

Card A.1   (James Montgomery Flagg poster)
BE PATRIOTIC
sign your country's
pledge to save the food.
U.S. Food Administration.

Card A.2   Mrs. Woodrow Wilson was the
first woman to sign the food
pledge of the Food Administration

Card A.3   (facsimile of Mrs. Wilson's card)
Here's the very card that
Mrs. Wilson signed.

Card A.4   There are four great problems
FOOD—men—money—ships.
If we fail in one we shall have
lost the war.
But we shall win with *your* help.

Card A.5   LEARN TO SUBSTITUTE
FISH is good food.
Eat it *instead of Meat.*
Corn is good food.
Use it instead of *Wheat.*[31]

Series B, similar in tone and content but containing only four slides, was to be screened the week of 21 October. The newsreel film of Wilson and Hoover described earlier was released during this week, and posters heralding "Food Will Win the War" and "Official Pictures of the United States Food Administration" were distributed to exhibitors.[32] The Food Administration wrote to exhibitors explaining the campaign and noting that after these "attractive" posters arrived, "we should like to have them framed and kept permanently on exhibition in the theaters."[33] The lobby of the theater—like every home in the nation—would be graced with a certificate of membership in the USFA. The Four Minute Men, local public speakers under the auspices of the Committee on Public Information, were also scheduled to deliver talks on the need for a "vast home army for conservation" in theaters during the week of 21 October.[34]

The Second Pledge Card Drive, which was designed to enlist the housewives of the nation in the Food Administration's conservation efforts, was highly successful. Ten and one-half million pledge cards were signed, and the same number of window cards were distributed.[35] The film industry contributed to this successful outcome by visibly aligning itself with food conservation efforts. Long after the campaign ended, exhibitors displayed the colorful posters and framed certificates (with the theater's name inscribed "preferably by a good penman") to remind patrons of their patriotism.[36]

By January 1918, the Film Division of the Food Administration added filmed advertisements called "trailers" to its arsenal of advertising methods, and in May short films called "picturettes" were also being distributed, with stars appearing in both. By this time the film exhibitor was the key purveyor of food conservation propaganda.

The Food Administration continued to search for ways to involve more and more exhibitors in their campaigns. John C. Flinn, a colleague of Friend's at Famous Players-Lasky, contacted John Wylie, the editor of *Moving Picture World*, about the best way to get Food Administration propaganda into the trade papers. Flinn's report to Friend helps position the Food Administration's use of the film industry relative to the use of other governmental departments.

> *Moving Picture World* and other trade papers, he [Wylie] is quite sure,
> will be very liberal in the space devoted to the Food Administration
> Committee. Whether it will be possible to obtain free pages for
> advertising matter is extremely doubtful he says, because if all the
> committees—he added jokingly—were as active as the chairman of the
> Food Committee it would require as many pages as committees to meet
> the situation.

Wylie also offered to continue to run a special column in his paper devoted to publicizing the activities of all the film industry committees working with Washington.[37]

The one criticism of the job Arthur Friend had been doing came in regard to the use of stars in the USFA's trailers and picturettes. R. C. Maxwell, head of the Education Division's department of outdoor advertising, complained to Edgar Rickard, Hoover's assistant, about the "ordinary" quality of the slides and films. He wanted more "live interest" in this propaganda, and thought that stars like Mary Pickford and Douglas Fairbanks were "patriotic enough to lend their talent in these pictures."[38] Friend had, however, made some use of the voluntary services of movie stars. Marguerite Clark appeared in the picturette "A Lesson in Saving Food by Marguerite Clark," Elsie Ferguson appeared in "Practical Hooverism," and Mabel Normand appeared in "Assisting Mr. Hoover." May Irwin, a Universal star, independently produced a film called "May Irwin Loaf," demonstrating the proportions of wheat to be used when baking bread, and she offered it to the USFA. Unfortunately, guidelines governing those proportions changed while the film was in production, so that the Food Administration could not give the film its official approval.

Occasionally the Food Administration intervened in the realm of commercial film production. These interventions fell into one of two categories: official endorsements by the USFA of commercially produced motion pictures, and censorship. When Mr. and Mrs. Sidney Drew's film *The Patriot*, produced for Metro, was reviewed, it was not only endorsed but recommended. When Lyda Flager, the Home Demonstration Agent in Waukesha, Wisconsin, wrote the Food Administration requesting a movie to show during the February 1918 Food Conservation week in her city, Mrs. A. I. McCreary of the Food Administration replied: "The film *The Patriot* was written and produced by Mr. and Mrs. Sidney Drew. It is on the subject of food conservation and has been approved by the U.S.F.A."[39] Not all films gained such approval. An undated evaluation of the Food Administration, apparently written in the spring of 1918, suggested that other films had been offered to the Food Administration and refused endorsement, perhaps too hastily. "The files show a number of very good films were not given our approval simply because no one took enough trouble to properly suggest or make changes."[40] The second type of intervention by the USFA was less positive. In at least two known cases, the Food Administration contemplated censoring a film. A letter from the Food Administration to J. H. Hecht of the CPI requested that *The Public Be Damned*, a film about the inflation of food prices, be squelched. "This picture is not entirely in accord with the present policies of the Food Administration and we have been trying to secure its suppression. We would appreciate whatever you can do to assist us."[41] This letter was written in May 1918, however, and the film had been in distribution since June 1917. Even if the film were to have been pulled from distribution, it would already have enjoyed wide exhibition, so it was allowed to run. The Food Administration also asked the CPI to suppress a film produced by Fox (and initially endorsed by Herbert Hoover) called *Cheating the Public*, but the CPI simply advised Ben Allen, head of the USFA's Education Division, that he should write Fox and tell them to "quit it."[42] This relatively mild response serves as an indication of the government's level of concern over the subversiveness of these films.

The use made of all branches of the film industry by the USFA offers evidence of the extent to which the industry was able to aid the war effort. Although organized and orchestrated at the national level by NAMPI's representative Arthur Friend, the food conservation campaign was implemented at movie houses throughout the country from the Unique Theater in Nashwauk, Minnesota, to the Rialto Theater in Manhattan. The message of the Food Administration was not glamorous, but straightforward. Short films entreated viewers to "Observe Tuesday and Saturday as porkless days and make every day a fat and sugar saving day."[43] Movie stars donated films illustrating breadmaking techniques and posed for pictures in the absolutely utilitarian uniform of the Food Administration. Like other retail merchants, movie theater managers advocated food conservation through posters and certificates tactics promising "to knit the neighborhood house more closely to the bones of the community."[44] Thus it is neither surprising nor coincidental that in the summer of 1917 NAMPI was elected to membership in the U.S. Chamber of Commerce. The industry, through its different branches as well as through its trade association, advanced its own development while aiding the government.

NAMPI Aids the Treasury Department

Inasmuch as the [War Cooperation] Committee has been securing the moving picture material for the Treasury Department at actual cost, and is always ready to submit all plans and ideas to the Treasury Department for O.K. before going ahead with them, I consider the present arrangement, so far as the Liberty Loan is concerned, highly satisfactory, and to the best interests of the Treasury Department from the standpoint of functional economy, efficiency in distribution, effectiveness and all around service.

Office of the Director of Publicity, War Loan Organization, May 1918[45]

Cooperation with the government's efforts on the homefront cast both national and local members of the film industry in a favorable light: it offered

Fig. 4.2. Movie stars like Billie
Burke enhanced their public images
as they participated in the war effort.

local film exhibitors the opportunity to validate their businesses within
their communities, and it offered the film industry at the national level the
chance to garner good publicity and so enhance its image. If the movie
industry worked hard for the cause of the Food Administration, it proved
equally committed to the efforts of the Treasury Department during its
Liberty Loan Campaigns.

NAMPI named Adolph Zukor, of Famous Players-Lasky, Marcus
Loew, of Loew Enterprises, Jules E. Brulatour, of Eastman Films, Walter
Irwin, of Vitagraph, and George Spoor, of Essanay, to its War Cooperation
Committee, which was assigned to the Treasury Department. While information regarding the activities of the Food Administration as it worked
through the motion picture industry must be gleaned from archival documents, film industry cooperation with the Treasury Department can be
found in the news, entertainment, rotogravure, and even the comics sections of the country's newspapers. The Treasury Department employed
plenty of "live interest" in its propaganda. Stars lit up the Liberty Loan
Campaigns, and the publicity their efforts gained intensified the glow.

The United States government held five bond drives, four during the
course of the war, and a fifth, the Victory Bond Drive, after the Armistice.
The film industry participated in each one of these campaigns. On 23 May
1917, a month before the announcement of the formation of the War Cooperation Committee, Brady met with "important movie people" in response to a request from William McAdoo, Secretary of the Treasury, for
film industry aid in promoting the First Liberty Loan.[46] The film industry
participated in this publicity effort in a variety of ways: movie stars spoke
on behalf of bond sales, advertisements were run in trade journals, and
film exhibitors added phrases promoting bonds to their newspaper ads.
Slides and short films also carried the Treasury Department's message.

For the first Liberty Loan, 30,000 slides carrying phrases furnished by
the Liberty Loan Publicity committee and 13,000 slides accompanied by a
letter from Secretary of the Treasury McAdoo and NAMPI president Brady
were distributed by NAMPI. Also distributed were 8,000 copies of a short
film showing President Wilson delivering his "historic message to the
American People to do their duty."[47] During the second bond drive, 100
prints each of five star-studded shorts were distributed free of charge, and
in October alone 17,500 sets of slides, 3 slides to a set, were distributed to
as many theaters.[48] For the third Liberty Loan, NAMPI released 17,200
trailers, 17,200 sets of posters, and a "splendid patriotic film contributed
by Douglas Fairbanks."[49]

The film industry's efforts did not go unnoticed. Fannie Gordon, a movie reviewer for the *Milwaukee Journal*, praised NAMPI's contribution to the fourth Liberty Loan campaign: "Since the United States entered the war, the moving picture industry has been one of the government's most powerful allies in giving publicity to those things which Uncle Sam deemed it necessary to get to the people. . . . " She put the citizens of Milwaukee on notice to anticipate a series of short advertising films, featuring fifty of the industry's most prominent stars.[50] One of these was Charlie Chaplin's contribution, entitled "The Bond, A Liberty Loan Appeal." In this short film, Charlie experiences four types of bonds: friendship bonds, bonds of love, bonds of matrimony, and finally Liberty Bonds. In the final encounter, Chaplin stands between figures representing Uncle Sam and Industry. In something of a chain reaction, Chaplin buys a bond from Uncle Sam, and Industry furnishes a soldier with a rifle; Chaplin buys another bond and a sailor is equipped. Next we see an allegorical figure of Liberty. Just as she is about to be cut down by a figure representing the Kaiser, he is vanquished by the soldier of Uncle Sam. Then Chaplin hits the Kaiser over the head with a huge mallet bearing the words "Liberty Bonds" and the picture is over.[51] Even after the war ended, film stars such as Mary Pickford continued to aid the Treasury Department by doing "film talks." A memo to the Secretary of the Treasury describes how, "at the end of each of her plays during 1919 she will appear in ordinary dress and talk thrift, [and] this publicity will be very effective among movie patrons."[52]

Movie stars not only lent their images to publicize the Liberty Loan, they also lent their voices by speaking at Liberty Bond rallies. On 24 June 1917, the rotogravure section of the *New York Times* published a photograph of Mary Pickford addressing a crowd. It was captioned, "Mary Pickford's eloquence wins San Francisco audience in Liberty Bond Appeal. Two million dollars were subscribed by audience which packed city auditorium to hear the Little Screen Star."[53] Douglas Fairbanks made a pitch for bonds at Chicago's main train station on LaSalle Street. "He is trying to get subscriptions of $1,000,000 worth of bonds and has passed the halfway mark."[54] On 30 December 1917 the *Chicago Tribune* printed a letter of thanks received by Marguerite Clark from Oscar Price, director of publicity for the Liberty Loan. It read in part: "It is my pleasant duty to express to you in behalf of Secretary McAdoo, the very sincere appreciation of the Treasury Department for the assistance and cooperation you gave the Second Liberty Loan."[55]

In the third Liberty Loan, Mary Pickford, Charlie Chaplin, Douglas

Fairbanks, Marguerite Clark, and William S. Hart segmented the country, with Hart staying in the West, Pickford going to the East Coast, Chaplin to the South, and Clark working in the Midwest. Marie Dressler opened the Third Bond Drive with a speech on the Capitol steps in Washington, D.C. The *Milwaukee Journal* described the scene: "You buy bonds, she's saying, On to Berlin."[56]

It was not only in the area of bond sales that film stars and other movie industry personnel enhanced their image and that of the motion picture industry by boosting the war effort. The actress Theda Bara, belying her image as a vamp, stamped "Buy a bond and help the cause of humanity" across all the fan photos she sent out.[57] Like many other film exhibitors, Frank Hall, manager of the Broadway Theater in New York City, devoted more space in his ad for the film *The Bar Sinister* to hawking Liberty Bonds than to the selling points of the film.[58] On 28 April 1918, the *New York Times* reported that many in the film industry, including Marion Davies ($6,000 worth), Mabel Normand ($3,000 worth), Madge Kennedy, and Mary Miles Minter, were "capitalizing on their popularity for the benefit of the government," buying Liberty Bonds.[59] Harold Edel, the manager of the Strand Theater in New York City, like his less illustrious colleague Mr. Hall, invested a week's gross receipts in this Bond Drive.

Before the Third Liberty Loan Drive, the Motion Picture Committee sent a request asking distributors to print slogans "boosting the Liberty Bonds" on all one-sheet posters published between the sixth and twenty-seventh of April 1918.[60] The Committee suggested sentiments ranging from "Buy Liberty Bonds" to "Liberty Bonds—Safe and Patriotic" and "Every Liberty Bond Smashes a Hun."

On 13 October 1918, Famous Players-Lasky ran a full-page ad in the *New York Times* picturing Columbia superimposed on a motion picture palace, urging movie-goers to "LEND THE WAY THEY FIGHT—BUY BONDS TO YOUR UTMOST," and quoting a letter from William McAdoo:

> The great motion picture industry has been conspicuous in its enthusiastic support of these enterprises. Mr. Zukor and his associates have represented your organizations in its relations with the Treasury Department and have given unstintingly of their time, talent and labor to help the Liberty Loan and War Savings appeals before the American people.[61]

Fig. 4.3. Famous Players-Lasky advertisement in the *New York Times*, 13 October 1918. Demonstrating practical patriotism, Famous Players-Lasky advertised its own contribution to the war effort while urging American citizens to buy Liberty Bonds.

The film industry, coordinated by the War Cooperation Committee, went "over the top" to promote the sale of Liberty Bonds. Many of the specific examples cited here were covered in the *New York Times*, but many others, including the *Chicago Tribune*, the *Milwaukee Journal*, and the *Minneapolis Tribune* also contained these sorts of ads and articles. That the pictures of stars in patriotic guises and articles about their contributions to the war effort were placed by their own or their studio's press agent, is to a certain extent irrelevant. Their names, faces, and actions were kept before the public, printed in that medium of mass communication most people relied upon for their news of the war. Established strategies of image building and publicity were simply adapted to the situation at hand.

NAMPI Aids Other Governmental Departments

The National Association of the Motion Picture Industry is about to
institute a fruit and shell saving campaign in motion picture trade
papers to help provide material for manufacturers of charcoal for Army
gas masks. Two hundred peach pits or seven pounds of nut shells make
one mask.

Forward: Journal of the Wisconsin State Council of Defense[62]

Examining the cooperation between NAMPI and the Food Administration and the Treasury Department illustrates the sorts of homefront activities in which the various branches of the film industry participated during the nineteen months of United States involvement in World War I. A brief summary of some of the work of the other departments to which NAMPI assigned industry representatives shows the broad spectrum of industry involvement with the war effort.

The War Department

On behalf of the War Department, the American Protective League requested travelogue films from distributors like George Kleine in the spring of 1918. The American Expeditionary Force had reached the Western Front by early 1918 and the Germans launched a major offensive that spring, bringing them within fifty miles of Paris. Thus the APL's request "for immediate use for intelligence purposes [of] photographs, drawings and descriptions of bridges, buildings, towns and localities . . . occupied by the German forces in France, Belgium and Luxembourg, and likewise in that part of Germany lying west of a line running north and south through Hamburg," was particularly urgent.[63] The German's Somme and Aisne-Marne Offensives, which culminated in Allied victories at Cantigny on 28 May, at Chateau-Thierry on 25 June, and Belleau Wood on 25 June, cut right through the part of France pictured in film the War Department requested.

The Red Cross

Stars aided the Red Cross. The 30 December 1917 rotogravure section of the *New York Times* printed a photograph of Douglas Fairbanks and Charlie Chaplin serving as footmen to Mary Pickford in a pageant benefitting the Red Cross.[64] Later that month, Fairbanks raised ten thousand dollars for the Red Cross at a "Wild West Entertainment" staged in Los Angeles.[65] William S. Hart donated his sombrero, with his autograph on the hatband, to the war relief efforts of the Red Cross.[66] For the Second War Fund Drive of the Red Cross, NAMPI distributed a narrative film entitled *The Spirit of the Red Cross*. In New York City, in a week in May 1918, a star was to appear at every theater in town to boost the fund drive, and a special matinee was held in every theater on Saturday morning at 10:00 A.M., with all proceeds going to the American Red Cross Fund.[67]

In Addition . . .

The United States Civil Service Commission, the United States Department of Labor, and the Department of Agriculture all requested that epilogues be attached to feature films requesting support for their programs.[68] P. A. Powers, treasurer of Universal, was appointed chairman of a Commission on Training Camp Activities. "Mr. Powers said yesterday that the appointment of the Committee would mean that thousands of feet of film would be placed at the disposal of the Government and that the soldiers and sailors would see the best motion pictures made by all the producing companies."[69]

In August 1918, a committee of NAMPI was formed to aid Fuel Administrator Garfield find ways to help the film industry conserve fuel and to educate the public, "in conservation by screen propaganda."[70] On a less grand scale, motion picture exhibitors aided the United States Army's "pit and shell" drive. *Forward*, the paper of the Wisconsin Council of Defense, reported particularly good results among midwestern theater managers:

"One house in Indiana obtained four barrels of peach stones at one afternoon matinee.[71]

The United States Army's pit and shell drive, the United States Food Administration, the Treasury Department, and the Red Cross, among other agencies and government departments, benefitted from the cooperation of the film industry during World War I. The film industry benefitted too. The National Association of the Motion Picture Industry facilitated government-industry relations and increased its own membership during 1917 and 1918. Stars and other industry personnel, working through NAMPI, became identified by their war work as well as their movie making and achieved wider recognition and a brighter image. Not everyone, however, affiliated with this trade association. George Kleine forged his own link with the federal government and came to the aid of his country as he protected the interests of his business.

George Kleine Aids the Government

FEDERAL OFFICERS IN CHARGE OF THIS RECRUITING CAMPAIGN HAVE
SEEN AND ENDORSED THIS THREE-REEL FEATURE, "THE STAR SPANGLED
BANNER," AND WILL CO-OPERATE IN EXPLOITING IT. THIS CO-OPERATION
IS A MIGHTY FORCE. . . .

advertisement for The Star Spangled Banner (1917)[72]

George Kleine was a gadfly in the film industry. He railed in the trade press and to the Priorities Committee of the War Industries Board about excessive star salaries, general inefficiency, and waste.[73] George Kleine refused to join NAMPI, objecting that it was composed of men who wished to satisfy "either personal vanity or business interests."[74] He worried about fiscal responsibility. "Another reason [for not joining] is the absence, so far as I am aware, of any accounting for the large sums of money that have been contributed and further sums that are being asked for."[75] When NAMPI assessed the George Kleine System a membership fee of five hundred dollars, Kleine pencilled "NO" into the margin of NAMPI's letter.[76] His final objection was more philosophical. Kleine didn't believe that one trade organization could attend to the needs of such a diverse constituency as the film industry. "In my judgement there should be one [trade organization] for producers, one for distributors and one for exhibitors, each independent of the other and co-operating in those matters in which their interests are identical."[77]

Although he was not a member of NAMPI, George Kleine remained on its mailing list, and his company did participate in the War Cooperation Committee's initiatives. He also acted independently of NAMPI, however. While most of NAMPI's activities were tangential to feature-film production and distribution, Kleine's were not. As distributor for the Thomas Edison Company's last feature, *The Unbeliever* (Alan Crosland, 1918), Kleine worked directly with Colonel A. S. McLemore of the United States Marine Corps to produce and promote this film intended to aid military recruiting.[78]

The cooperation among Kleine, Edison, and the Marine Corps began before the United States entered World War I with collaboration on a three-reel narrative film, *The Star Spangled Banner*. It was released on 10 June 1917, just after the United States entered the war, and was timed to coincide with a Marine Corps recruitment drive. *The Star Spangled Banner* served as a dry run for the collaboration among Kleine, the Edison Company's McChesney, and McLemore for the six-reel feature *The Unbeliever*, released in February of 1918.

The Unbeliever *(Crosland, 1918)*

> On Monday noon, February 4, I am to have luncheon with Colonel
> McLemore and Major Parker of the United States Marines and about
> thirty-five or forty Publicity Sergeants who will be here from various
> sections of the country. . . . One of the things to be discussed is the
> co-operation of the Marine Corps in connection with the exploiting of
> "The Unbeliever." Major Parker wants me to be in a position to tell him
> just what we would like to have them do in co-operation with your
> [George Kleine System] offices, so I will appreciate it if you will tell me
> by return mail exactly what instructions or requests I should pass on to
> them.
>
> *L. W. McChesney, 24 January, 1918*[79]

The Unbeliever was adapted from "The Three Things," a novelette written by popular author Mary Raymond Shipman Andrews. Serialized in the November and December 1915 issues of *Ladies' Home Journal,* it was reprinted by Little, Brown in 1915, 1916, 1918, and 1924.[80] Published before the United States entered the war, "The Three Things" told the story of Phil Morton, a rich young man with three failings—he did not believe in God, he hated all Germans, and he felt superior to people in the working class. In the film version, which was scripted and produced after the

United States entered World War I, Phil enlisted in the Marines. Through a series of wildly improbable coincidences, terrible wounds, and dumb luck, he came to appreciate religion, democracy, and some Germans. He also fell in love with a brave Belgian girl—from the working class.

The Unbeliever was made possible by the cooperation of the United States Marine Corps. Much of the film was shot at the Marine cantonment in Quantico, Virginia, with the Marines, under Colonel A. S. McLemore, providing men, uniforms, "bunks and chow," and locations. "Generally the Commanding Officers are with us the whole way, and now a ray of optimism is active in spite of our heartbreaking delay in getting underway."[81] The weather had not cooperated and helmets for the soldiers' costumes were late in arriving, but nevertheless shooting ended around 23 November, and the film was completed in early December.[82]

The Marines, represented by Colonel A. S. McLemore, also played an important role in the promotion of *The Unbeliever*. Their goal—as it had been with promotion of *The Star Spangled Banner*—was to encourage enlistment among young men attending the film. To this end, Marines performed in live acts which preceded some screenings of the film. In Chicago, under the supervision of retired Marine Corps Lieutenant Frederick Kensel, Marines were part of the "Patriotic Prelude" to *The Unbeliever*.[83] As a medley of patriotic songs, including "Keep the Home Fires Burning," "The Halls of Montezuma," "The U.S. Spells US," and "When the Great Red Dawn is Shining," were played, the curtain rose on a camp of Marines about to embark for France. Next, local tenor Hardy Williamson sang, and the Marines in twos or in fours marched off stage. Then the screen was lowered and the first scene of *The Unbeliever* played. This was followed by another live presentation in which Chicago contralto Ida Gardner sang goodbye to the tenor, and the movie ran to its conclusion.

A similar prologue was staged when *The Unbeliever* played at the Liberty Theater in Seattle, Washington. Two Marines blew their bugles in front of the theater. Inside the house, the auditorium was darkened; a bugle sounded assembly; the tramp of feet was heard, and a line of soldiers carrying bayonets appeared over the top of the dug-out built around the footlights. Answering the assembly call, there was a rattle of guns and the sound of gunfire. This was followed by "The Star Spangled Banner," and *Motion Picture News* reported that the audience was on its feet while the theater rang with cheers and whistles as the first scenes of *The Unbeliever* appeared.[84] Between shows, Private Hollister, who claimed local fame by having hiked from Portland, Oregon, to New York to enlist, gave recruitment talks.

The five-week run of *The Unbeliever* at the Majestic Theatre in Detroit typified the way the film was marketed with the help of the Marine Corps. One week before it opened there, the manager of the Majestic announced his coming attraction as a film that would be something special: "Coming Sunday, March 10, 'The Unbeliever.' Endorsed by U.S. Government Officials and some of Detroit's Leading Businessmen, Educators, Ministers, and Club Women as the Greatest War Drama Ever Presented."[85] At midweek, Detroit citizens were primed to expect verisimilitude: on 7 March, the movie column of the *Detroit Free Press* reminded readers of Marine Corps involvement in the production, named the stars (Raymond McKee and Marguerite Courtot), and announced that Marjorie Kay, "a Detroit girl, who worked with the American ambulance service in France [would] sing, and [that] there [would] be other special features."[86] In the advertisement on the day of the film's opening, theater manager McGee included testimonials from some of the leading citizens who had been invited to its preview. Local attorney Henry Ledyard was quoted: "It is the greatest war film I have ever seen." Dr. A. G. Studer, Secretary of the Detroit YMCA added his endorsement: "It is fascinating in its realism and as a lesson of the common brotherhood of man, is compelling and abiding." The advertisement also quoted the Secretary of the Detroit Board of Commerce, a representative of the Detroit United Railway, the city's acting major, the chairman of the War Advertising Committee of the Adcraft Club, and Dr. Leo M. Franklin.[87] On 11 March McGee hosted a second special showing, and the *Detroit Free Press* reported that "most of the seats [were] taken by members of the Michigan war boards, state government and city officials, United States military officials and members of the state guard."[88] On 12 March an article in the news section of that newspaper proclaimed that " 'Military Night' at the Majestic was a spectacular event." It was, in fact, attended by members of the Army, Navy, and Marine Corps, as well as Detroit's police commissioner and a "capacity assemblage of citizens . . . [and] Mayor Marx and Colonel W. G. Latimer, Commander of the Five Hundred and Fiftieth Michigan State troops and members of the regiment saw themselves on the screen in a review of the troops before Governor Sleeper and military officials shown as a prelude to 'The Unbeliever.' " Also in attendance were 350 uniformed soldiers, Major F. E. Phelps, Commander of the local Army recruiting office, Captain F. E. Martin, in charge of Marine Corps recruiting for the district including Detroit, A. B. Jewitt of the Ford Motor Company, and George Kleine and M. E. Smith "of Chicago, representing the Edison Company, producer of the picture which was made under the auspices of the Marines and sponsored by the United States government."[89] On 18 March, a week into *The Unbeliever*'s run, "The Reel Players" assured Detroit's citizens who had not yet seen the film that "the picture was offered Sunday in precisely the same manner as a week ago. Some of the short preliminary films, such as the resume of current events in the pictures, have been changed, but that is about all."[90] As before, the program would include Marines marching across the stage as if they were boarding a ship to France. In addition, the "Reel Players" wrote, "Miss Kay sings 'Throw Me a Kiss Over the Sea[,]' the orchestra provides special music and the whole production forms a fitting prelude."[91]

A clear pattern of cooperation between film distributor and Marine Corps emerges from these descriptions of particular exhibitions of *The Unbeliever*. Stage shows incorporating soldiers of the Corps functioned to link real Marines with movie Marines, enhancing narrative credibility and heightening the drama of the film, particularly because the young men performing onstage might in the near future be living the lives of their filmic counterparts. In fact, real Marines did play roles in the film, did go to France, and ultimately did fight at Chateau Thierry and Belleau Wood—a fact which Kleine also incorporated in later promotional campaigns for this film.

The Marines simultaneously entertained movie audiences and pursued their goal of sparking young men to enlist. The layout of the advertisement that ran in the *Detroit Free Press* during the *Unbeliever*'s "Fourth Tremendous Week" included the image of a Marine drawn by illustrator James Montgomery Flagg.[92] The soldier resembles Raymond McKee, the actor who played Phil, and this same image appeared on one of the recruiting posters Flagg created for the Marine Corps during World War I. In the poster the Marine stands before an American flag while the text proclaims a message consonant with the movie's theme: "First in the Fight—Always Faithful—BE A U.S. MARINE!"[93] The advertisement for *The Unbeliever* which ran in the 24 March issue of the *Detroit Free Press* noted that McKee had enlisted "and soon sails for France."[94] The film's star had, it seems, fallen under the sway of his promotion and performance. Part of his service to his country included starring in a film produced for the War Department

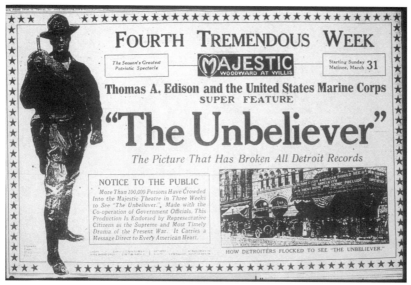

Fig. 4.4. Advertisement for *The Unbeliever* in the *Detroit Free Press*, 31 March 1918.

Commission on Training Camp Activities. A poster bore the smiling face of Sergeant Ray McKee playing Billy Hale, "The Boy Who Kept 'Fit To Win.' " This film was "the first motion picture to tell the truth about the cause and effect of venereal disease."[95]

Stage shows were not the only avenue traveled to spur enlistment. Kleine deployed his network of film exchanges in the service of the Corps. In a memo dated 7 June 1918, he tied the promotion of the film directly to the conduct of the war, highlighting the valor of the Marine Corps.

> The Chicago Tribune, Friday June 7, has its main headline on the front page
> "U.S. MARINES GAIN TWO MILES" . . .
> Let you and your UNBELIEVER customers watch the papers and help them to take advantage of such glorious news items in publicity. . . .
>
> Has "THE UNBELIEVER" stimulated enlistments in your territory?[96]

Upon receipt of this memo, Kleine System exchangemen from around the country responded. The reply made by Mr. Schaeffer of the Denver office was typical.

Fig. 4.5. James Montgomery Flagg's illustration of a soldier who resembled Raymond McKee was used in 1918 to promote both *The Unbeliever* and Marine Corps recruitment efforts. Courtesy of the National Archives.

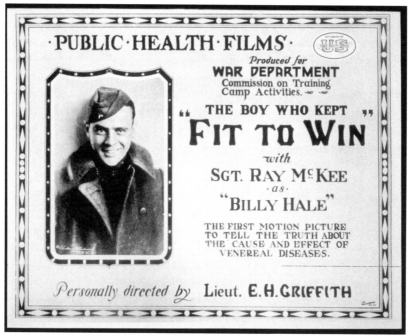

·PUBLIC·HEALTH·FILMS·

Produced for
WAR DEPARTMENT
Commission on Training
Camp Activities.

" THE BOY WHO KEPT "

FIT TO WIN

with

SGT. RAY McKEE

·*as*·

"BILLY HALE"

THE FIRST MOTION PICTURE
TO TELL THE TRUTH ABOUT
THE CAUSE AND EFFECT OF
VENEREAL DISEASES.

Personally directed by Lieut. **E.H.GRIFFITH**

Fig. 4.6. Raymond McKee, star of *The Unbeliever*, enlisted and went to work making hygiene films for the War Department. Courtesy of the American Social Health Association, Social Welfare History Archives, University of Minnesota–Twin Cities.

> I just called Capt. J. C. E. Guggenheim of the local Marine station and he says that as a result of the UNBELIEVER'S run at the Rialto Theatre May 26th to June 5th (11 days) that he secured at least one hundred recruits. . . . During THE UNBELIEVER'S run, they had a regular recruiting station in the lobby of the Rialto Theatre. . . . [97]

Kleine also promoted *The Unbeliever* by following the progress of the Marine extras from the 78th, 79th, 80th, and 96th companies who had acted in the film and heralding their achievements. It was a sad business. McLemore informed Kleine that these companies—which had arrived in France in time to fight in the major Allied offensives in the spring and summer of 1918—had "suffered casualties in killed and wounded amounting to nearly eighty percent."[98] Kleine planned to add a "Roll of Honor" to the beginning of *The Unbeliever*,[99] and McLemore approved of the idea. "Such a picture," he suggested, should bring home to the audiences of 'The Unbeliever' more vividly than anything else, what these men have gone through, who a few months ago 'played' the game of war before the movie camera."[100] Before he created this new prologue, however, Kleine wrote to the mayors of these soldiers' hometowns. The Kleine System was following its own advice—watching the papers and using war news to its advantage in publicizing *The Unbeliever*. Kleine relayed information gained from McLemore to the mayor of Macon, Mississippi, about one of its native sons, Warren Sessions: "Serg. Warren Sessions, in the action near Vierzy on July 19, [was cited for bravery] for fearlessly exposing himself to the heavy machine guns in order to steady and encourage his men when their advance had been checked.[101] Kleine sent a similar letter to Mayor D. E. Waterston of Perry, Missouri, applauding the valor of one of its own, Sergeant Moss Gill. The mayor responded appreciatively, writing, "This is the first information we have had as to the particular circumstances under which Sergenat [*sic*] Gill was wounded and I desire to thank you for your thoughtfulness. . . . " Mayor Waterston offered Kleine a bit of praise in return. "Let me say that 'THE UNBELIEVER' was shown here and that it was the unanimous verdict of our people that it was the greatest war picture ever shown here."[102] Kleine also forwarded a copy of this series of letters to Colonel McLemore who added his thanks to Waterston's. "It is a tribute both to Sergeant Gill and 'The Unbeliever' and your thoughtfulness in sending me the letter is appreciated."[103]

George Kleine, the Edison Company, and the Marine Corps also cooperated when *The Unbeliever* encountered censorship trouble—in Chicago. The film ran afoul of Major Funkhouser, Chicago's infamous movie censor, as well as Shailer Matthews, a professor of divinity at the University of Chicago who served on the city's Thrift Stamp Committee, and James A. Davis, a private citizen. I have shown how the cooperatively conceived promotional strategies for the film gave the Marines, the Edison Company, and the Kleine System control, centralized at the national level. Even potentially quirky local exploitation stunts were standardized by the tips-to-exhibitors columns in trade papers and by the close relationship between Kleine's exchangemen and theater managers. The unpredictability, however, of idiosyncratic complaints like the ones in Chicago constituted a challenge to national distribution. The stakes in these cases were high. Kleine's distribution strategy for *The Unbeliever* involved opening the film in large theaters in major cities.

We could no doubt obtain a great number of $15.00 and $25.00 bookings immediately, but we are pressing hard in every important city to get an engagement in the principal house, not so much for the direct income as because of the indirect effect upon follow-up prices. . . . it will increase the ultimate earnings of the film.[104]

As seen in the case of *The Little American,* problems in Chicago meant problems in the multi-state Chicago territory. Any controversy would also very likely be covered by the major exhibitor trade papers, including *Moving Picture World,* which had a Chicago reporter, and so might affect bookings nation-wide. Additionally, there was the threat of national censorship; Shailer Matthews had forwarded his particular objections to the Department of Justice. A man like Matthews, wrote George Kleine, "can do a great deal of harm puddling with his atom of a brain in public affairs."[105] This film represented a significant investment, and Kleine could not risk interference in its distribution. He, McChesney, and McLemore took each complaint seriously.

Each case was different. Funkhouser wanted a scene showing a German officer shooting a woman and child removed. Shailer Matthews objected to a scene in which Phil, wounded, finds himself in a hospital, his bed in between the beds of two Germans. Christ walks through the scene, and the intertitle reads, "Love your enemies." James Davis found a variety of problems with the film which he felt made it function as pro-German propaganda, including German officers being too well dressed, German brutality being attributed to Prussian influence, German commoners being shown in too sympathetic a light (they appreciate violin music), and a flag-raising ceremony which did not conform sufficiently with military protocol. Kleine and his opposite number at Edison, McChesney, took up each complaint, primarily with Hinton Clabough of the Secret Service, who was stationed in the Federal Building in Chicago. The only change made to the film, however, was the elimination of "Love your enemies."

Kleine's strategy for defending *The Unbeliever* was to fight local attacks with local praise. Addressing himself to Davis's objections, Kleine wrote Clabough of the ecstatic reception *The Unbeliever* had encountered in Detroit. "Experience is the best teacher and must knock out all finespun theories that run counter to it." Pencilled in at the top of this letter is the note "McLemore Thank you. You have rallied to our support in great shape. LWMc"[106] Apparently McLemore, the Marine liaison, corresponded with Clabough, and McChesney, Edison's representative, was also in on the action. No record exists in the Kleine papers or in public sources like newspapers or trade papers to indicate Clabough's reaction either to the letters of complaint or to the letters of defense, and Kleine's letters reveal no evidence of governmental pressure for change. Instead the decision to remove the offensive title seemed to have been Kleine's. "Without taking into account the idiotic attitude of the Shailer person, the point has been made—I believe at the preliminary Detroit show—that the 'Forgive your enemies' title is rather out of place. . . . "[107] No other changes called for by Funkhouser or Davis were made, and the film played in Chicago, opening at the Auditorium Theater.

In the fall of 1918, during the final weeks of World War I, Kleine and Colonel McLemore collaborated on the text for a "Roll of Honor" that would name soldiers who had acted in the film and subsequently fought overseas. Once more cooperation was cordial, and once more it yielded mutual benefits. In December Kleine wrote McLemore, "I cannot refrain from congratulating you and your Department upon the fact that public sentiment is crystallizing into the judgment that the work of the Marines was the vital factor in turning the war to victory."[108] McLemore responded in January 1919, after reading the script for the "Roll of Honor. "I think this is good business for you, and it is additional good advertising for the Marine Corps. I thank you for your courtesy."[109] *The Unbeliever* remained in distribution through 1919.

Conclusion

We are taking this opportunity to place before you the important part which the Motion Picture Industry has played in co-operation with the various departments of the Government in disseminating patriotic propaganda through the medium of the 17,500 motion picture theatres scattered throughout the United States.

These facts are further placed before you for consideration in connection with the classification of the industry in its relation to the war activities and in the firm belief that you will establish a rule that the motion picture industry is essential in every particular to the successful conduct of the war program.

"War Achievements of Motion Picture Industry Set Forth in Brief Presented to Federal Officials by National Association,"
July 1918[110]

It is clear that the film industry—including both those companies represented by NAMPI and those few companies who did not join the organization—played a significant role in the United States' propaganda efforts on the homefront during World War I. Government officials and historians alike judged the work of the War Cooperation Committee of NAMPI successful and important. It is also clear that the film industry benefitted from such well-organized and whole-hearted cooperation.

NAMPI made material gains in its membership in 1917–1918. By August 1919, 93 companies were listed as members, including 47 producers and 15 distributors controlling 500 exchanges.[111] The war also engendered a unanimity of purpose that helped these different sectors of the industry, each with its own agenda, cohere. Their cohesion ended soon after the Armistice, however. In December of 1918, the Exhibitors Class split from NAMPI to form a separate organization.

Acting on behalf of the industry, NAMPI had rallied its governmental supporters to gain exemption for the film industry workers from the Army's Judge Advocate General Enoch H. Crowder's "work or fight" order. Armed with letters of support from George Creel, Herbert Hoover, and William McAdoo, NAMPI won classification as an essential industry from the War Industries Board. NAMPI had also successfully lobbied the Fuel Administration to allow film exhibitors to remain open on that one day a week when other businesses were forced to close to conserve fuel. During the winter of 1918, when the Fuelless Monday order was in effect, exhibitors benefitted from what became for them, in effect, a three-day weekend.

Over the course of the war, NAMPI defeated most state and all federal attempts at censorship through its lobbying efforts and through a voluntary agreement allowing the National Board of Review to screen and approve all films for release. Less concrete were the benefits the film industry gained from the wealth of publicity its war-related activities enjoyed. Stars, producing companies, NAMPI, and local exhibitors, all received press coverage as they participated in the war effort. The film industry and the reformer were, for however brief a period of time, on the same side. As the image of the film industry improved, its potential for attracting a wider audience increased. World War I offered the film industry a greater number of selling points in advertising its product. Moviegoing not only offered entertainment—important enough in this time of stress—but included in the price of admission a war tax that went directly to the government. The theater functioned as a rallying point for the community. It was the place to be informed and inspired by the government's Four Minute Men, the place to be reminded about specific food conservation tactics, the place to contribute to the Red Cross. In their advertising, exhibitors plugged these reasons for coming to the theater as heartily as they promoted the feature film being shown. Film producing companies also sent current movies overseas to be shown to soldiers.

Trade associations were primarily protective alliances which also helped to standardize business practices and foster good public relations with the consumer. [112] The National Association of the Motion Picture Industry followed these general guidelines and functioned with special effectiveness during the months from April 1917 until November 1918. As a result, both the government and the film industry benefitted.

5

The U.S. Film Industry at the End of World War I

And so it has occurred to us that our imperious guests, Mars and
Bellona, are not to blame for all of our troubles. In fact, like every other
evil, war has brought some blessings in disguise. . . .
                                            Variety, *25 October 1918*[1]

THE ARMISTICE ENDING World War I went into effect at eleven o'clock
on the morning of 11 November 1918. Kenneth White, a soldier stationed
in Limoges, France, described the scene for his mother at home in Wisconsin. "Bells ringing, people parading, and everybody letting loose after four
years of war. They are willing to give the Americans plenty of credit too for
bringing the war to a speedy close. The American soldier stands aces high
in France today."[2] In Chicago on that day crowds poured into the
McVickers Theater to watch Charlie Chaplin play a soldier in *Shoulder
Arms*. Doughboy Charlie destroyed an enemy trench, won the love of a
Belgian girl, and captured the Kaiser—in his dreams. Nevertheless, Kaiser Bill was booed, and Chaplin, like his real-life counterpart, stood "aces
high" on Armistice Day.[3]

Waging war had required the United States to expand and mobilize its
fighting force rapidly. Ten million men complied with the new Selective
Service Act and registered for the military draft; 2.8 million of them between the ages of eighteen and forty-five were called up in 1917 and 1918,
and 52,000 of these soldiers—including some who acted in *The
Unbeliever*—died in battle. Despite the absence of these men from the
work force, the domestic economy grew during World War I. More women
went to work, orders for war materiel increased, and corporate profits
tripled between 1914 and 1919.[4] Inflation and labor unrest would follow
the peace, but those difficulties were still several months in the future.

While the workplace and the domestic sphere were disrupted in the
eighteen months from April 1917 through November 1918, they were not
significantly diverted from their prewar course. Neither was the film in-

dustry. United States participation in the war had been too brief to cause massive change.[5] Life and most businesses continued as troop ships crossed the ocean and women planted victory gardens, knitted socks for soldiers, and revised their bread recipes to conserve wheat. Throughout the war, movies offered the American public both momentary diversion from the inconveniences and anxiety of homefront life and a way to participate in the war effort. Theater managers showed newsreels and documentaries about the conflict, housed recruiting stations in their lobbies, collected peach pits for use in gas mask filters, and encouraged their customers to buy Liberty Bonds and War Savings Stamps. The feature films headlining their bills were produced by an industry determined to take a leadership role in spreading the government's message to its citizens but equally guided by prewar aesthetic and business strategies.

The film industry continued to evolve during the World War I era, sparked by both preexisting and war-related causes. Companies grew horizontally, absorbing their competition, and they also expanded vertically, bringing the ability to produce, distribute, and exhibit films into one firm. Such growth came at the expense of the smaller or unaffiliated enterprises. Famous Players-Lasky not only gained production companies like Morosco and Pallas, it also took on the capacity to distribute its product by acquiring Paramount in the summer of 1916. Then, in 1920, on the strength of a line of credit from the Wall Street banking firm Kuhn Loeb, Famous Players-Lasky began buying theaters.[6] First National was formed in 1917 by combining regional theater chains to finance film production and subsequently distributing those films among its members. By war's end, the film industry had incorporated big-business methods, vertically integrating, building theater chains, and creating an oligopoly which would last until 1948. Film producers, exhibitors, and stars like Charlie Chaplin worked hard—spurred on by developments that were sometimes—but not always—war-related.

Film Production

Cause and effect figures will prove that our over-production and too
many exchanges are the highway to economic disaster. . . .
Motion Picture News, *12 October 1918*[7]

During World War I producers continued to release fewer pictures, following a trend that had begun sometime between 1911 and 1914, when the industry adopted the feature-length film as its standard product. Studios cut the number of movies—both shorts and feature-length films—they manufactured between 1916 and 1919. *Variety* reported a decrease from 2,200 subjects and 4,850 reels in 1916 to 1,525 subjects and 4,056 reels in 1917, and these numbers were further reduced to 1,010 subjects and 3,171 reels of film for the 1917–1918 period.[8] The number of feature films dropped from 885 to 876 between the production year of September 1917–August 1918 and the succeeding 1918–1919 season. In the 1919–1920 season, the total decreased even more substantially, to 645.

This decline in the number of features produced in the fall of 1918 and released in 1919 was the result of several distinct causes, not all of which were war-related. One of these was the pandemic of Spanish Influenza, which was particularly virulent in October and November of 1918, causing studios to cut back their production schedules or close entirely for four weeks.[9] While the steady decrease in the number of films produced during the years 1916–1918 might be said to reflect only the effects of influenza, however, or the impact of diminished foreign distribution, the continuing decline in production into 1920 indicates the existence of a deliberate production strategy.

Beginning with the 1917–1918 season, columnists writing for the exhibitor trade papers informed theater managers that "fewer and better" pictures would be made in 1918 and 1919.[10] The buzzwords "fewer and better" and "fewer and bigger," had also been used as producers adopted the feature-length film in the early to mid-1910s as part of a production strategy designed to increase profits.[11] Touted as a boon to the exhibitor, decreased production would eliminate the "cheap picture," and all branches of the film industry would enjoy the benefits of greater attendance generated by word-of-mouth advertising. It was less prominently pointed out that these fewer but better pictures would also have higher rental costs, resulting in the need for longer runs at increased admission prices. This particular production initiative resulted in a change in the operation strategies of many smaller exhibitors, as it brought about the end of the daily change of film programming.

Concurrent with this decline, however, film industry discourse also highlighted the *increase* in the number of independent production companies formed by stars and prominent directors during the months of United States involvement in World War I. *Wid's Yearbook 1918*, for example, gave the matter of independent production extended consideration when it published the responses to a question it posed in a previous issue. "What," it had asked, "is the most important event of the Sept. 1917–

Aug. 1918 production season?" J. S. Dickerson, manager of the Watkins Opera House in Watkins, New York, and Maurice Tourneur, film director, agreed in their assessment. In Tourneur's words: "The big event here is the breaking away of stars and directors from producing organizations. . . . This departure from the old system means individuality. . . .[12]

Among the independents were marginal figures within the film industry, producing a single film and then disbanding. It was another group, those prominent stars and directors with more ambitious long-term goals, whose numbers increased more significantly over the course of U.S. involvement in WWI.

There were several nonwar-related economic causes for an increase in independent film production during the mid-1910s, including the institutionalization of the multiple-reel film, and lower taxes. Additional factors encouraging independent production were the demand from exhibitors for 104 films yearly to satisfy the needs of a twice-weekly change of programs, and the inability of the studios to meet that demand completely; the capability of stars, who, because of the income derived from their own high salaries or from their ability to attract other investors, were able to finance their own production companies; and the availability of distribution outlets like First National to handle independently produced products. As a result, independents were responsible for one-third of the features produced between 1916 and 1918.[13]

The trend toward independent production by stars and directors was under way well before the United States entered World War I in 1917, but the period from late 1918 through 1919 saw an especially remarkable increase in the number of independent producers, suggesting that the increase in independent productions was in at least some respects war-related.[14] Among the factors involved was a press agenting practice common at the time that publicized high salary as a selling point to differentiate their stars from ordinary mortals. In the context of wartime sacrifices, this practice prompted several unwelcome repercussions both inside and outside the film industry.

As early as 20 April, 1917, *Variety* juxtaposed the high salaries of industry personnel with the threat of high war taxes to be imposed by the government.[15] In May of that year, the *New York Times* also covered the issue of high salaries and named the stars causing the commotion.

> New contracts have been made and new companies organized, and
> while there has been no diminution in the size of salaries, no press

agent blurb about the millions paid to the World's Greatest Comedian or the Queen of the Movies has made the welkin ring. . . .

Now a war tax that promises to devour large slices of great incomes is impending, and between the threat of it and the probing of the state tax commissions the proverbial camel would pass through the needle eye more quickly than boastful figures through the lips of a movie magnate.[16]

Chaplin and Pickford—the high-salaried individuals alluded to here—benefitted from the tax advantages open to them through independent production.

But it was not only the promise of greater creative autonomy and the threat of a tax on 40 percent of their income that spurred independent production in 1918–1919. Another cause was—or at least seemed to be—an economic problem. Both the trade press and the popular press carried stories linking high star salaries and wartime conditions to a slump in industry profits, and the film industry's immediate response was to cut or threaten to cut salaries. As early as May 1917, Vitagraph did cut some salaries by 25 percent. *Variety* reported the story and the affected worker's reactions. "Some of the photoplayers claim Vitagraph is using the war as an alibi for cutting salaries. . . . Several directors were among those of the Vitagraph forces hard hit and they quit rather than work on for the reduction."[17] Early in 1918 other film producers, including Carl Laemmle and Samuel Goldwyn, also took the opportunity to blame poor business returns on "inflated" salaries.[18]

Independent production, however, was not viewed as competition by the producing studios, since the independents often distributed through established companies such as Artcraft, Pathe, Mutual, and Goldwyn, and the addition of their films to the product pool took pressure off the producing studios. The independent producer incurred the greater financial risk, and the distributor shared in any profits through a distribution fee. Finally, the prewar and wartime trend of vertical integration of the film producer and distributor and exhibitor kept the independent producer from posing a serious threat to the likes of Famous Players-Lasky or Fox. In the conclusion of an article on the growing phenomenon of the theater chain in 1917–1918, Wid Cumming, editor of *Wid's Yearbook*, cautioned that successful independent production "is not as simple as it might seem. . . ."[19] Independent producers needed access to theaters, particularly the highly visible, well-publicized first-run theaters if their films were to prove profitable. Increasingly over the course of 1917–1918, but especially in the postwar period, such critical exhibition outlets were controlled by integrated corporations such as First National and Famous Players-Lasky. Thus, the effects of the war would play a greater part in shaping the film exhibitor's business in the 1920s.

Film Exhibition

Altogether combinations of circumstances have worked against
the exhibitor and many of the smaller theaters have been having
a hard time.

Moving Picture World, *9 February 1918*[20]

During World War I, Darwinian rhetoric announcing "the survival of the fittest" was often applied to the film exhibitor by motion picture trade journalists.[21] Those exhibitors who proved fittest were most often the owners of large theaters in cities and movie houses organized into chains. The war years were not, on the whole, profitable for the small, independent, or rural exhibitor. These businessmen and women, enjoying a much smaller profit margin, felt the impact of wartime policy and regional idiosyncrasy acutely. The experiences of Chicago's exhibitors illustrate the nationwide developments in movie exhibition.

In January 1918, after the country had been at war for nine months, James McQuade, the Chicago correspondent to *Moving Picture World*, reported a decrease in the number of movie theaters in the city since 1914. His study, based on the records of the Chicago License Commission, showed that 312 theaters seating three hundred people or less had applied for licenses in 1914. In 1915 that number declined to 258; 1916 saw a loss of 28 more small theaters, and by 1917 only 172 theaters of this size took out licenses. During this same time, however, larger theaters were being built, and McQuade noted that although the total number of theaters in Chicago had decreased from 500 in 1914 to 393 in 1917, seating capacity for the city had decreased only by 2,156 seats. He further observed that several large theaters were currently under construction; thus, "the total seating capacity of Chicago picture theaters [would] considerably exceed that of any period in the past."[22] In Chicago and other cities the trend in movie-going led away from the smaller, neighborhood, subsequent-run theaters and toward patronage of the newer, more elaborate first-run houses.[23]

Motion Picture News also noted the decline of the small neighborhood theater in Chicago. Its reporter faulted exhibitor business practices, especially the daily change of film and an over-saturation of theaters in some neighborhoods, suggesting that there were simply too many theaters in competition for a constant or shrinking body of consumers.[24] Larger theaters, which typically programmed films with bigger stars for longer runs, were in a better position to maximize profits for their programs. The wartime production strategy of "fewer and bigger" pictures—that is, films with higher rental fees—indicated the more general industry-wide tendency toward concentration: fewer and bigger films, fewer and bigger producing studios, fewer and bigger movie theaters.

Like smaller theaters in Chicago, movie houses in towns and rural areas suffered during World War I. In asking, "Why the Falling Off?" *Moving Picture World* noted a decline in attendance at theaters outside of the big cities. The affected exhibitors proposed a variety of causes, from wartime policy to industrial trends: " 'We haven't any coal." . . ."So many young men have gone to war we have a noticeable decrease in attendance of young people." . . ."Too many big features." . . ."Too many and too high war taxes.' "[25] Theater-owners had already been assessed a tax under the provisions of the 1916 Revenue Act, but once the United States entered the war, the government needed new monies and so levied new taxes. War taxes on raw film, positive film, and admission prices went into effect in November 1917, and by December the trade papers recorded exhibitors' reactions to this added cost of doing business. Film producers passed the tax on raw and positive film on to the exhibitor. Producers and distributors, through their exchanges, translated these taxes into a charge of 15 cents per reel per day to be paid by all exhibitors regardless of the size of their theater.[26]

An exhibitor in Portland, Oregon, explained the smaller theater managers' objections: "It charges the small exhibitor the same flat rate as it does the big fellow, while the margin of profit to the small theater is greatly smaller than that of the larger house."[27] This claim was corroborated by reports from exhibitors in Brooklyn; New Orleans; Reading, Pennsylvania; Washington, D.C.; and St. Louis.[28] The reports often linked war taxes, a decrease in audience (particularly young men on account of the draft), and the necessity of maintaining a low admission price, and it was frequently noted that smaller theaters were most adversely affected. Journalists commiserated with the theater-owner. "This poor fellow can't figure out how he can do business in his home town charging, say, an admission of 10 cents."[29] Small theaters in city neighborhoods, small towns, and rural areas, whose audience base was already eroded by young men going onto the service, did not have the option of raising ticket prices as did the larger city theater relying on a "transient trade." The small theater could not afford to lose even a few customers to a higher price of admission.[30]

In addition to publishing the reports sent in by local film exhibitors, *Moving Picture World* surveyed the state of film exhibition in the United States and Canada. In February 1918, the trade journal published the results of its study, in an article entitled "World Correspondents Describe Business Conditions." Its findings reinforced the dichotomy existing between the health of large and small theaters. For instance, although conditions in Cleveland were manageable for the first-run theaters, this was not the case for smaller businesses.

> The neighborhood houses . . . continue below normal. . . . Outside of Cleveland, throughout the smaller cities of northern Ohio, there has been little improvement, the slump starting Nov. 1. Many very small towns, with one or two theaters, are opened one or two nights a week and about 15 have closed.[31]

The *Moving Picture World* survey noted the practice of reducing the number of shows per week. Michigan houses cut back. These exhibitors experienced lower attendance due to extreme cold and snow; the weather problems were magnified by a coal shortage because of government regulation of this important resource in many parts of the East and the Midwest. Still, the reporter noted, "Most of the smaller theaters throughout the state are running only a few nights each week even under normal conditions."

Regional idiosyncrasies reinforced a trend favoring the larger, urban theater. In Des Moines, Iowa, exhibitors benefitted from the military patronage of an army cantonment; the theaters throughout the rest of the state, however, felt the effects of cold weather and coal shortages. "There have been approximately 150 theaters closed in Iowa in the last 120 days. . . . Many of the theaters now open are running but from 1–3 nights a week in the small country towns." The reporter predicted that many of these small theaters now closed would open again in the spring. This hopeful assessment nevertheless pointed out the vulnerable and precarious position of the small and rural film exhibitor.

Texas did not have the burden of cold weather. Instead, drought accounted for the demise of "perhaps 75 houses in the smaller towns." The dry spell also affected theaters in rural areas of California, yet "business conditions in the moving picture industry in the San Francisco territory are regarded as being quite satisfactory."

Much the same was true of Kentucky for the period throughout 1917 and into early 1918. Louisville theater managers benefitted both from the higher employment in the local manufacturing industry due to war orders and from the presence of between 25,000 and 50,000 soldiers stationed at Camp Taylor near the city. In rural areas, however, "a number of theaters have been forced to close this winter due to lack of fuel. . . . many power plants have been down frequently on account of lack of fuel. In addition the roads have been impassable. . . ."[32]

While *Motion Picture News* urged exhibitors not to listen to the "calamity howlers," the combination of strains—felt by all exhibitors—most adversely affected small and rural exhibitors. *Moving Picture World*'s survey covered a period of time through early 1918. The exhibitor besieged by bad weather might at least look forward to spring. Spring, however, would be succeeded by a traditionally slow summer season and in 1918 that summer season would be followed by an unpredicted and catastrophic influenza pandemic in the fall. In other words, even without the war, April 1917 through November 1918 would have been a difficult time for film exhibitors, especially smaller exhibitors. The war tax, the draft, and wartime regulation of such materials as coal were more burdensome for the small or unaffiliated theater manager than for the manager of a theater in a regional chain, or the manager of a large theater in a city.

The decline of the small exhibitor's power and position within the United States film industry during the nineteen months of American involvement in World War I was intensified by the continuation of a trend that would accelerate after the war ended: the development and expansion of theater chains. *Wid's Yearbook 1918*, covering developments in the industry from September 1917 until August 1918, included the following note: "Gradually in the past few years there has been a decided tendency toward the accumulation of several theaters by one individual or corporation, particularly the tying up of all the best houses in one city."[33] The article was followed by five and one-half pages listing by state and by city the theaters comprising each chain. In *Wid's Yearbook 1920*, this listing had increased to eight and one-half pages in a reduced type size. The expansion of existing theater chains and the cooperation of independently owned theaters in booking circuits was held up as a positive advance in business management by the exhibitors trade press. Commenting in July 1917, a writer for *Moving Picture World* reported,

> In almost every city today we find certain exhibitors who are owners of a chain of theaters embracing from six to twelve and in many cases there are many more, including links in different cities. In almost every instance these places of amusement are in exterior and interior architecture an attraction and a credit to the community where they are located. We are convinced that this chain system is only another indication of a more stabilized phase of the industry developed by serious-minded business men.[34]

Operating theaters using the latest management practices, instilling a sense of professionalism in exhibitors, and firmly establishing movies as the predominant form of entertainment within a community were the goals set for theater-owners during the war years. Additionally, given the array of stresses felt by the film exhibitor in 1917 and 1918, it is not surprising that a development touted as "stabilizing," would encounter little resistance either rhetorically or actively. Contemporary business historian Howard T. Lewis suggested that exhibitors also saw in theater chains a parallel to the mergers and consolidations taking place in other businesses.[35] Frank Rembusch, an Indiana exhibitor, added another, more pragmatic reason for exhibitors to combine: "[the] Paramount Company would dominate the market if exhibitors didn't get together."[36]

Exhibitors wanted the leverage such economies of scale could provide as they bargained with distributors in the face of rising film rental fees accruing to the fewer and better pictures. In Chicago, Alfred Hamburger increased the number of theaters in his chain from eight in 1916 to twelve in 1917, and had an additional three houses under construction. In 1917 the Ascher Brothers added six theaters to their chain of nine, and Lubliner and Trinz added four theaters to their chain.[37] In Minneapolis, Ruben and Finkelstein expanded their theater chain in the Twin Cities and earned comparison with other big city peers like Hamburger, the Ascher Brothers, and Marcus Loew: "The week of April 7 [1917] the Minnesota exhibitors opened their 8th and the Twin Cities' largest theater . . . and also purchased their 9th theater. . . . Ruben and Finkelstein now own the 5 largest theaters on Hennepin Ave. . . ."[38] *Moving Picture World* reported that the "Tendency among Theaters to Combine," in St. Louis would

". . . pave the way for a struggle in the very near future of 'survival of the fittest' among several syndicates."[39] The theaters would be tested by more than prevailing business trends and the exigencies of a wartime economy, however. The pandemic of Spanish Influenza in the fall of 1918 would literally threaten the lives of many in the industry, including film producers, exhibitors, and actors.

Spanish Influenza

Because of the deplorable epidemic of influenza that has gripped the entire country, even unto its most remote corners, the clock of the motion picture industry has been stopped as of October 14.
　　　　　　　　　Moving Picture World, *26 October 1918*[40]

Film land is full of gloom and germs.
　　　　　　　　　Moving Picture World, *9 November 1918*[41]

The movies faced another challenge just as the war was ending—the pandemic of Spanish Influenza. This disease, also known as "grippe," or "grip," required film industry reaction to a situation with no business precedent. The flu affected the operations of all branches of the industry in a way the war never had—it closed them down. Spanish Influenza broke in three waves. The first took place among soldiers fighting in Europe in the spring of 1918; the second hit American shores in late August 1918, leaving few families in the United States unaffected; and the third struck in 1919. The flu killed twenty million people worldwide, and more than four hundred thousand in the United States. More soldiers died of the flu than died in battle in World War I. Most vulnerable were people between the ages of twenty and forty-five.

While the film industry had two years to watch the progress of the war and to strategize its response prior to April 1917, Spanish Influenza allowed no planning time. The flu was caused by an air-borne virus, and it had no effective treatment beyond bed rest, keeping warm, and avoiding crowds. No vaccine prevented infection, and the disease was highly contagious. For example, four thousand new cases were reported on a single day in Cincinnati.[42] To ameliorate conditions, theaters, schools, and churches in cities and towns across the country were closed by order of local and state public health officials in October.

Moving Picture World's lead editorial for the week of 26 October blared, "PRODUCERS DECIDE TO CLOSE UP SHOP, Shutting of Theaters in

Districts Where Grip is Spreading leads national Association Members to Take Action—Reports from Affected Communities."[43] By then the flu, which began in the East, had reached the Midwest. Movie houses in North and South Carolina, Maryland, Georgia, Kentucky, Michigan, Indiana, and Iowa closed. On 2 November, *Moving Picture World* trumpeted, again in large, upper case letters, "INFLUENZA EPIDEMIC WORKING WEST." Boston's theaters had reopened, but San Francisco's were now closed.

Although it was difficult to be optimistic in the face of these closings—hard to apply the precepts of practical patriotism—the industry tried. Throughout November, trade papers reported that exhibitors around the country were taking advantage of their time off to re-decorate their theaters.[44] In Dallas, Texas, some managers adapted by turning their lobbies to other purposes. P. G. Cameron of the Crystal Theater transformed his into a vegetable market.[45]

Reacting to the loss of so many exhibition outlets, the Los Angeles production studios closed or cut by half their production for five weeks, laying off actors and technicians. Distributors with time on their hands reorganized the stock on their shelves. At no time had the war incapacitated the film industry as much as Spanish Influenza did.[46] The Armistice came just as the country was emerging from its bout with the flu. At the end of November, A. H. Giebler, the Hollywood correspondent to *Moving Picture World* rejoiced, "the germs are fleeing like the Germans." In the midst of all this turmoil, Charlie Chaplin's war comedy, *Shoulder Arms*, opened in cities around the country.

Charlie Chaplin's *Shoulder Arms* (First National, 1918)

Shoulder Arms was Chaplin's second film for First National. His work history, progressing from actor to director to producer and, finally, to founding member of United Artists, reflects the general career path for big stars in the industry of the time, and illustrates the trend toward an increase in the volume of independently produced films. In switching from Keystone to Essanay in 1915, Chaplin negotiated a higher salary and the right to direct his own pictures. He moved to Mutual in 1916, this time for higher salary for fewer pictures—twelve two-reelers. In moving to First National in 1917, the deal was not for more money—at least not for higher salary—but, rather, for even fewer pictures: Chaplin's contract called for eight films to be made in eighteen months. He was now an independent producer enjoying the attendant benefits of greater creative autonomy as well as financial gain, and he was still, through First National, distributed to major theaters in the United States.[47] The culmination of this steady progress toward independent production came in January 1919, when Chaplin, Pickford, Fairbanks, and D. W. Griffith created United Artists to distribute their movies.

Chaplin's career from 1914 through the 1920s also illustrates the movement from the single-reel to the feature-length film that was taking place during these years. His Keystone films were mainly one-reelers, those for Essanay and Mutual two-reelers. Chaplin's move to First National saw him producing films ranging from two through six reels: two-reelers were *A Day's Pleasure*, *The Idle Class*, and *Pay Day*, for the period December 1919–April 1922; three-reelers were *A Dog's Life* and *Sunnyside*, April 1918 and June 1919; *The Pilgrim*, February 1923, was a four-reeler; and the six-reeler *The Kid* was released in February 1921. This mixed lot of shorts and features may be explained by the requirements of the comedy genre where humor may be more easily achieved in a shorter format and by the fact that after 1919 Chaplin was trying to finish up his contractual obligations to First National so that he could begin making movies for United Artists. His U.A. films produced in the 1920s, *A Woman of Paris*, *The Gold Rush*, and *The Circus*, were eight, nine, and seven reels long, respectively.

Shoulder Arms, a three-reel comedy, opened in New York two weeks before World War I ended. Charlie Chaplin, the Little Tramp, had gone to war. The film's release also coincided with the inexorable movement of Spanish Influenza from the East Coast to the West. Therefore the topicality of the war and the timeliness of the flu met in the promotion of *Shoulder Arms*. Neither of these grim realities dampened the ardor of Chaplin's New York fans. *Shoulder Arms* proved so successful that Harold Edel, the twenty-nine-year-old managing director of the Strand, alluding to the flu, extended the run a second week. "We think it a most wonderful appreciation of 'Shoulder Arms' that people would veritably take their lives in their hands to see it."[48] Ironically, this "appreciation" was published in *Moving Picture World* on 9 November, seven days after Edel succumbed to Spanish Influenza.

Shoulder Arms opened at the Circle Theater in Indianapolis on 3 November, the day after the theaters in that city reopened following a three-week ban on public performances. The flu and the war had shared the front page of the *Indianapolis News* throughout October. While headlines charted the defeat of Germany's armies, sub-headlines reported the num-

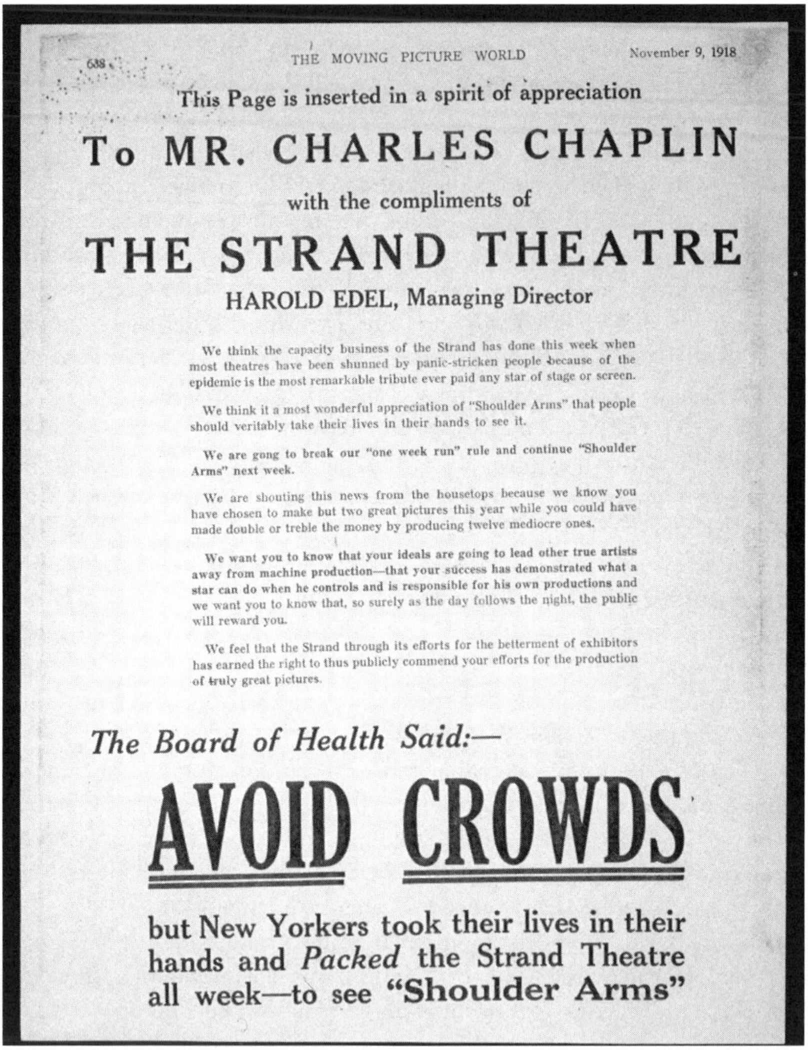
688 THE MOVING PICTURE WORLD November 9, 1918

This Page is inserted in a spirit of appreciation

To MR. CHARLES CHAPLIN

with the compliments of

THE STRAND THEATRE

HAROLD EDEL, Managing Director

We think the capacity business of the Strand has done this week when most theatres have been shunned by panic-stricken people because of the epidemic is the most remarkable tribute ever paid any star of stage or screen.

We think it a most wonderful appreciation of "Shoulder Arms" that people should veritably take their lives in their hands to see it.

We are gong to break our "one week run" rule and continue "Shoulder Arms" next week.

We are shouting this news from the housetops because we know you have chosen to make but two great pictures this year while you could have made double or treble the money by producing twelve mediocre ones.

We want you to know that your ideals are going to lead other true artists away from machine production—that your success has demonstrated what a star can do when he controls and is responsible for his own productions and we want you to know that, so surely as the day follows the night, the public will reward you.

We feel that the Strand through its efforts for the betterment of exhibitors has earned the right to thus publicly commend your efforts for the production of truly great pictures.

The Board of Health Said:—

AVOID CROWDS

but New Yorkers took their lives in their hands and *Packed* the Strand Theatre all week—to see "Shoulder Arms"

Fig. 5.1. Advertisement in *Moving Picture World* placed by Harold Edel, manager of the Strand Theater in New York. Ironically, Edel fell victim to Spanish Influenza only days before this advertisement was published.

ber of new cases of Spanish Influenza in the city. Readers on 17 October were cheered to see the headlines "Lille Occupied," "Haig Strikes Le Cateau Sector," "Retreat of 17 German Divisions Almost a Rout," "Germany Bending," and "More Pressure Says Lansing." A bit farther down the page came more sobering news: "Influenza Ban May Be Extended," which meant the closing of many public venues. Below this was printed the daily flu casualty list: "Civilian Population, new cases 415, total 3,352; new deaths 15, total 49."[49] On 23 October 1918, 415 new cases were reported for a total of 4,777, and the death toll had risen to 256.[50] Thus on Saturday, 2 November, the first day the ban was lifted, Indianapolis's theater managers collaborated on an advertisement. Entitled "Mother and Jim, Lettie and Me," its text linked war, flu, and the movies. All three were timely.

> We had a family reunion last night, Jim came home from camp. Big Surprise No. 1. Lettie read in the paper that shows were open, Surprise No. 2. And when Jim asked mother to go she said, "I guess so," Surprise No. 3. We went Saturday, in the front row. Great Show![51]

By Monday, 4 November, the Spanish Influenza was no longer newsworthy; the war once again dominated the front page: "Terms of Armistice open to the Austrian and Hungarian Territory for an Attack on the Huns," "Hostilities Cease on Italian Front," and "Yankees and British Seek to Cause Hun Disaster."[52] Charlie Chaplin's *Shoulder Arms* opened for a week-long run at the Circle Theater on 3 November. Echoing the military rhetoric of the front page, the announcement for the film ballyhooed that Chaplin had "Captured the Town—Ask Any of Yesterday's Happy Patrons."[53]

The advertising campaign launched by S. Barrett McCormick, manager of this large downtown theater, was held up as a model by *Moving Picture World*. The trade journal especially admired the way McCormick sold the film with a blend of timeliness—the imminent ending of the war—and the established star power of Chaplin. As in the case of *Joan the Woman*, the exhibitor exploited his flexibility (in a way the film producer never could) to respond to the events, changing daily, as the Armistice approached. As the reporter for *Moving Picture World* noted: "Mr. McCormick had the town watching for his advertising to see what [of a newsworthy nature] was coming next."[54]

On Wednesday, 5 November, Republican victories in state and local

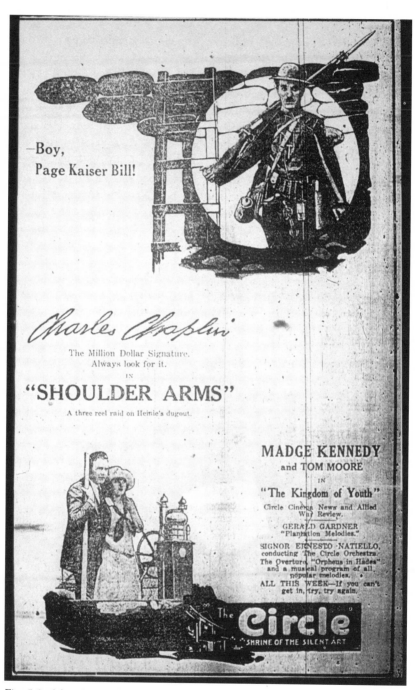

Fig. 5.2. Advertisement for *Shoulder Arms* in the *Indianapolis News*, 6 November 1918. The manager of the Circle Theater followed the principle of timeliness as he tied promotion of the film to fast-breaking events at the end of the war.

elections in Indiana were overshadowed by headlines applauding, "Allies Driving Ahead on First of 200 Miles," and "Prisoners Taken in Italy Will Total 500,000." On the movie page, McCormick featured a grimacing Charlie alongside text reading "Say—Who Said Soft Peace."[55] On 6 November, election news got top billing in the headlines: "Republicans Will Control Next House, Returns Indicate," and "Senate Complexion in Doubt." Still, war news was presented in upper case type: "ARMISTICE DELEGATES LEAVE BERLIN FOR WEST FRONT." In this issue, Charlie, in full military regalia, looked out at the reader and the advertising copy commanded, "—Boy, Page Kaiser Bill!"[56] The high point of McCormick's campaign, when he was best able to exploit war news to his advantage, happened on 7 November, the day a reporter for United Press International misinterpreted a French cease fire and wired his New York office with the message, "Urgent. Armistice Allies Germany signed smorning [*sic*]. Hostilities ceased two safternoon [*sic*]."[57] McCormick alluded to the "false armistice" in that day's ad for *Shoulder Arms,* slipping in the jibe, "This is a war picture but it was not filmed by the United Press."[58] *Moving Picture World* was equally gleeful over the quick thinking of this exhibitor when it devoted two pages to documenting McCormick's campaign for *Shoulder Arms* in early December—here was a man and a method to be emulated. The fact that the article, including all the ads McCormick had run, plus commentary on the effectiveness of their type style, size, and copy, ran nearly a month after the true Armistice, attests to the institutional sanctions then operative regarding the use of timeliness to sell movies. McCormick's only "regret" might have been that the war ended two days after the film closed. The manager of the McVickers Theater in Chicago was luckier.

Shoulder Arms opened in Chicago on Armistice Day, 11 November 1918. Its review in the *Chicago Tribune* heralded "A Great Picture with a Great Man on a Great Day." The film's reviewer described the audience in the theater: "They streamed in waving flags, throwing confetti, and wearing strange patriotic headgear, rakishly awry. When the favorite's name was flashed upon the screen, greeted it with a rousing cheer."[59] The "gathering" continued at multiple theaters throughout Chicago at least until the end of December. It had a particularly long life as a reissue, playing in 1922, 1927, 1943, 1959, 1963, 1971, and 1986. *Shoulder Arms* did not languish on distributors' shelves, the ironically happy result of the ending of the war. While timeliness—first the flu and then the end of the war— were used to sell *Shoulder Arms* to movie-goers in New York, Indianapolis, and points between, once the flu threat abated and the war ended, the

Chaplin persona became the main talking point for exhibitors. Who was Charlie Chaplin, and how did *Shoulder Arms* fit into the mix of films available to the public in November of 1918?

On 20 October, the day *Shoulder Arms* opened at the Strand in New York City for its prerelease run, Guy F. Lee, whose verse appeared daily in the *Chicago Tribune*, published "The Little Fellow."

The Little Fellow

The Serb is back; the Belgian
    Is marching home once more;
The Finn is nearly finished
    With German peace and war;
And Luxembourg the trampled,
    For years by fear held mute,
Arises, David-like, to give
    The giant Hun the boot.

It won't be long till all of them,
    These infants of the earth,
Shall have their chance to breathe and grow
    Mid safety, hope and mirth,
Take heart! Down-trodden children
    Among the lands of men:
The Little Fellow's coming
    Into his own again![60]

These "little fellows" were countries, but the allusion in the verse is to Chaplin. Chaplin, Charlie, the Little Tramp, the Little Fellow, the Little Feller, was a ubiquitous sign in popular culture by 1918. Children jumping rope chanted, "Charlie Chaplin went to France / To teach the ladies how to dance, / Heel, toe, around we go, / Salute to the captain, bow to the Queen, / Turn your back on the old submarine."[61] Allied soldiers made the Little Tramp mascot of their companies and sang "The moon shines bright on Charlie Chaplin" to the tune of the popular contemporary song "Red Wing."[62] Other film makers tried to cash in on Chaplin's fame by imitating him. In fact, though, when *Shoulder Arms* itself was plagiarized by a film called *Charlie in the Trenches*, Chaplin sued.[63]

Shoulder Arms joined *The Yellow Dog, The Border Wireless, Vive La France, Battling Jane, America's Answer, Private Peat, The Last of the Kaiser, or the Prussian Cur, The Life of General Pershing,* and *The Hun Within* as the war-related fare available to Chicago's movie-goers. However, while these ten films had war-related content, twenty-one others did not. And, although their numbers increased over the course of the war, films with war-related content never dominated other films in release. The most popular film of World War I, however, was D. W. Griffith's epic war drama *Hearts of the World*. Comedies comprised a small proportion of all war-related film production in the United States in 1917 and 1918, and *Shoulder Arms* was the only comedy among the ten war films playing in Chicago the week it opened. But in describing *Shoulder Arms* before its release, *Moving Picture World* did attempt to reassure its exhibitors that the humor in the movie did not detract from "the dignity of soldiering, but rather embellishes that dignity with a new viewpoint."[64]

Exhibitors showing *Shoulder Arms* could feel assured that they would not offend those among their clientele who may have had loved ones at the front. Walter K. Hill, the film reviewer for *Moving Picture World*, raised another issue of propriety implicit in the fact that Charlie Chaplin made a comedy about the war. "In all this, Chaplin never stoops to a single vulgar act. Right to the finish he plants a sturdy kick right were everybody in the audience will want to extend their own complements [sic]."[65] In pointing out the controlled nature of Chaplin's physical comedy, Hill alluded to a debate that had been circulating about the nature of Charlie Chaplin's comedy since he began to attain star status in 1915.[66] By 1918 Chaplin had refined his screen persona to meet the objection made by proponents of the genteel tradition that he was vulgar. To counter claims that he was an uncouth and uneducated "low comic," he fashioned for himself the image of a serious artist. Hill's review indicated that at least a trace of the old concerns remained. Chaplin, perhaps aware of this problem of perception "signed" the advertisements for his film "Charles," not Charlie Chaplin.

Publicists and trade journalists may also have felt the need for cautious handling of *Shoulder Arms* for the reason that Chaplin had not enlisted in either the British or the United States military. The charge of slacker had been leveled against him as early as 1914 and again after American entry into the war. He countered these charges in at least three ways: he contributed money to the British war effort; his studio issued a press release in June 1917 that he had registered for the selective service but had been turned down because he was underweight; and he helped the United States Treasury Department raise money during its Liberty Bond drives. In fact, Chaplin's Liberty Loan film *The Bond* was released during the fourth Liberty Loan Drive in September and October 1918, shortly before the pre- release of *Shoulder Arms* at the Strand. Chaplin, along with less controversial stars like Pickford, Fairbanks, Hart, Marguerite Clark, and Marie Dressler, also helped raise money for the Third Liberty Loan in April 1918, by speaking at Bond rallies in the South.

In "Advertising Aids for Busy Manager," *Moving Picture World* advised exhibitors to feature Charlie Chaplin as "Doughboy Charlie," and offered as appropriate and expeditious such advertising tag lines as "Putting the Silver Lining to the Clouds of War," "When Chaplin Laughs the World Laughs with Him," and "The Man Who Has Sent Waves of Laughter around the World." Selling points for *Shoulder Arms* foregrounded the war and Chaplin's proven ability to make the world laugh. Echoing contemporary cliches, "Putting the Silver Lining to the Clouds of War" conjured up contemporary standards like "Keep the Home Fires Burning." Singers of the song and publicists for the film agreed: "There's a silver lining through the dark clouds shining, / Turn the dark clouds inside out 'til the boys come home." Exploitation hints encouraged exhibitors to handle this Chaplin film as they had handled previous Chaplin films—with store window tie-ins and look-alike contests. The film's timeliness could also be exploited. "This time make them copy the military equipment Chaplin carries and offer a prize to the best equipped soldier."[67]

Contemporary critical reviews of the film in the trade papers and in the New York and Chicago newspapers were quite positive.[68] Both in and between their lines, these reviews posed reasons for the film's popularity. The *Chicago Herald* noted: "*Shoulder Arms* is very, very funny. Mr. Chaplin with his sad seriousness, makes a delicious doughboy. . . . It's a bravely jolly little picture, excellently done. . . ." The reviewer for the *New York Times* began by quoting an audience member.

> "The fool's funny," was the chuckling observation of one of those who
> saw Charlie Chaplin's new film, *Shoulder Arms*, at the Strand
> yesterday—and, apparently that's the way everybody felt. There have
> been learned discussions as to whether Chaplin's comedy is low or
> high, artistic or crude, but no one can deny that when he impersonates
> a screen fool he is funny.[69]

Chaplin the actor had established his patriotic bona fides through his work selling War Bonds, and movie-going citizens of Chicago may have seen *The Bond* in the month before they saw *Shoulder Arms*. Chaplin the actor, despite some lingering doubts about his artistry, had been accepted into the ranks of the genteel. In December, as *Shoulder Arms* was in wide release throughout Chicago, Mae Tinee, the movie columnist for the *Chicago Tribune*, told her readers how Helen Keller, "the famous blind girl," and her companion Mrs. Sullivan Macy, had visited Chaplin in Hollywood. "After dinner the party went to view Mr. Chaplin's latest picture, *Shoulder Arms*. The scenes as they flitted by were telegraphed to the blind girl by Mrs. Macy's finger on the palm of her hand."[70]

Charlie, as screen persona, had also established his popularity among movie-goers and film distributors. First National's 1917 contract with Chaplin paid one million a year and a $75,000 bonus upon signing. The Charlie of *Shoulder Arms*, that sadly serious private, that "funny fool," the character with whom audiences in Chicago, on Armistice Day, could be "spontaneously confidential," was familiar. Although he was dressed in military garb and outfitted with "such equipment as a soldier never dreamed of" instead of his usual baggy pants and cane, this "delicious doughboy" traced his lineage from the Little Fellow. And that Little Fellow was, at least in 1918, a secure and cheering and ever adaptable presence in American culture. "The moon shone bright on Charlie Chaplin," so the soldiers sang.

Conclusion

Give us movies and more movies. We can not get enough. They have
helped us to win the war.
Homer Croy, Moving Picture World, *30 November 1918*[71]

"What's playing," said the Man-in-a-Hurry to the girl in the box office.
"The Great Victory, Wilson or the Kaiser? The Fall of the Hohenzollerns."
"I haven't finished celebrating, either," said the customer as he grabbed
his change.
Moving Picture World, *14 December 1918*[72]

As film historian Janet Staiger points out, "If there was a 'golden age' of the studio, it was in full operation by 1918."[73] It was not only the studio system's mode of production which had been established; the foundations for the structure of the film industry, at least through 1948, were also set. Economic power was vested in the large integrated, or soon-to-be integrated, companies within all branches of the film industry. The traces of the future oligopoly were present. Prewar trends such as independent production, decreases in the number of small theaters, and increases in the numbers of theaters in chains, continued and accelerated over the months of American involvement in World War I. The industry emerged from the war a big business, its stock bought and sold on Wall Street.

It had also become a reputable business. One of the abiding benefits for the film industry of its participation in the war effort on the homefront was an enhanced public image, an effect that was felt in both tangible and intangible ways. The most prominent movie stars like Chaplin and Pickford, as well as lesser lights, had the opportunity for increased public exposure. They travelled the country speaking on behalf of Liberty Bonds; they appeared in picturettes for Herbert Hoover's United States Food Administration; they were featured regularly in the photogravure sections of newspapers working in their gardens, knitting for soldiers, and donating ambulances to the Red Cross. These photo opportunities helped weave film personalities even more tightly into the fabric of popular culture. They became homefront heroes and heroines, and the goodwill they garnered almost certainly added to the audiences for their films. These activities also may have helped to forestall potential criticism when their private lives got messy. When Pickford and Fairbanks divorced their mates to marry each other in March 1920, the public which had responded so generously to their Bond Drives reveled in their union. [74]

William Gibbs McAdoo, Secretary of the Treasury, Director-General of the Railroad Administration, and son-in-law of President Wilson, had met Pickford, Chaplin, and Douglas Fairbanks during their work on the Third Liberty Loan. [75] He would serve as counsel to United Artists, formed in 1919. The film industry also won the aid of Republicans. Will Hays, Republican Party chairman, and postmaster general in Warren Harding's administration, would join the film industry in 1922 as its point man—heading the Motion Picture Producer and Distributors Association. His task was to quell any federal censorship of the movies. Hays did his job well, with the industry instituting its own self-regulation.

Thus, World War I provided the film industry with the opportunity to enhance its goodwill with its market—the American public—and to win the goodwill of those in positions of power in the government. When Woodrow Wilson embarked for France to attend the Peace Conference, he carried fifteen movies with him for entertainment. "The Famous Players-Lasky Corporation received a wire from Washington November 28 to supply the motion pictures. . . ." The work of Douglas Fairbanks, Mary Pickford, D. W. Griffith, and Dorothy Gish, among others, sailed with the American delegation on board the *George Washington.* [76]

6

The War Film in the 1920s

The screen must keep up with the times. . . . Let us move along in
American Style with ingenuity, with originality, with sound judgment,
with subtle humor, with pictures of manhood such as marched away to
France, types of true womanhood, either that or be down and quit too
flat for an upright art.

Louis Harrison Reeves, Moving Picture World,
14 December 1918[1]

AN EDITORIAL IN the *Moving Picture World* in November 1918 reflected upon the ending of the First World War. Its lead sentence conjured
a curious, homely metaphor. " 'Well, that's finished,' as the old lady ex-
claimed as she wound up the last ball of carpet rags for the new rug on the
sitting room floor. Yes; we mean the war."[2] A rug of this kind, crafted from
remnants by traditional methods, is an apt image for the way the United
States film industry continued to incorporate World War I into its movies in
the decade following the Armistice. The war provided scenarists, directors, set designers, and actors with plots, settings, and bits of business to
be molded in accordance with conventional narrative construction and
stylistic practice into movies about World War I. In addition, the narratives and mise-en-scenes of westerns, comedies, dramas, and mysteries
were also shot through with references to the conflict which had absorbed
the public's interest throughout 1917 and 1918.

Although it was over, the war and subsequent peace negotiations were
never far from the public attention in 1919 and the early 1920s. Headlines
announced that President Wilson had fallen ill on 25 September 1919
while campaigning in Colorado on behalf of the Versailles Treaty he had
helped craft in Paris, and eight days later that he had suffered a massive
stroke. The United States Senate voted to reject the Treaty that November,
unable to reach consensus on Article X—the provision establishing a
League of Nations. On 19 March 1920 a second vote yielded the same
outcome. The League became a campaign issue in 1920 as Warren Har-

159

ding, the Republican's candidate, opposed United States membership in the League, and James Cox with his running mate, Franklin Delano Roosevelt, favored it. Cox and Roosevelt were defeated.

Nevertheless, the new Republican administration did respond to a rising urgency in the country to protect and ensure world peace. In 1921 Charles Evans Hughes, Harding's secretary of state, convened the Washington Conference to discuss arms limitation. With representatives from Great Britain, Japan, France, Italy, China, Portugal, Belgium, and the Netherlands, he helped to negotiate a series of treaties addressing naval disarmament and other issues. In 1926, the United States joined the World Court, sponsored by the League of Nations, and in 1928, ten years after the Armistice, this country along with sixty-one other nations signed the Kellogg-Briand Pact. That agreement renounced war as "an instrument of national policy." Shortsightedly, perhaps idealistically, it contained no means of enforcement other than world opinion; its provisions would be grossly violated in less than ten years.

In addition to foreign policy issues, which kept it prominent in the news, the Great War was the focus of memoirs and novels. *With the Yankee Division in France*, by Frank P. Sibley, *New England in France, 1917–1918*, by Emerson Gifford Taylor, *History of the Yankee Division*, by Harry A. Benwell, and a number of regimental histories were printed in 1919 and 1920 alone.[3] In 1919 popular novelist Mary Roberts Rinehart published *Dangerous Days*, her tale of industrial espionage and a rich young man's decision to enlist. Rupert Hughes, soon Captain Hughes, wrote *Patent Leather Kid*, in which a young, unpatriotic boxer is drafted, achieves heroism in battle, and is reunited with his love, in 1917; it was reissued in 1919, 1926, and 1927, and was made into a film starring Richard Barthelmess in 1927. John Dos Passos published *One Man's Initiation* in 1920 and *Three Soldiers* in 1921. e e cummings' *The Enormous Room* came out in 1922, and Willa Cather won the Pulitzer Prize that same year for *One of Ours*, her story about a Nebraska farm boy who dies in France in 1918. Edith Wharton published *A Son at the Front* in 1923.[4] These books manifested a range of attitudes about the war. They were written by men with combat experience, as well as man like Hughes who, for medical reasons, never saw battle. Women like Cather who had never left the United States published novels about the war, as did the expatriate Wharton, who had lived in France since 1906 and had worked for the Red Cross in Paris. Thus, in 1919 and through the early 1920s, war and the peace remained in the headlines, on the bookshelves, and in the minds of the American public. The fresh memories of the battlefield and the home-front fostered contemporary interest in the political results of the Great War. These memories also provided iconography, plot twists, themes, costumes, and characters for movie-makers in the immediate postwar period.

The continued timeliness of the war was one of several factors accounting for the release of war-related films already in production in late 1918 and the planning of future films for 1919. Although there was debate in early December 1918—as there had been during the early months of the war—about the advisability of producing movies with war stories, in general the trade papers advocated their production. Louis Harrison Reeves, *Moving Picture World*'s critic and feature writer, chided exhibitors: "Millions upon millions of intelligent and true-hearted Americans are deeply interested in events of these four years. . . . The screen must keep up with the times."[5] Harry Rapf drew on historical precedent to champion war films. In late December, he reminded *Moving Picture World*'s readers that after the Civil War many plays and vaudeville sketches had used that conflict as raw material. In the present time, he argued, as long as the narratives followed convention and included "a Good Love Story," the Great War would provide a ready source of drama and comedy. In fact, the film industry would be out of step with the rest of the mass media if it did not utilize the war in its products. "Every newspaper has headlines referring to soldiers and war material; war is the basic idea of cartoons and editorials, why should the movies be different?"[6]

Distributors charged with selling films to exhibitors hedged their bets. In their advertising for movies featuring the war, they tried a number of tacks to ensure a successful run. First, some advertisements foregrounded the fact that, since the Armistice had been signed, people could enjoy watching war stories without worrying about loved ones at the front. In late November and throughout December of 1918, the pages of motion picture trade journals featured advertisements based on this theme. "The War is Over. Happiness and Health Resumed. Show Your People 'The Road to France.' " *To Hell with the Kaiser* was sold on the promise that "It was great before. It is greater now." And, "Now that their Minds at ease, show your Patrons this mighty History of the War, Crashing Through to Berlin."[7]

Movie-goers might also be persuaded to buy tickets to see historical treatments of the war. What had been a contemporary story in October and early November became a period piece in December. In fact, *The Cavell Case*, the story of the execution of British nurse Edith Cavell by the Germans in 1915, was touted as being "permanent as history." It also adhered

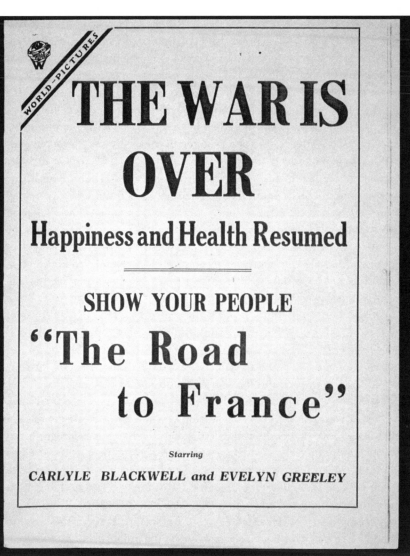

Fig. 6.1. Luring the audience. When World War I ended, exhibitors used a variety of appeals to lure audiences to the theater to watch war movies. Above, an advertisement that ran in *Moving Picture World*, 7 December 1918.

Fig. 6.2. Advertisement in *Moving Picture World*, 7 December 1918.

to Harry Rapf's admonition to include heart interest. "It is a drama of man vs. woman that is rooted in the basic struggle between justice and tyranny—the struggle that has returned civilization as a victor."[8] The Famous Players-Lasky campaign for D. W. Griffith's *The Greatest Thing in Life* asked the question, "When the happy millions finished celebrating

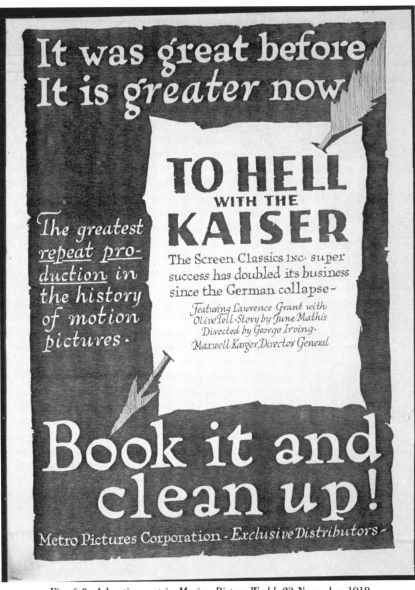

Fig. 6.3. Advertisement in *Moving Picture World*, 23 November 1918.

Victory, what next did they want?"[9] The answer, of course, was a movie that pictured what it had been like "over there."

Still, in case some audience members might be wary of war, distributors hustled to convert their copy for peace time. Even though the advertisement for *The Unpardonable Sin* featured the menacing silhouette of a German soldier advancing toward a young girl—one of the major motifs in WWI propaganda posters—the text read, "Not a WAR STORY But—a story of the sacrilege of womanhood that made any red blooded man FIGHT."[10] *Variety,* noting that war-related comedies, such as *Shoulder Arms* and *The Geezer of Berlin* were proving quite popular in the early postwar period, still advised "Killing War Advertising," while not necessarily killing war dramas and comedies. Instead, they proposed shifting emphasis from the war to some other feature of the narrative. *Lafayette, We Come* was an example of the way a wartime drama could veer "away from the strife angle." In its new advertisements "reference to the war is omitted, with the mystery end of the story played up."[11] One doubts, however, that such obfuscation really worked. Lafayette, a Frenchman who helped the thirteen colonies in the Revolutionary War, was inexorably linked with the World War. Arriving in France, the commander of the American Expeditionary Force, General John J. Pershing, placed a wreath on Lafayette's tomb. He acknowledged the American debt to France and promised its repayment. "Lafayette," he said, "we are here."[12] An audience could not miss the film title's referential meaning.

Timeliness, however, was only one explanation for the persistence of the European War in the movies during 1919. Celebrating the end of the war, relegating the war to the historical past, and directing attention away from its presence in new releases were signals of a basic fact about feature film production in the late 1910s: an industry which took almost fifteen months to convert one-fifth of its feature production to war-related stories could not demobilize over night. Add to this inertia the estimate of six months production time for a feature film, the number of films in various stages of production in November 1918, and exhibition schedules calling for a weekly change of feature, and it is clear why 1919 saw at least fifty-four war-related feature films in release.[13] While the industry did take audience preference into account, it also had to contend with its own mode of production. Film advertising and promotion, on the other hand, could respond more quickly to new events (as we saw in the promotion of *Shoulder Arms* in Indianapolis). It was also less expensive for film companies to

Fig. 6.4. "Remember Belgium." The Hun could do no worse than threaten the virginity of a young woman. The image of bestiality advancing on innocence was a potent organizer of nationalist sentiments. Courtesy of Walter Rawls, *Wake Up America.*

change their "paper"—posters and advertisements—than to re-write scripts or re-edit films.

There was a significant drop in the number of features identified by the trade as war films in the early 1920s, sinking to a low of about nine new feature films in 1921. Still, the war was never a taboo subject for film narratives—as it was never taboo for published fiction and nonfiction— nor was it absent from newspaper headlines. The film industry, ever calculating its risks, produced an expensive, prestige picture about the war within three years of the Armistice. *The Four Horsemen of the Apocalypse*, based on Vincente Blasco Ibáñez's popular 1918 war novel, projected Rudolph Valentino, the tango, and the Great War onto the screen in March 1921.

The producers of *The Four Horsemen of the Apocalypse* relied upon conventional strategies for ensuring the success of this film. It was based on a popular novel, "read probably in all the four corners of our land," and it exploited the spectacular in its mise-en-scène. Reviewers of the film praised the special effect of the four biblical horsemen: Conquest, Fam-

Fig. 6.5. The Hun and the girl in a publicity image from *The Unpardonable Sin* that was used to illustrate the novel.

ine, War, and Death—galloping across the sky. "The Beast is a spiked
monstrosity belching forth fire and smoke. Each horseman is more terrible
in aspect than the one before. Riding together, they make a startling and
haunting picture and pave the way for the war-scenes that follow."[14] Discussing the quality of June Mathis's adaptation of the novel, the reviewer
for the *New York Times* highlighted the war scenes: "The part of the story
that is its reason for existence, the latter section dealing with the war, has
been treated adequately and in the intense spirit of the original."[15] *Life*'s
reviewer, Sherwood Anderson, rated it higher than *The Birth of a Nation*,
Joan the Woman, or *Hearts of the World*. He worried, however, that the
American public was still too much in thrall to the spirit of wartime propaganda to appreciate the film's message. "It is our belief that the film will
not be an unqualified success in the United States, where the entire war
now resolves itself into terms of Liberty Loan Drives and George Creel."[16]
The reviewer for New York's *Morning Telegraph* disagreed.

> It is right and proper that the greatest of war-pictures should come over
> two years after the war is over. The patriotism that swept the world in
> 1914 and 1915 has been turned into cynicism by bungling peace
> delegates, by exposures of money wasted on aircraft equipment and
> armament, and by squabbling politicians.[17]

The Four Horsemen of the Apocalypse ran for five weeks at New York's Lyric
Theater, then moved to the Astor for an additional eleven-week run. It
played twenty-seven weeks at the LaSalle Theater in Chicago, six weeks at
the Stillman Theater in Cleveland, and seven weeks at the Garrick in
Philadelphia. This film also marked the beginning of Rudolph Valentino's
short-lived celebrity, and its popularity hinged on his performance. Thus,
a new timeliness characterized by a national reappraisal of the United
States role in the Great War, spectacular mise-en-scène, and an emergent
star all contributed to the success of the film. After *The Four Horsemen of
the Apocalypse*, movies continued to prompt Americans into "keeping the
war in mind."[18]

The numbers of war-related features began to increase slightly in
1922, 1923, and 1924. The year 1925 saw evidence of a resurgence of
interest on the part of the film industry in producing stories about the Great
War. In that year no fewer than twenty-eight films with war-related narratives, including the popular roadshow attraction *The Big Parade*, were
released. The trend continued with thirty-five war movies being produced

in 1926.[19] The success of roadshow attractions such as *The Big Parade* and *What Price Glory?* sparked production of a spate of less expensive feature films, set during World War I, by most of the major film studios.[20] It also prompted the reissue of *The Four Horsemen of the Apocalypse* in 1926, and Chaplin's *Shoulder Arms* in 1927. *The Big Parade* and *What Price Glory?* were running in New York in August 1927, the week *Wings*, discussed later in this chapter, opened.

The war also found its way into a variety of genres whose films told contemporary stories. Threaded through the narratives and mise-en-scènes of two-reel comedies, westerns, and big-budget dramas were reminders—as if the audience had ever really forgotten—that the Great War had been fought, that its effects were still felt. *Rolling Stone*, a Billy West comedy released in 1919, revolves around a jailbird who falls in love with the warden's daughter. Near the end we see Billy's two babies, in their cradle, dressed in military uniforms. Billy reads a newspaper, its headline—"Wilson Sees End of War." Another two-reel comedy, *The Detectress*, circa 1919, featured Gale Henry traversing "Dirty Alley." An intertitle explains, "Dirty Alley was as peaceful as no mans land on a busy day." In the 1920 comedy *Hold Me Tight*, director Slim Summerville catapults one of the actors through a billboard reading, "Come Through New War Savings Stamps." A 1921 Toonerville comedy, *The Skipper's Narrow Escape*, based on the cartoons of Fontaine Fox, notes that if only some of the Skipper's raisin cider moonshine had made it to France during the war "the Germans would have quit." The plot of a 1924 comedy, *Hold Your Breath* is based on the premise that a woman's brother never fully recovered after being gassed "over there"; so, in order to keep the family solvent and housed, the woman needed to take over his job. Still another example is the 1928 short comedy *Vacation Waves*. In it, Edward Everett Horton, a train conductor who has just been shot in the backside, yells "War is over but if you shoot me again I'll start another one."[21]

Comedy was not the only genre to incorporate references to the war into narratives and mise-en-scène. *The Stolen Ranch*, a 1926 western directed by William Wellman, shows two army buddies, Frank and Breezey, who survive the "inferno" of the war. The war cemented their friendship, and that friendship "was the net profit taken from Flanders Fields." Frank still suffers from shell shock, however, so Breezey must protect him from sudden loud noises. The two return home to find that Frank's ranch has been taken over by bad guys—presumably slackers who did not fight in the war. The film concludes only when Frank has regained his land, won his girl, and recovered from his war neurosis. The mise-en-scène of *The Stolen Ranch* includes flashbacks to the battlefields where Frank and Breezey fought. Its iconography includes coils of barbed wire, airplanes flying overhead, bombs exploding, trenches, and skeletal trees—a visual shorthand that had, by 1926, come to signify the Great War.[22]

In addition to the way the war insinuated itself into the narratives and mise-en-scènes of genres far removed from the trenches, Eric von Stroheim's *Foolish Wives* (1922) incorporated the war, in the form of a wounded veteran, into the thematic fabric of a big-budget drama. The soldier's long-suffering presence in the background of many of the scenes in this film stands in sharp relief to the "foolish" wife, her ineffectual husband, and the evil Count, played by Stroheim. Commenting on the expensive "rich and splendid" Monte Carlo sets that Stroheim erected in California, the reviewer for the *New York Times* failed to notice the veteran who constituted a significant motif of that setting.[23] In 1922, perhaps, former soldiers were too familiar a part of the landscape of contemporary life and film to warrant mention. They were common, thus unremarkable elements in the narratives and mise-en-scènes of a variety of movies.

Timeliness, Convention, and the World War I War Film of the 1920s

The Big Parade: ". . . told by a soldier who became an artist."
Literary Digest, *6 March 1926*[24]

The conventional story of the Great War was told by way of a variety of characters—men and women, Americans or Europeans, combatants and those on the homefront. It was situated in hospitals behind the front lines, offices in Washington, D.C., YMCA canteens, and small towns in the Midwest, and in time periods before, during, and after the war. The immediate postwar period when the survivors came home, led quickly to the 1920s, when journalists, scholars, and ordinary folk began to question United States participation in the war that had been fought to make the world safe for democracy, adding further perspectives. In fact, permutations of these elements and situations existed in many of the films that Hollywood produced in the 1920s.

In *The Four Horsemen of the Apocalypse*, for example, Valentino plays Julio, a young Argentinean with a French father, who is living in France at the outbreak of the war. His cousins have a German father. Most of the narrative time takes place in the period before Julio joins the fighting, and the love story at the heart of the film is the engine that drives its narrative. *The Child Thou Gavest Me* (Associated First National Pictures, 1921), on the other hand, was an after-the-war story in which a young woman, raped an impregnated by an unknown soldier while serving as a nurse in Belgium, finds that the man she plans to marry was, in fact, her assailant. They reconcile and with their child create a family. A lighter note was struck by *Don't Write Letters* (Metro, 1922). In this film a short man enlists, but, instead of seeing combat, is assigned to work as a cook. He misrepresents his war-time career to the girl he loves, but she reciprocates his affection anyway.[25] Of the films touching in some way on the diverse experiences of World War I, those receiving the most critical attention in the 1920s, and those that served to influence the war-related films that would come in the 1930s and during World War II, were movies that showed the experiences of the doughboy and the flyer in combat.

Pictures including King Vidor's *The Big Parade* (Metro Goldwyn Mayer, 1925), and Raoul Walsh's *What Price Glory?* (Fox, 1926), replaced D. W. Griffith's *Hearts of the World* as the quintessential World War I war films of the 1920s. In addition to proving that movies about the war, with predominantly male casts, could pull in an audience—*The Big Parade* ran for two years at the Astor Theater in New York—these films built on foundations of narrative and mise-en-scène visible in Chaplin's 1918 comedy *Shoulder Arms*. They focussed on the ordinary soldier, his bleak and muddy life in the trenches, and scenes showing basic training, mail call, and soldiers going over the top. While reiterating certain narrative characteristics—for example, sequences depicting life before and after the war, or including a love story within their plot structure—typical of war-related pictures released during the war (like *Joan the Woman, The Little American, Hearts of the World,* and *The Unbeliever*), the war films of the 1920s also displayed striking innovations. They were told from the soldier's point of view and foregrounded battle over any other wartime experience.

The function of women also changed dramatically. War-related films made during the Great War followed the tradition of *Birth of a Nation*, in which the Civil War became the stuff of family melodrama, and sexual threats to the "Pet Sister" and Elsie Stoneman served to motivate significant moments in the plot. In the narrative logic of World War I vintage movies, the worst thing the enemy could do was rape or threaten to rape Angela, Virginie, or the Belgium girl rescued by Chaplin's uniformed Little Tramp. D. W. Griffith's *Hearts of the World,* the most popular war film of 1918, reached its climax as The Boy saved The Girl from assault by a

German officer. Combat films made in the 1920s eliminated or significantly reduced the role of women as causal agents in their narratives.
Characters like Melisande and Charmaine still appeared in *The Big Parade* and *What Price Glory?*, but a clear divide was created between the
"love story" and the war scenes. Now, mothers and sweethearts lived on
the homefront where they wrote letters, and were, most often, faithful; if
overseas, they drove ambulances or served as nurses. They might also be
French villagers providing love and comfort behind the lines. Still, in most
films made in the mid-1920s, war was defined as combat, and women were
well out of the fray.

These new film narratives were not without precedent. *What Price
Glory?*, a play by Maxwell Anderson and Laurence Stallings that opened in
the fall of 1924, was especially influential. Reviewers likened it to Dos
Passos's *Three Soldiers* in essays heralding a new way of telling war stories
that was "tougher" and more "hard-boiled."[26] Critics writing about the
play applauded its "realistic" characters. Chords struck in the discussions
of Anderson and Stallings's work echoed through the journalistic writing
on the combat films which followed in its wake. A review in *The Woman
Citizen* opened by proclaiming *What Price Glory?* the most talked-about
play of the season. It was dramatic fiction that had "the feel of the thing."[27]
Reviewers noted roughness in language and actions, as well as in the
costume and makeup of the actors. Its style was fit to convey the un-
adorned truth of the ordinary soldier. The theater program for *What Price
Glory?* begged tolerance for the "speech of men under arms." Profanity
was justified on mimetic grounds. This was how soldiers talked. A review
in the *Literary Digest* praised the play for colloquial dialogue.

> In a theater where war has been lied about, romantically, effectively—
> and in a city where the war play has usually meant sugary
> dissimulation—'What Price Glory' may seem bold. The audience is
> asked to bear with certain expletives which, under other
> circumstances, might be used for melodramatic effect, but herein are
> employed because the mood and truth of the play demand their
> employment.[28]

Mordaunt Hall, reviewing the 1926 film adaptation noted that "no profanity is seen in the text of this picture, but one can readily tell from the
movements of their lips what these two Marines are calling each other."[29]
There was the perception that this play was different from what had come
before, that it was raw, but also truthful.

The identical sentiment was expressed one year later when *The Big Parade* opened in Boston. The reviewer for the *Boston Transcript* praised this film and damned all its cinematic predecessors. "To watch it unroll is to realize anew all the shallow bombast, all the flatulency and all the saccharinity with which previous picture-makers have encumbered the trade of war." Instead, he placed Vidor's film within the newer tradition of "tough" stories about realistic doughboys, "soldiers nearer convention than Dos Passos's, less professional than Kipling's, and somewhat less pungent than Stallings's own marines in *What Price Glory?*"[30] New standards for realism—affecting even the makeup of the protagonists—in the depiction of war were being set and applied across theater, literature, and film.[31]

Thus, it is significant that the most influential war films of the 1920s, and the novels and plays they resembled, were written by a relatively small number of men who had served in the military during World War I. It is equally important that the actual screenplays were credited to more established Hollywood writers. The review of *What Price Glory?* in *The Woman Citizen* concluded by linking verisimilitude with authorial experience: "Laurence Stallings, who, with Maxwell Anderson, wrote it, was a captain of marines, and lost a leg and won years of pain as a result of Belleau Wood. He ought to know."[32] Stallings provided the story for *The Big Parade*—in which a young soldier loses a leg in a battle like Belleau Wood. John Monk Saunders, Second Lieutenant in the Signal Corps Aviation Section, contributed the story for *Wings*, *The Legion of the Condemned* (Paramount, 1928), and *The Dawn Patrol* (First National, 1930), and Maxwell Anderson, co-author of *What Price Glory?*, adopted Erich Maria Remarque's *All Quiet on the Western Front* for the screen. The stories these men told, based on their experiences in the war, were transformed into scenarios by other men and women, veterans not of combat, but of Hollywood.[33] The result was an accommodation of the conventions of war films to date, and with the need of the film industry to appeal to a broad audience, not only former soldiers or men. Typically, therefore, these war films of the 1920s included a romantic subplot featuring established female stars.

The combat films of the 1920s were also different in tone from 1917–1918 movies with war-related plots. *Big Parade*, *What Price Glory?*, and, as we shall see, *Wings*, were perceived at least by movie critics, as being ambivalent in their attitude toward the war. Even a perfunctory glance at titles like *The Big Parade* and *What Price Glory?* finds an irony absent

from *The Little American* or *The Unbeliever*.[34] Jim Apperson, the young rich
man who enlists in "the big parade"—the war—after being surcharged
with enthusiasm by the rousing martial music he hears in a recruitment
parade, comes limping home at war's end. He has lost a leg; his two
buddies—a riveter and a bartender—are both dead. Jim's fiancee has
taken up with his brother, who stayed home. The price paid by Apperson
for a dubious glory is indeed high, and he knows it. An intertitle late in the
film fairly shouts, "What the hell do we get out of this war? Parades—who
the hell cares?"

  What Price Glory? was released as a roadshow in the year following *The
Big Parade*. It tells of two career soldiers, Quirt and Flagg (Victor
McLaglan and Edmund Lowe), who spend most of their time, and much of
the movie, competing for the affections of women in China, the Philip-
pines, and finally in France. Although its ads promised that "Women Love
It's [sic] Daring—Its Romance and Its Uproarious Humor," the film also
had, in addition to its quizzical title, a "tragic note."[35] This included what
the reviewer for the *New York Times* called the "Trench of Death"—a shell
explodes in a trench and buries all the men positioned there. The scene
closes on an image of bayonets spiking up through the rubble. The film's
thematic terrain is equally bleak. After one of the young soldiers, an artist
who spends much of his onscreen time writing home to his mother, dies in
Flagg's arms, an intertitle describes a setting fraught with poignant irony:
"And all night long that wounded sniper in a tree screams for mercy. You
talk about honor and courage and a man bleeds to death in a tree over your
head." Soon after, Quirt screams—in intertitle—"What Price Glory
Now?"

  These influential films, plays, and novels voiced a belief, broadly felt
in American culture by the mid-1920s, that the government's wartime
propaganda had been false. Stories of atrocities perpetrated in Belgium by
bestial German combatants were unfounded, and the more high-toned
metaphorical description of this war as the Great Crusade of Civilization
against Autocracy was at odds with the soldier's experience. In November
1924, the month after *What Price Glory?* opened in New York, an essayist
writing in *The Independent* even castigated the songwriters of World War I
who followed the government's line; their lyrics "did not merely lack con-
viction; they denied reality":

> Did not those able authors [the songwriters] demonstrate over and over
> again that the south of France was full of armless orphans, that the
> Germans used their dead for lubricating oil, that the enemy morale was

Fig. 6.6. Advertisements from *Moving Picture World.* The prepared advertising for *What Price Glory?* took pains to target
women.

at its last gasp! . . . certainly, some of the deadliest work of the war was done with the Pen.

The best songs of the war, the author argued, were "Tipparary," "Madelon," and "Smiles," not the "work of the Bronx School and their bleatings about Duty and Country and Baebie and Daddie and George Washington and the Flag."[36] In a 1927 essay, Lawrence Stallings made similar claims about the "yawping patriotism" and "cant" of the "slaves of Tin Pan Alley." He valued the irreverence of the parodies the soldiers sang. "Over There," for example, became "Underwear," and "Mademoiselle from Armentieres" gave rise to as many verses—few suitable for print—as there were companies.[37] The standard for songs, plays, and movies was authenticity, and this was the sole domain of the combatant.

Popular culture was not the only place where Americans questioned the veracity of propaganda themes designed to win their support for the Great War, and where they more generally questioned the efficacy and morality of the war itself. In 1927 the *American Mercury* published two articles—"The Higher Learning Goes to War" and "The Historian Cut Loose"—that criticized the role professors and universities had played by helping to prepare and disseminate information designed to win support and cooperation with the war effort.[38] Professional historians were especially faulted for lending the credibility of their discipline to the service of the state.

American Mercury also published E. T. Saintsbury, a very angry former Four Minute Man, in the fall of 1927. His complaint reflected a disappointed idealism: he had believed the message that the war would make the world safe for democracy and that this victory would be manifest in an egalitarian society back at home. "For a year and a half I had sweated and exhorted in every school-house, church, and movie-parlor in the country . . . expounding our Sacred Principles to the citizenry." Saintsbury, a superintendent of schools using information provided by scholars working for the Committee on Public Information,

> had pointed out the absolute solvency and dependability of Uncle Sam as a creditor, and damned the Central Powers, especially Germany, before many a bucolic movie audience, thus filling the space between a Fatty Arbuckle masterpiece and the thirteenth instalment of "The Diamond from the Sky." I had predicted, six times a week, the virtuous triumph of our arms, and set forth our duties as lay members of the proud forces that were struggling to maintain civilization against the Hun.

As a Four Minute Man, he had shared the stage with the local bank president and others of the "Old Guard." With them, he had fomented the superpatriotism that enabled his county to go "over the top" in contributions to war bond drives. On Armistice Day, however, he began to sense that "the dictum that the war was a Great Leveler" was false. He was not invited to speak at the local rally. "But now, on the night of the Big Parade, I found myself once more a poor pedagogue—and him a banker, and hence an eminent man." Saintsbury concluded on a note presaging the congressional committee hearings held from 1934–1936 into the activities of the "merchants of death"—financiers and corporations that had profited from United States involvement in World War I: "I was an interested spectator when the notes given for Liberty Bonds began to fall due. . . . I knew how the patriotic country bankers were going to profit." He was repaid the rate of eighty-three cents on the dollar for his investment in Liberty Bonds.[39] It was into this context of public debate and disillusionment about the U.S. government's management of World War I that *Wings* debuted at the Criterion Theater in New York City, 12 August 1927.

Wings (Paramount, 1927)

Go, Get 'Em: The True Adventures of an American Aviator of the Lafayette Flying Corps Who Was the Only Yankee Flyer Fighting over General Pershing's Boys of the Rainbow Division in Lorraine, When They First Went "Over the Top"

> The title of a book by William Wellman (1918)

John Monk Saunders is responsible for the story. . . , a conventional narrative that serves its purpose as a background for the remarkable scenes in the air.

> Mordaunt Hall, review of Wings, New York Times,
> 13 August 1927[40]

The eyes of the world are on aviation. A Paramount Picture, "Wings," is the sensation of New York.

> advertisement, Saturday Evening Post, 19 November 1927[41]

From the eminence of an orchestra chair one joins the flight of furybirds.

> review of Wings, New York Morning Telegraph,
> November 1927[42]

Wings opened to standing-room-only crowds thirteen years to the month after the guns of August first sounded in Europe. The anniversary of the beginning of the war coincided with the film industry's new show year. One month later, the *Leviathan*, a German ship which had been captured during the war, trailed by a fleet of fifteen smaller vessels, sailed from New York for France carrying some twenty-five thousand Americans who had participated in the Great War. They were returning ten years after the United States entered the conflict to visit the places where they had fought. In the late summer of 1927, former doughboys, sailors, flyers, and their friends and families who had served on the homefront also had other venues where they could refresh, share, and perhaps reshape their memories of the war. When veterans, like the editor of *Aviation*, R. Sydney Brown, Jr., a former lieutenant in the Royal Flying Corps, went to see *Wings*, the movie produced a visceral, if nostalgic response.

> When the war pilot sees the hero take off in the familiar "Spad" and two minutes later "dog fighting" in a Curtis "Hawk," or sees the hero send a "Gotha" down in flames when in truth it is a post-war Martin bomber that goes down he may smile to himself and think of S.E.5s and Camels and Fokkers, etc., but he experiences the old kick of half fright, half exultation, and grips the arms of his seat in suspense just as much as the novice who is sitting next to him and learning all about the art of warfare for the first time.[43]

Though the fall of 1927, World War I was both timely and evocative. For the film industry, the war was a mine rich in stories and settings—and in this sense Paramount was following a popular trend. In any case, the *Christian Science Monitor* noted this development in its review of *Wings*: "In answer to the resounding broadside that M.G.M. made with its "Big Parade," Paramount has shot another super-special production into the filmy air. . . ."[44] When *Motion Picture News* surveyed the fall season, it was circumspect in its judgment of these films, observing, "There is war on Broadway." *The Patent Leather Kid* had opened 12 August to join *What Price Glory?* then playing at popular prices at the Roxy (with a cast of two hundred for its prologue), and the *Big Parade* at the Astor Theater. The article concluded by wondering "just how much war stuff even Broadway [could] digest all in one dose."[45] In October, the same columnist reported data that began to answer the question he had posed in August: "The box office career of *What Price Glory?* is being followed with interest. There were predictions when it opened [in 1926], that it had limited appeal, because it was not a woman's picture, and therefore could not succeed on a big scale." Not so, the writer noted. It had done well in both cities and rural areas. In New York, it had enjoyed a twenty-six week run at the Sam Harris Theater. At that point, scheduled for a three-week stay at the Roxy, *What Price Glory?* had grossed 408,152.45.[46]

There was another salient trend in both popular culture and the motion picture industry in 1927 that might have forecast the popularity of *Wings*—a fascination with aviation. *Wings* was one of the first films to exploit the narrative possibilities of war in the air and Paramount doubled the sales value of its war-related timeliness by tapping the "air-mindedness" of the U.S. public in the late 1920s. The nation as a whole had seen an increase in the number of airports built across the country. On a smaller scale, department stores throughout the United States were sponsoring model airplane building clubs and holding competitions in which hundreds of children, girls as well as boys, took part. Schools incorporated aeronautics into their curricula. And, not surprisingly, the advertising industry also took to the air. The sky provided the largest billboard of all.[47]

Motion picture producers participated in this trend, setting both war-related and nonwar-related movies in the air. In August 1927, the same month that *Wings* opened, *Variety* reported a spate of airplane movies. Under a headline warning of an "Air Film Flood," it noted, "Pathe is rushing completion of its airplane picture *An Ace in the Hole*. . . . The drive is directed primarily against Paramount's *Now We're in the Air* . . . and Universal's *The Flying Mutt*. . . . Warner Brothers is also making an airplane story."[48]

Film exhibitors exploited and augmented the lure of aviation to fill their theaters. A ten-thousand-dollar aircraft beacon was installed on the roof of the Keswick Theater in Greater Glenside, Pennsylvania. The manager of the Hennepin-Orpheum Theater in Minneapolis promoted *The Flying Fleet* by sponsoring a contest to see who could define the most aeronautical terms. Five thousand handbills listing the terms to be defined were dropped by airplane over the city, and a sixteen-year-old boy won the contest by defining 1,107 terms. H. M. Addison of the Great Lakes Theater in Buffalo, New York, not only dropped 50,000 handbills from the sky over his city, in the lobby of his theater, he also erected a booth to sell airmail stamps, and mounted a display of real airplane parts alongside model planes built by the *Buffalo Evening News* model building club.[49] Throughout the mid-1920s, the trade papers encouraged managers to connect with airports whenever possible and predicted, "Airports in their desire to stimulate interest in their towns and surrounding communities, as well as to attract customers for short flights will gladly cooperate in such tie-ups if approached properly."[50] Aviation-related ballyhoo benefitted both the theater manager seeking an audience and the airport operator promoting the business of air travel.

Wings differentiated itself from the standard airplane movie by the magnitude of its spectacle and its corresponding rental price. (As late as 1929 exhibitors were still complaining about its cost: "Too close a split caused us to record a poor showing at the box office. . . . 'prestige,' that intangible and illusive thing that film peddlers prate about, fails utterly to provide beefsteak for our tables"[51]). It was the quintessential big picture replete with airplane stuff," "trick stuff," and "real stuff;" it definitely appealed to the "circus instinct." A writer for *Motion Picture News* predicted, " 'Wings' will fly right into the roadshow class easily."[52] Paramount had calculated the odds of making such an expensive film as *Wings*, estimated to cost upwards of $2,000,000, shrewdly.[53]

In the late 1920s, aviation was personified by Charles Lindbergh, who had flown *The Spirit of St. Louis* solo from Long Island to Paris in May 1927. Serendipitously for the publicists at Paramount, aviation, Lindbergh, and the war were notes in the same chord. As he was being driven to his hotel after landing at Le Bourget, Lindbergh stopped to put flowers on the grave of the unknown soldier. In Paris, he was celebrated before an audience made up of World War I flying "aces." Before returning to a ticker tape parade in New York City in June, "Lindy" visited Brussels and London, and in each city, he laid a wreath at the tomb of the unknown soldier. In his first day in London, Lindbergh attended a ceremony commemorating that nation's war dead.[54] In August, as *Wings* turned them away at the door, Lindbergh, an international hero, was back in the United States. He was flying to airports around the country demonstrating the safety and efficiency of air travel, stoking both contemporary enthusiasm for aviation and a continuing fascination with the Great War.

Wings incorporated the celebrity and credibility of Lindbergh directly. The film opened with a series of intertitles designed to cue its audience to connect aviation and the Great War, the present and the recent past. First a quotation from Charles Lindbergh was superimposed on a cloud-filled sky, marked by the black shapes of birds' wings: "On June 12, 1927 in Washington, Colonel Charles A. Lindbergh paid a simple tribute to those who fell in the war." The second intertitle followed: " 'In that time,' he said, 'feats were performed and deeds accomplished which were far greater than any peace accomplishments in aviation.' " The third intertitle dedicated the

Fig. 6.7. Cover of *Motion Picture News*, 3 March 1918, showing *40,000 Miles with Lindbergh*. Movies tapped the American public's interest in aviation and Charles Lindbergh by exhibiting documentaries like *40,000 Miles* and feature films like *Wings*.

film, in words superimposed over the image of the Winged Victory, a cross-shaped grave marker encircled by a wreath, and a low-angle view of clouds and sky: "To those young warriors of the sky, whose wings are folded about them forever, this picture is reverently dedicated." The fourth intertitle then moved its audience into the diegetic world of the film. Behind the line "A small town—1917—youth and the dreams of youth" was a low-angle view of a castle on a hill—a metaphor for the realm of the imagination as well as a visual equivalent of the medieval rhetoric associated with flyers and World War I's air war.[55]

Wings told the story of John Powell (Charles Rogers) and David Armstrong (Richard Arlen), two young men from the same small town who enlist, go through training camp together, and quarrel over a girl back home. The frame story, which begins before U.S. entry into the war and closes after the Armistice, depicts the romantic rivalry between Powell and Armstrong. It also establishes the social hierarchy in their town. Armstrong and Sylvia, the object of both mens' desire, are part of the upper crust, while Powell and his next-door neighbor Clara Preston, played by Clara Bow, are part of the middle class. In what Mordaunt Hall, the *New York Times*'s reviewer, acknowledged as the one unconventional scene in the narrative, Powell—mistakenly believing that Armstrong has been killed—takes off in a rage and shoots down a German plane, which his friend, not dead at all, has commandeered. Armstrong dies, and Powell, now grey about the temples, returns home to a parade in his honor and the difficult task of returning David's small teddy bear to his grieving, aged parents. He has also come to realize that the girl he loves is not the wealthy and ethereal Sylvia, with her long, loose hair and flowing gowns, but his effervescent short-haired and shorter-skirted neighbor who shares his love of cars and planes.

The distribution plan for *Wings* followed the Broadway roadshow strategy. Success at the Criterion was crucial, because Paramount would use data gathered from the New York run to sell *Wings* to exhibitors across the country, first as a roadshow and again when the film went into general release. Promotion began five days before its opening, one day before advance tickets went on sale. Two of the main themes in the 1927 advertising campaign for the film were the timeliness of the picture and its authenticity. Specifically focussing on aviation and the creative contributions of veterans to the making of the film, publicists applied promotional principles established as early as the 1910s. Dominating the ad in the *New York Times* on 7 August were images of airplanes angling toward the center from

Fig. 6.8. Aviation and autobiography were used to sell *Wings*
in this advertisement in the *New York Times*, 14 August 1927.

each corner, chasing the smoke from their forward guns, speed lines dashing off their wings. The text set the scene and sold the credibility of the film's makers: "Duel with the aces in desperate battle, revel with them in Paris cafes! The war-drama of the air made by men who were war-birds and who bring to life the thrilling story of themselves and their comrades."[56]

Over the next five days, the timeliness of aviation and the realism attributed to the film because of the participation of former airmen in its production (including Saunders, who provided the story, Wellman, who had flown with the Lafayette Flying Corps, Arlen, one of the stars who had flown with the Royal Flying Corps in Canada, and the stunt flyers who manned the planes) were joined by selling points highlighting narrative elements less time-bound. On 8 August, readers of the *New York Times* learned that the film was a "melodrama"; on the ninth the film was celebrated for offering "young love"; and on the eleventh the film's producer, director, and the writer of the story (but not the screenplay) were heralded. By 13 August, the day after it opened, *Wings* was touted as "The sensation of the year!"[57]

Reviewers of the film in newspapers and the trade press reinforced the focus on timeliness and verisimilitude begun by Paramount, and included the responses from aviators and veterans in their articles on *Wings*. Mordaunt Hall quoted a conversation he had overheard in the lobby of the Criterion on opening night.

> After the exhibition of the first half of this absorbing subject, Commander Richard E. Byrd was noticed in the lobby talking to Jesse L. Lasky and the words of the hero of the North Pole and transatlantic flights evidently pleased the producer. As the Commander turned to re-enter he remarked:
> "And I wouldn't say so if I didn't think it."

Hall also eavesdropped on the less prominent, including a "young officer of Uncle Sam's flying force," who found the plane crashes "a real bust-up." In addition, Hall noted that "some of the incidents are based on memorable occurrences during the great war, notably the one in which Powell plunges through the air seeking vengeance on the enemy for having, as he thinks, slain Bruce Armstrong, his buddy."[58] The *Literary Digest* cited Major George A. Vaughn, Jr., a "war ace" who corroborated that men as young as those portrayed by Arlen and Rogers had flown in World War I. "One of the boys in my squadron was only sixteen," he offered.

"The boys really looked like war flyers."[59] When Epes Winthrop Sargent analyzed the film for *Moving Picture World*, his article, "The Box Office Lowdown on the Paramount Spectacle," was followed by "What War Fliers Think of the Technical Achievement." Two veteran pilots agreed with the judgement of Charles P. Porter of the 147th Aero Squadron, recipient of Distinguished Service Cross, Croix de Guerre, and the Oak Leaf: "After viewing "Wings" . . . I know that no one need miss seeing the actual manner in which our Air Force conducted its warfare in France."[60] Buttressing assessments by individuals that *Wings* showed the air war as it actually had been was information about the cooperation of the Army in the making of the movie by providing locations, soldiers, and logistical support at Fort Sam Houston in San Antonio, Texas, where *The Big Parade* had also been shot.

While professional reviewers and former flyers agreed on the visual splendor and accuracy of the "air stuff," there was also a consensus on the ordinariness and even the implausibility of the *Wings* narrative. The film told an "average tale." The ending was "improbable," and, "like so many screen stories, much too sentimental, and there is far more of it than one wants."[61] Epes Winthrop Sargent attempted to account for the dichotomy. He felt the filmmakers had allowed scenes of fighting to supersede narrative convention.

> It has been demonstrated in previous productions that the most successful war play makes war itself the background rather than the reason. The war, as such, is so far greater than any of the personal elements arising from the struggle that it will blanket, almost completely, any intimate plot in which a handful of contestants are concerned.[62]

This description of the "successful war play" fits both *What Price Glory?* and *The Big Parade*, in both of which more screen time is spent off the battlefield than on. Even the combat sequences in these films were set mainly in trenches and in command posts, enclosed spaces which functioned like rooms and foregrounded the actors. In *Wings*, however, Sargent noted, "At the moment when the plot is rushing to its climax, the war in all its immensity, is cut into the plot, and the titanic struggle reduces the flyers to merely one of the components of the mighty whole."[63] Visual and aural spectacle wrested attention from the human agent. This violated the norms of classical Hollywood cinema in place since 1917, norms which

Sargent had been influential in disseminating since the 1910s in his weekly columns for *Moving Picture World* and in his screenwriting handbook, *The Technique of the Photoplay.*[64]

Technology contributed to the dwarfing of the actors. To film the scenes in the air, specialized portable cameras were attached fore and aft in the planes, as well as on the wings. These cameras were a type most often associated with documentary shooting and included the Akeley, which had been used by the Signal Corps during the war, and the Eyemo, developed by Bell and Howell in 1925 for use in newsreel photography.[65] The aerial point of view shots these cameras provided, stunning in themselves, were enhanced in well-equipped theaters by a special lens system called the Magnascope, which magnified the screen image. Used only in scenes of aerial dog fights, when the curtains would open wider and the image would expand to fill the screen, this device contributed to the film's spectacle. In addition to Magnascope, Paramount also used recorded sound to heighten the effect of its airplane scenes. Special machines behind the screen recreated machine-gun fire and the take-off noises of airplanes, the latter with different sound effects to distinguish between the American and the German planes.[66]

Wings was highly successful in New York. A. Griffith Grey, head of the roadshow department at Paramount, credited the film with setting a new precedent for Broadway exhibition. It was the first film to achieve sizeable advance ticket sales, in excess of thirty thousand dollars. By the first week in September, seats were being reserved three weeks ahead. Grey, on his way to prepare for the presentation of *Wings* in Chicago, agreed with critics that there was "amazing public interest in aeronautical matters, stirred by the wonderful flights of Lindbergh, Byrd, Chamberlin, and others." Again the film would be breaking new ground, this time as the first movie ever to play in an Erlanger house. Here, too, the exhibition would be grand. "There will be Magnascope or triple sized screen, the wonderful sound effects to create the illusion of planes firing machine guns and crashing to the earth in flames and an orchestra of twenty-eight."[67] In Los Angeles, where it opened at the Biltmore Theater on 15 January 1928, *Wings* was the first picture to command a ticket price of $2.20.[68]

Throughout 1928 and into 1929, aviation continued to be popular, and war movies set in the air, like *The Legion of the Condemned*, which reunited John Monk Saunders, William Wellman, and Gary Cooper, *Lilac Time* [First National, 1928] and *The Sky Hawk* [Fox, 1929] followed in the

Fig. 6.9. Advertisement from *Motion Picture News*, 30 June 1928, showing *The Legion of the Condemned*. The war in the air became a popular staple in the late 1920s and into the 1930s.

Fig. 6.10. Advertisement from *Motion Picture News*, 22 September 1928, showing *Lilac Time*.

wake of *Wings'* success. In September, as the 1928–1929 show year started, *Wings* was finishing its first year at the Criterion and its roadshows were touring the larger cities in the United States. Although Paramount advertised that its films for this new season were "in tune with these changing times," both this individual company and the film industry were actually continuing trends which had brought profit and prestige in the past year. There was, however, one striking addition—recorded sound.[69]

In February 1927, while *Wings* was in production, Paramount, along with Loews, Universal, First National, and Producers Distributing Corporation, was signatory to the Big Five Agreement. This agreement bound companies to study the existing sound technology for one year and then to jointly adopt the same system. These companies were not trying to halt or route the coming of recorded sound. Instead they employed cautious business tactics: forming alliances, minimizing disruption to their well-established mode of production, and lessening the odds of choosing a technologically inferior sound system.[70] Warner Brothers and Fox did not sign the pact, and *Don Juan* was released with a recorded score in August 1926, *Seventh Heaven* on 2 May 1927, *Sunrise* on 23 September 1927, and *The Jazz Singer* on 6 October 1927. These films, with their innovative use of sound, were very popular, and could lay claim to both timeliness and realism.

Wings was emblematic of the way in which Paramount, one of the most prosperous film companies during the 1920s, made the transition to the production and exhibition of pictures with recorded sound. The film was, in fact, an early sound film; Paramount had simply not advertised the fact. In March 1928, however, the month following the expiration of the Big Five Agreement, *Motion Picture News* announced that Paramount had cooperated with General Electric to create the special sound effects of planes and machine guns used in *Wings*. "The sounds," they explained, "come from another film which runs parallel to the one showing the picture." The new system required additional personnel in the projection booth as well, including an electrical engineer trained by General Electric. "If anything went wrong with the intricate machine, he alone could repair it.[71]

Instead of foregrounding this innovative use of sound, however, the advertising of *Wings* highlighted its more familiar elements: realism, the war, the air, and the romance. Mordaunt Hall's review of *Wings* in the *New York Times* described the sound used in the film, but simply noted it in passing.[72] Thus, while promoting aviation, with its well-established public interest, Paramount made the choice to enter *Wings* into competition with other airplane movies, other World War I movies, and other silent roadshow attractions, instead of competing in the area of the newer, less-refined, and less-accessible sound technology. Paramount did not feature recorded sound as a selling point in its promotion of *Wings* until May 1928, when it heralded the upcoming season in its trade paper advertising in statements like the following: "Before release to picture houses, *Wings* will be synchronized with music score and the sensational sound effects that have made its exhibition the talk of the nation."[73] The reason for this belated trumpeting was a good one. It was still sensational aerial cinematography, not "sensational sound effects," that had made *Wings* the talk of the nation.

Paramount's behavior was fitting, however. Being "in tune with these changing times" meant following the lead of a cultural conductor, not altering the tempo of the score. In its handling of the war, also, Paramount adhered to popular consensus. The film did not gloss over the horror of battle; soldiers, including one of the heroes of the film, died. And also in keeping with contemporary sensibility, *Wings* provided an "authentic" view of the conflict by telling a story authored, and directed, and acted by veterans. Even though it was the weakest part of the movie, the narrative evoked admiration for brave deeds and sorrow for lost life, for "sad memories of good comrades 'gone west,' " without anger, rancor, or bitterness. One reviewer even remarked that *Wings* delivered "a curiously effective message for peace."[74] Another, noting that it "carrie[d] a strong if incidental message for peace," summed up the strengths and weaknesses of the film: "For the public, it is and will be, a grand show. The airplane stuff overshadows everything else, dwarfs the love story, shoves it into the background but who cares?"[75]

Wings impressed the motion picture community, receiving one of the first Academy Awards for outstanding production in 1927. In addition, the success of *Wings* and other airplane pictures brought the movies praise from the aviation industry. In September 1928, a dinner was held in New York City to honor the film industry, represented by executive officers of the Motion Picture Producers and Distributors Association (the descendent of the National Association of the Motion Picture Industry), for the "large role played the motion picture in the development of aviation." At this dinner, Will Hays, former postmaster general of the United States, former chairman of the Republican Party, and the head of the M.P.P.D.A., presented Major Lester D. Gardner, president of the Aeronautical Chamber of Commerce, with a print of *40,000 Miles with Lindbergh*. Gardner then visited England, France, and Belgium, countries that Lindbergh himself had visited after his historic flight, presenting the heads of government of those countries with this record of American accomplishment. Copies of the film were also to be given to the governments of Cuba, Mexico, and other Central American countries.[76] *Wings* had found widespread favor with the public at home. After playing over a year on Broadway, it bridged film's passage to sound in 1928, and even in 1929 exhibitors reported *Wings* was doing good business. C. W. Becker, manager of the Electric Theater in Bunwell, Nebraska, recommended the film to his colleagues: "Best picture to date as far as general appeal is concerned. Good in any house. All we gained was prestige."[77]

Conclusion

By the 1920s, the film industry had arrived. The movies had adapted well to the exigencies of doing business during the Great War. To the job of creating and exhibiting quality movies profitably, it had added the missions of raising public morale, schooling its audiences in the behaviors deemed necessary by the government to win the war, and contributing its resources—personnel, pictures and theaters—to the war effort on the homefront. The industry was rewarded for its practical patriotism in a variety of ways. In the production of *Wings*, for instance, Paramount had the help of the War Department, which provided planes, flyers, and the facilities of Kelly and Brooks Air Fields in San Antonio, Texas. More generally, participation in the war on the homefront had burnished the film industry's image and secured its place as entertainment for the growing middle class. A favorable business climate, free of any federal censorship regulations, also accrued to the film industry in the 1920s.

The U.S. film industry fit comfortably into the business world of the 1920s. In its strategy of integrating production with distribution and increasingly with exhibition, and of expanding into overseas markets (where classical Hollywood cinema became the standard which other national cinemas both emulated and rebelled against), the major film companies continued to develop in synchronization with companies in the mainstream of American industry in the 1920s. Famous Players-Lasky, for example, experienced steady growth throughout the decade. In 1924, it calculated its fixed assets at $8,248,044.04, in 1925 at

$8,952,181.39, in 1926 at $10,046,337.18, and, for the first nine months of 1927, at $10,800,000. By 1927, Paramount Famous Lasky owned all the stock of Publix Theaters Corporation and had forty-five exchanges handling the United States and Canadian markets alone.[78] These advances reflect the general advance of the industry, as business enterprise and as popular art, and the benefits the industry received for its participation in the war effort.

The Great War affected the way the film industry portrayed war. The conventions governing the way Hollywood told war stories changed from the prewar period through 1917 and 1918 and into the 1920s, but these changes were fairly contained. After 1919 women played a less vital role in the narratives of war-related movies, and the climaxes of the plots most often occurred on the battle field. Two films of 1929 are the exceptions proving the rule that war was now a man's enterprise. *Battling Sisters* (Lupino Lane Comedy Corporation) parodied the conventional war film of the 1910s. In this comedy short, set in the future of 1980, men and women reversed traditional gender roles, with women going to war, and men staying home. The film included a farewell scene—an allusion to *The Big Parade*, where the men followed the truck carrying the women soldiers away. Its high point came as the enemy officer, a female—threatened the purity of the man at home. He was saved, of course, in the nick of time, by his wife.[79] The second film, *She Goes to War* (United Artists), was a drama directed by Henry King in which the conventions of the 1920s combat film prevailed. An adaptation of Rupert Hughes's 1925 novel, this film simply replaced the typical male soldier with a woman. Like Jim Apperson in *The Big Parade*, she was wealthy; like him she bonded with a small group of ethnically and socially diverse women. The press book for the film included articles attesting to the presence of General Charles P. Summerall on the set where "he little dreamed he was to be taken back to France and to the scenes that were indelibly seared on his memory." The War Department allowed Fort Leonard Wood, in Maryland, to be used as a set during filming of the battle sequence which included a tank that is immersed in flames. Even the film's music was authentic: "The score will for the first time in film history form a singular record of famous American peace and war songs since the days of the Civil War." Although press material said *She Goes to War* presented the Great War "from the woman's point of view," narratively and stylistically it resembled its 1920s male-oriented predecessors.[80]

One of the main differences between war films made during the war and those made in the middle 1920s was the participation of veterans in nearly all phases of the creative process of the later films. Their stories and experiences encountered the Hollywood conventions of narrative and style, as well as the established strategies for film distribution and exhibition. Thus, like earlier war films, those made in the 1920s usually began before the war and ended back at home, and they contained a love story. The love story, relegated to a subplot and set within the framing story, was also a way to provide a female star to ensure there were women in the audience. Clara Bow was the best known of the three leading players in *Wings*, but as *Moving Picture World*'s Sargent noted, although "Miss Bow is capital . . . her opportunities are limited."[81] The love story also functioned thematically; its sweetness accentuated the brutality of the battle scenes.

Before the 1920s, war had been a necessary evil undergone in order to save the honor and chastity of women, to make the world safe for democracy, and to end all wars. In the 1920s, it was not so clear why men went "over there." In *The Big Parade*, Jim is swept away by a parade and stirred by its martial music. In *What Price Glory?* Quirt and Flagg are career soldiers fighting for a living; in *Wings* John wants to fly planes. Accounting for a change of tone in the description of war from the early to the mid-1920s, a reviewer of *The Big Parade* referred to "literature of the first reaction" to the war. Alluding to Dos Passos and to Stallings and Anderson's *What Price Glory?*, he commented that the characters in these works "appear entirely obsessed by the steady irritation of everything from cooties to commanding officers." Jim, Bull, and Slim, the film's three main characters, had a broader range of emotions, and thus *The Big Parade* presented a "truer" picture of what war was like. Patriotism had been a sufficient selling point for the war movies made in 1917 and 1918, but in the 1920s it was the perception that war, especially the depiction of combat and life at the front, was represented authentically that most characterized public discourse. Publicists and critics pointed out veterans working on production teams. Mise-en-scene was held to a standard of verisimilitude, and any deviations from the vintage planes or tanks or elements of uniforms were noted. *The Big Parade* was praised in part because its sets were so crammed with the details of daily life that "there is hardly a false note for even the most skeptical doughboy to cavil at."[82] Sound effects of different types of planes taking off in *Wings* or a score comprising "songs of peace and war" in *She Goes to War* were likewise judged by a standard of authenticity. Even the audience at the theater was scouted for former soldiers whose responses could be cited in film reviews. The films of the 1920s provide a good illustration of the "second reaction" to the war, one distanced by time, mediated by narrative convention and the film industry's proclivities, and nuanced by the growing ambivalence, broadly felt in American culture, regarding U.S. participation.

7

Conclusion: Practical Patriotism

I look ahead to a prospect of infinite potentialities; to a future too great
to be foreseen, but which we must carve for ourselves out of the material
at hand.

Adolph Zukor, December 1917[1]

AFTER THE UNITED STATES had been at war for eight months, Adolph
Zukor, president of one of the fastest growing film production and distribution companies in the United States, wrote that better films and greater
profit for filmmakers and theater managers would grow from the service
that the film industry tendered to its customers and to its country in that
time of crisis. Movies would entertain audiences, thus lightening the nation's mood and diverting its citizens from "constant contemplation of the
gigantic drama, greater than any we may hope to depict, which is spread
upon the great screen of Europe." Seizing the moment, the newly formed
National Association of the Motion Picture Industry quickly rushed to help
the government spread its "information and propaganda" (not a derogatory
term in 1917) to the large numbers of Americans who went to the movies
every week. NAMPI touted this effort as, simultaneously, it expanded its
own membership. Service would have a payback, Zukor believed, and in
his assessment we hear once more the principle of practical patriotism: "In
giving of the best that is in us, we shall be best serving ourselves and our
industry."[2] By any measure, this proved to be the case.

Over the course of the Great War the film industry refined its product,
and in the 1920s it set an international standard for filmmaking. It also
continued along a path of corporate growth toward oligopoly which helped
to ensure its profitability in the succeeding decade. There was no
government-initiated censorship of the films, and, in fact, key figures in
the government, like Will Hays, went to work for the film industry in the
1920s. The war did not divert the development of the craft or the business
of filmmaking from its prewar course. As Zukor said, the industry would
secure its future prosperity using material at hand.

195

At the same time, Zukor's vice president, Jesse Lasky, prophesied the important role movies would play after the fighting ended. He wrote, "This great war will be told on the screen for future generations in addition to being written in books,"[3] and he, too, was right. While movies about the war never dominated the release schedules of film distributors, they did become a staple throughout the late 1910s and the 1920s, even though both their function and their form changed over time. Before the United States entered the conflict in April 1917, films told stories of the need for preparedness as well as the need to refrain from mixing in the problems of Europe. After American entry, movies like *The Little American, Hearts of the World, The Unbeliever,* and *Shoulder Arms* showed movie-goers bestial Huns, endangered women, and brave, young American men. These films stirred feelings described then as patriotic, enhanced citizen support for the government's war effort, and in some cases actually spurred military recruitment. Increasingly during the 1920s those films defined as war pictures portrayed soldiers in combat—in the trenches and in the air. Here war was not depicted as a noble enterprise. In fact, in films like *The Big Parade, What Price Glory?,* and *Wings,* it replaced the Hun as enemy. Still, the Great War on the screen did offer young men the opportunity to act in noble ways.

Movie houses, also, played a significant role entertaining, informing, and rallying communities to the government's cause during World War I. Following the dictums of trade journalists and writers of theater management handbooks, exhibitors worked to carve out and secure a niche for their theaters within the cultural life of their neighborhoods, towns, and cities, and the war was readymade for such a business strategy. Of course, theater managers showed feature films, newsreels, and short comedies to their audiences, but they also provided public speaking forums for the Four Minute Men of the Committee on Public Information, additional recruitment stations for all the armed services, and collection points for peach pits needed in the gas masks worn at the front. These businessmen and businesswomen sold War Savings Stamps along with movie tickets, and provided music while their customers sang "Over There," and "Keep the Home Fires Burning." Such activities were promoted by the trade, including its most prominent members, because they showed both good business sense and good citizenship. In the end, all these strategies succeeded, so that the film industry prospered into the 1920s, when it laid further claim to the war as the raw material for its narrative films.

On the ten-year anniversary of the Armistice, Herbert C. McKay, dean of the New York Institute of Photography, helped promote a documentary film produced jointly by the Departments of War and Navy and the Eastman Kodak Company. "We begin to feel the approach of age," he wrote. McKay encouraged his readers, especially those who owned 16mm projectors, to commemorate 11 November 1928 by watching *America Goes Over.* This five-reel film was authentic, not like "the most florid of staged reproductions, with heavy rolling smoke and exaggerated dramatic gesture. . . ." Instead, one knew that "the aerial encounters are not staged stunts—the twisting, swirling plane which falls is bearing a human being who is going to death or capture." McKay offered two reasons for watching this film. First, it provided a way to honor the veterans of the war and those who died in combat. It also functioned as history. "We, who were only youngsters at the time, face the fact that a new generation is rising—a generation whose privilege is to learn, in some infinitesimal degree, the sacrifices made by the immortal A.E.F."[4] The film industry, which also had the cooperation of the government in making *The Big Parade* and *Wings,* among others, sold its feature films on the same promise of honor and historical truth. I suspect that more young people watched *Wings* in a theater in 1928 than watched *America Goes Over* on a home projector. Those coming of age in the late 1920s and 1930s based their image and their understanding of the Great War, in part, on the movies they saw on Saturday afternoons.

Intellectual historian George Mosse has grappled with the effects of incorporating World War I into the popular culture of Europe and to a lesser degree into that of the United States in the years following the war. Examining the design of cemeteries and war memorials, postcards, plays, and movies, he argues that when the war was mediated in these ways the result was "the myth of the war experience" that valorized the fallen soldier as a martyr to the cause of a holy state. As a result, soldiers' deaths became not simply understandable but acceptable and heroic. Mosse spelled out the political consequences of this transformation of war into the stuff of popular culture.

> The Myth of the War Experience was central to the process of brutalization [in German politics] . . . providing nationalism with some of its most effective postwar myths and stories. The Myth of the War Experience also attempted to carry the First into the Second World War, to establish an unbroken continuity which would rejuvenate the nation.[5]

War films have been the most durable legacy of the participation of the U.S. film industry in World War I. When Adolph Zukor wrote that the "gigantic drama" of war could not be captured on a movie screen, he was right. Instead, in the 1920s, the conventions of narrative filmmaking processed the stories reported or imagined by men and women, many of whom had seen the conflict first-hand. Film conventions also evolved, and audiences left movie theaters with a consistent set of images and themes representing an increasingly distant war. Movies and movie-going, stars, stories, and showmanship all jostled other manifestations of the Great War in our popular culture to shape an abiding memory of World War I.

NOTES
SELECTED BIBLIOGRAPHY
INDEX

NOTES

Introduction

1. For a discussion of public sentiment in the United States and of Woodrow Wilson's reasons for staying out of the war until April 1917, see the prologue to David M. Kennedy, *Over Here: The First World War and American Society* (New York: Oxford University Press, 1980), 3–44.

2. George Kleine to Union Trust Company, September 1915, George Kleine Collection, Library of Congress, container 66.

3. Kleine to Congressman Fred Britton, 6 April 1917, George Kleine Collection, container 66.

4. Kleine to Newton Baker, 23 June 1917, George Kleine Collection, container 65.

5. Kleine to George Creel, 25 September 1918, George Kleine Collection, container 65.

6. Kleine to Creel, 14 July 1918, George Kleine Collection, container 65.

7. Kleine to Brigadier General Fuller, *The Star Spangled Banner* file, George Kleine Collection, container 65.

8. Kleine, circular 109a, 19 September 1918, George Kleine Collection, container 66.

9. *The Unbeliever* file, George Kleine Collection, container 67.

10. See, for example, Kleine to Kendall Banning, Director of Moving Pictures, Committee on Public Information, 11 August 1917, and Kleine to Baker, 23 June 1917, George Kleine Collection, container 65.

11. The term "practical patriotism" comes from an advertisement for *The Bar Sinister, New York Times*, 3 June 1917, sec. X. The manager of the Broadway Theater in New York City was offering a Liberty Bond worth fifty dollars in a sweepstakes for his audience. The ad described this combining of entertainment and support of country as practical patriotism. The advertisement also urged theater-owners across the country to follow his lead. "One Bond given away daily in each of America's 16,000 picture theatres would place $5,000,000 a week in Uncle Sam's pocket and give strength to his mighty blows."

12. My study closes with the coming of sound and the onset of the Great Depression. These two significant events in film history and American history

create additional pressures on the organization of the film industry and the development of the war film genre. For more information on World War I films made in the 1930s and early 1940s, see Thomas Doherty, *Projections of War: Hollywood, American Culture, and World War II* (New York: Columbia University Press, 1993), and Jeanine Basinger, *The World War II Combat Film: Anatomy of a Genre* (New York: Columbia University Press, 1986).

Chapter 1. The U.S. Film Industry and the Coming of War, 1914–1917

1. "Facts and Comment," *Moving Picture World* 21.7 (15 August 1914): 931.

2. Woodrow Wilson, quoted in John M. Cooper, Jr., *Pivotal Decades: The United States, 1900–1920* (New York: W. W. Norton, 1990), 227.

3. For more information on U.S. reaction to the war in Europe, see Cooper, *Pivotal Decades*, and Nell Irvin Painter, *Standing at Armageddon: The United States, 1877–1919* (New York: W. W. Norton, 1987).

4. For a discussion of the range of isolationist positions, see John Milton Cooper, *The Vanity of Power: American Isolationism and the First World War, 1914–1917* (Westport, CT: Greenwood Publishing, 1969).

5. Painter, *Standing at Armageddon*, 295.

6. Cooper, *Pivotal Decades*, 251–252.

7. *Moving Picture World* 21.10 (5 September 1914): 1343. The phrase was used by the editor in "Facts and Comments," as he continued to discuss the trade potential of the war in Europe.

8. Cooper, *Pivotal Decades*, 11, makes the point that "an enormous wave of business consolidation had gathered during the mid-1890s, and in six years between 1897 and 1903 the wave broke over the United States fundamentally altering the shape of the American economy." Thus the movement to consolidate within the film industry needs to be understood within the larger context of business practice in the United States in the early part of the 20th century.

9. Robert H. Wiebe, *The Search for Order, 1877–1920* (New York: Hill and Wang, 1967), 12.

10. "Special" signified a film that was more expensive to produce, often required higher ticket prices, and was promoted as prestigious and out of the ordinary. It was distinguished from the "standard" feature, which was the industry's stock-in-trade.

11. "Diplomats see Farrar in Film: First Showing of New Lasky Motion Picture 'Joan the Woman' Given in Washington: Star Wires Regrets," *New York Telegram*, 22 December 1916, in the *Joan the Woman* scrapbook, vol. 273, Cecil B. DeMille Collection, Brigham Young University Library (hereafter cited as DeMille Collection).

12. Chronological record for 1916, *Moving Picture World* 31.1 (6 January 1917): 58–60. *Moving Picture World* reported that Famous Players and Lasky combined 28 June 1916, Morosco and Pallas were absorbed 20 October 1916, Cecil B. DeMille was named president of the Oliver Morosco Photoplay Company and vice-president of Pallas Pictures Company 11 November 1916, and Famous Players-Lasky acquired controlling interest in Paramount 8 December 1916.

13. Epilogue, *Joan the Woman* script, p. 2, box 1228, folder 3, DeMille Collection. The film itself survives at the George Eastman House in Rochester, New York, and a copy of the Eastman print on videotape exists in the DeMille Collection.

14. DeMille to Lasky, 17 June 1916, box 238, folder 14, DeMille Collection.

15. Lasky to DeMille, 29 May 1916, box 238, folder 14, DeMille Collection. A portion of the DeMille correspondence from 1916 and 1917 is collected in *The Demille Legacy*, ed. Paolo Cherchi Usai and Lorenzo Codelli (Pordenone: Edizioni Biblioteca dell'Immagine, 1991). Where documents exist in both the BYU collection and in *The DeMille Legacy* I will provide both citations. This letter of 29 May is found in *The DeMille Legacy*, 338. *Joan the Woman* was the most expensive film DeMille directed until *Forbidden Fruit* in 1920; its grosses were higher than any film he directed until *Male and Female* in 1919.

This trend of making big features would change in the next year. In March 1917, Lasky wrote DeMille, "Our people here all agreed that we should produce two pictures of Farrar next season, of 6,000 feet each instead of one long picture, as planned." Lasky to DeMille, 10 March 1917, box 240 folder 1, DeMille Collection.

16. Lasky to DeMille, 9 June 1916, box 238, folder 14, DeMille Collection; *DeMille Legacy*, 360–361.

17. DeMille to Lasky, 17 June 1916, box 238, folder 14, DeMille Collection; *DeMille Legacy*, 372–373.

18. Lasky to DeMille, 9 June 1916, box 238, folder 14, DeMille Collection; *DeMille Legacy*, 366.

19. Lasky to DeMille, 27 June 1916, box 238, folder 14, DeMille Collection; *DeMille Legacy*, 384.

20. Ibid.

21. Ibid.

22. DeMille to Lasky, 12 July 1916, box 238, folder 14, DeMille Collection.

23. Ibid.

24. DeMille to Lasky, 17 June 1916, box 238, folder 14, DeMille Collection.

25. Lasky to DeMille, 21 July 1916, *DeMille Legacy*, 399.

26. Lasky to DeMille, 27 June 1916, box 238, folder 14, DeMille Collection; *DeMille Legacy*, 384.

27. DeMille to Lasky, 12 July 1917, box 238, folder 14, DeMille Collection.

28. Ibid.

29. "Mme Farrar's Joan of Arc in the New Spectacle of the Screen," *Boston Evening Transcript*, 5 February 1917; box 238, folder 23, DeMille Collection.

30. Friend to DeMille, 27 November 1916, box 238, folder 12, DeMille Collection.

31. Lasky to DeMille, 15 September 1916, box 238, folder 14, DeMille Collection; *DeMille Legacy*, 418.

32. Lasky to DeMille, 14 September 1916, box 238, folder 14, DeMille Collection.

33. Ibid.

34. Lasky to DeMille, 15 September 1916, box 238, folder 14, DeMille Collection.

35. Ibid.

36. DeMille to Lasky, 7 October 1916, box 238, folder 14, DeMille Collection; *DeMille Legacy*, 421.

37. Lasky to DeMille, 21 July 1916, *DeMille Legacy*, 403.

38. Lasky to DeMille, 6 January 1917, *DeMille Legacy*, 445.

39. DeMille to Lasky, 21 November 1916, box 238, folder 14, DeMille Collection; *DeMille Legacy*, 441. In silent cinema, the speed at which film was projected varied between fourteen and eighteen frames per second. In fact, the rate at which the film stock passed through the projector might vary within a film to create comic or dramatic effects or simply to match the speed at which the film was shot. With the coming of sound, projection speed standardized at twenty-four frames per second. For more information about this and other technical aspects of silent film, see Paolo Cherchi Usai, *Burning Passions: An Introduction to the Study of Silent Cinema*, trans. Emma Sansone Rittle (London: British Film Institute, 1994).

40. These points were conveyed in articles like Edward Speyer, "Farrar's Joan of Arc Likely to Interpret Maid of Orleans as a Fiery Tempestuous Saint," *Detroit News Tribune*, 29 October 1916; "Noted Producer and Prima Donna Place Wreath at Feet of Joan of Arc," *Salt Lake City Herald*, 12 October 1916; "Did Joan of Arc Use a Mirror?" *Homestead Pennsylvania Messenger*, 27 November 1916. These are all included in the *Joan the Woman* scrapbook, vol. 273, DeMille Collection.

41. Louella Parsons, "Secret of Geraldine Farrar's New Screen Triumph," *Columbus Dispatch*, 17 December 1916; vol. 273, *Joan the Woman* scrapbook, DeMille Collection.

42. "Geraldine Farrar as Joan of Arc, Photodrama on the Life of the Maid of Orleans Soon to be Shown in Forty-Fourth Street Theater—DeMille Selects Title 'Joan the Woman,'" *Moving Picture World* (30 December 1916); *Joan the Woman* scrapbook, vol. 273, DeMille Collection.

43. Ibid. Actually, DeMille added a couple of years onto Joan's age, either

through reliance on historical evidence of the time, or to give Farrar, not a girlish-looking actress, a bit of help. According to the chronology in Marina Warner, *Joan of Arc: the Image of Female Heroism* (New York: Vintage Books, 1982), xxi–xxii, Joan was either sixteen or seventeen when she waged the battles depicted in *Joan the Woman*. She was eighteen or nineteen when she was burned at the stake.

44. Ibid.

45. Advertisement for *Joan the Woman, New York Times*, 14 December 1916, sec. X.

46. Advertisements for *Joan the Woman, New York Times*, 16 December 1916, sec. X; 18 December 1916, sec. X; 19 December 1916, sec. X; 20 December 1916, sec. X; 21 December 1916, sec. X; 22 December 1916, sec. X; 23 December 1916, sec. X.

47. Advertisement for *Joan the Woman*, "Medieval and Modern France," *New York Times*, 19 December 1916, sec. X.

48. Advertisement for *Joan the Woman, New York Times*, 21 December 1916, sec. X.

49. Advertisement for *Joan the Woman, New York Times*, 22 December 1916, sec. X.

50. Geraldine Farrar, *Such Sweet Compulsion: The Autobiography of Geraldine Farrar* (New York: Greystone Press, 1938), 172.

51. *Joan the Woman* script, box 1128, folder 3, pp. 4–5, DeMille Collection.

52. Ibid.

53. David M. Kennedy, *Over Here: The First World War and American Society* (New York: Oxford University Press, 1980), 12, points out that "the electoral margin was disconcertingly narrow. A difference of fewer than 4000 votes in California would have removed Woodrow Wilson from the White House. And his party fared no better; though Democrats enjoyed a majority of nine seats in the Senate, the voters returned but 216 Democrats to the House of Representatives, along with 210 Republicans and 6 Independents."

54. Advertisement for *Joan the Woman, Moving Picture World* 31.8 (24 February 1917): 1124–1125.

55. Advertisement for *Joan the Woman, Moving Picture World* 31.9 (3 March 1917): 1286–1287.

56. Advertisement for *Joan the Woman, New York Times*, 25 March 1917, sec. X.

57. Advertisement for *Joan the Woman, Chicago Tribune*, 8 April 1917.

58. "Live Wire Exhibitors," *Motion Picture News*, 28 April 1917, pp. 2, 649.

59. George Blaisdell, "Joan the Woman Cecil DeMille's Great Spectacle Is Received with Enthusiasm at Its Opening in New York," *Moving Picture World* (1 January 1917); *Joan the Woman*, scrapbook, vol. 273, DeMille Collection.

60. "Diplomats See Farrar in Film, First Showing of New Lasky Motion

Picture 'Joan the Woman' Given in Washington, Star Wires Regrets," *New York Telegram*, 22 December 1916; *Joan the Woman* scrapbook, vol. 273, DeMille Collection.

61. "Spectacular Films for Holiday Week," *New York Times*, 25 December 1916, sec. X.

62. George W. Graves, "Current Releases Reviewed, 'Joan the Woman,' " *Motography*, 13 January 1917; *Joan the Woman* scrapbook, vol. 273, DeMille Collection.

63. "Tremendous Impressive Spectacle with Superb Moments," *Wid's Yearbook 1917*; *Joan the Woman* scrapbook, vol. 273, DeMille Collection.

64. Letterhead on correspondence dated 6 January 1917, box 240, folder 1, DeMille Collection; *DeMille Legacy*, 446.

65. Advertisement for *Joan the Woman, New York Times*, 31 December 1916, sec. X; advertisement for *Joan the Woman, New York Times*, 31 January 1917, sec. X.

66. Graves, "Current Releases Reviewed: 'Joan the Woman,' " *Motography*, 1 January 1917; Blaisdell, " 'Joan the Woman': Cecil DeMille's Great Spectacle Is Received with Enthusiasm at Its Opening in New York," *Moving Picture World*, 1 January 1917; "Tremendous Impressive Spectacle with Superb Moments," *Wid's Yearbook 1917*; *Joan the Woman* scrapbook, vol. 273, DeMille Collection.

67. Blaisdell, " 'Joan the Woman.' "

68. Alexander Wollcott, "Joan the Prima Donna," excerpt from "Second Thoughts on First Nights," *New York Times*, 25 February 1917, Sec. 3; cited in George C. Pratt, *Spellbound in Darkness*, (Greenwich, CT: New York Graphic Society, 1973), 241.

69. Frederick James Smith, " 'Joan the Woman' Humanizes History," *New York Mail*, 6 January 1917; *Joan the Woman* scrapbook, vol. 273, DeMille Collection.

70. Blaisdell, " 'Joan the Woman.' "

71. "Tremendous Impressive Spectacle with Superb Moments," *Wid's Yearbook 1917*; *Joan the Woman* scrapbook, vol. 273, DeMille Collection.

72. Peter Milne, "Joan the Woman," *Motion Picture News*, 6 January 1917; *Joan the Woman* scrapbook, vol. 273, DeMille Collection. The Catholic Church had begun the process of canonizing Joan of Arc. In 1903 she was pronounced "venerable," and in 1909 she was beatified. Sainthood would be conferred upon her in 1920.

73. "Mosk-Censorship," 24 April 1946, box 13, folder 9, DeMille Collection.

74. "Young Peasant Girl Named Perchaud Said to Hear Voices Like Joan of Arc," *New York Times*, 10 March 1917; "Joan of Arc Park," *New York Times*, 15 December 1918.

75. Kennedy, *Over Here*, 55–56.

76. Her autobiography, *Such Sweet Compulsion*, 155, includes a photograph

of Farrar garbed as Columbia with flag and shield flanked by two Red Cross nurses, taken at a Liberty Loan Drive Pageant.

77. Shauer to DeMille, 1 May 1919, box 240, folder 14, DeMille Collection.

78. Ibid.

79. Advertisement for *Joan the Woman, Moving Picture World* 31.13 (31 March 1917): 2022–2023.

80. " 'Joan the Woman' Income," box 240, folder 14, DeMille Collection.

81. David Pierce, "Success with a Dollar Sign: Costs and Grosses for the Early Films of Cecile B. DeMille," lists the costs on *Joan the Woman* as $302,976.26, and its gross as $605,731.30 (*DeMille Legacy*, 316.)

82. Shauer to DeMille, 1 May 1919, box 240, folder 14, DeMille Collection.

83. DeMille to Shauer, 8 May 1919, box 240, folder 14, DeMille Collection.

84. Shauer to DeMille, 7 June 1919, box 240, folder 14, DeMille Collection.

85. DeMille to Lasky, 16 October 1918, box 240, folder 11, DeMille Collection.

86. "Militia," *Moving Picture World*, 21 April 1917; box 13, folder 9, DeMille Collection.

87. "Militia," *Motion Picture News*, 28 April 1917; box 13, folder 9, DeMille Collection.

88. *Moving Picture World*, 16 June 1917; *Motion Picture News*, 23 June 1917; box 13, folder 9, DeMille Collection.

89. DeMille to Lasky, 14 August 1917; box 240, folder 1, DeMille Collection; *DeMille Legacy*, 538.

90. Ibid.

91. Telegram from Lasky to DeMille, 21 August 1917, box 240, folder 1, DeMille Collection.

92. Box 32, folder 1, DeMille Collection. On 8 March 1918, Captain Samuel A. Gibson, 12th Infantry, Intelligence Officer, wrote DeMille thanking him for "the courtesy and cooperation extended by you to a representative of this office on a recent call at your studio." On 13 March 1918, Second Lieutenant Thaddeus Knight, 63rd Infantry, Assistant Intelligence Officer, wrote DeMille, "Enclosed you will please find your credentials as a representative of the Intelligence Office in this district. I placed no official number on the card as yet and until such time as a number is given you will use your own signature."

93. For a thorough history of the American Protective League, see Joan M. Jensen, *The Price of Vigilance* (New York: Rand McNally, 1968).

94. U.S. Attorney General T. W. Gregory to A. M. Briggs, Chairman of National Directors, American Protective League, 16 November 1917, box 37, folder 1, DeMille Collection.

95. There is a particularly humorous exchange recounted in a report from 22 July 1918, as S.A. writing to F.K. (Fred Kley) told of suspicious comments voiced by a young girl on the lot. F.K. parenthetically asked who the young girl was and

discovered it was F.L.C. Report to F.K. from S.A., 22 July 1918, box 37, folder 1, DeMille Collection.

96. DeMille to Knight, 19 March 1918, box 32, folder 1, DeMille Collection.

97. T. R. Moss to DeMille, 13 August 1918, box 32, folder 1, DeMille Collection.

98. See Jensen, *Price of Vigilance*.

99. Memo from Knight to DeMille, 23 March 1918, box 32, folder 1, DeMille Collection.

100. DeMille to Lieutenant F. C. Lewis, 10 May 1918, box 37, folder 1, DeMille Collection.

101. Report on Mr. Paul Weigle to DeMille, 21 May 1918, box 37, folder 1, DeMille Collection.

102. DeMille to Lewis, 23 May 1918; Lewis to DeMille, 25 May 1918, box 37, folder 1, DeMille Collection.

103. DeMille to Lewis, 28 May 1918, box 37, folder 1, DeMille Collection.

104. "Second Report on Bryant Washburn," 15 July 1918, box 37, folder 1, DeMille Collection.

105. Ibid.

106. DeMille to Lasky, 14 August 1917, box 240, folder 1; Captain Gibson, 12th Infantry, Intelligence Officer, to DeMille, 8 March 1918, box 32, folder 1; DeMille to Lasky, 16 October 1918, box 240, folder 11, DeMille Collection.

107. Telegram, DeMille to Lasky, 4 October 1918, box 240, folder 11, DeMille Collection.

108. Lasky to DeMille, 6 November 1918, box 240, folder 11, DeMille Collection.

109. Lasky to DeMille, 14 November 1918, box 240, folder 11, DeMille Collection.

110. Ibid.

Chapter 2. The Films of World War I, 1917–1918

1. "New Film Plays," *Milwaukee Journal*, 9 June 1918, sec. 2.

2. Timothy Lyons, "Hollywood and World War I, 1914–1918," *Journal of Popular Film* 1.4 (winter 1972): 15–30; Michael T. Isenberg, *War on Film: The American Cinema and World War I* (London: Associated University Presses, 1981).

3. Isenberg, *War on Film*, 17.

4. Benjamin Hampton, *A History of the Movies* (New York: Covici-Friede, 1931), 173.

5. "The Exhibitors Tell What They Want," *Motography*, 9 March 1918, lead editorial.

6. In order to analyze the film industry's products of April 1917–November 1918, it is necessary first to compile a master list of films released during these months. The base list for this study is the "List of Current Film Release Dates" published weekly in the trade paper *Moving Picture World*. This exhibitor's weekly had a circulation of 17,200 in 1917 and 15,000 in 1918, figures closely mirroring the number of exhibitors in business during those years, according to *N.W. Ayer and Son's American Newspaper Annual and Directory* (Philadelphia: Ayer and Sons), 1917: 1253; 1918: 1280; and "Motion Picture Theaters in the United States and Canada," published by the Motion Picture Directory Company, 1917 or 1918 (National Archives, record group 4 [112 HC-A4, box 505]). For consistency, I am working from the list printed in the first issue of every month. Thus, for example, the listings for May 1917 reflect the films in release during April 1917. While these listings are not absolutely complete, there is much evidence for their representativeness: the numbers of the films listed (e.g., 557 in April 1917, 590 in April 1918, 496 in November 1918); the inclusion of all major producer-distributors and many states rights distributors; and the many types and lengths of films encompassed: five-reel drama, split animation, multiple-feature reels, and so on.

Next I sought to determine which films were war-related by virtue of narrative content or documentary topicality. In this sorting I used a rather large net, including not only *Crashing Through to Berlin*, *A Maid of Belgium*, and Mutt and Jeff's *Landing the Spy*, but also films such as *A Face in the Dark* ("It's a detective story with a secret service finish," said *Variety*, 19 April 1918, 45), *Sweetheart of the Doomed* ("The scenes are laid near Paris showing wonderful views of the European War," *Milwaukee Sentinel*, 22 April 1917, sec. 2), and *Darkest Russia* ("Timely, Vital!" *Milwaukee Sentinel*, 15 April 1917, sec. 2).

In compiling this subset of war-related films I used both primary and secondary sources. I included all films whose advertisements in the *New York Times* made reference to a link with the war. I also included films listed in a compilation published by the *Exhibitor's Trade Review* in July 1918 entitled "The Exhibitor's Catalog of War Pictures for 1917–1918" (20 July 1918). In addition, I included films which, as reviewed by the staff of *Moving Picture World* ("Critical Reviews") and in summaries of their plots ("Advertising Aids for Busy Exhibitors"), revealed some narrative relationship to the war. On the average, over this nineteen-month period, *Moving Picture World* summarized the plots of thirty-five films each week. Distributors in *Moving Picture World's* "List of Current Film Release Dates" sometimes specified a film as "topical" or as a "war drama." Secondary sources also providing titles included Jack Spears, "World War I on the Screen," vols. 1 and 2 (*Films in Review* 17 [May 1966]: 274–292; 17 [June–July 1966]: 354–365 and Timothy Lyons, "Hollywood and World War I, 1914–1918" (*Journal of Popular Film* 1.4 [1972]: 15–30). Because of the number and variety of my sources, this list of war-related films should be taken as representative rather than definitive.

7. "List of Current Film Release Dates," *Moving Picture World* 32.5 (5 May 1917): 858, 860, 862, 864. Newsreels included were by *Selig Tribune, Hearts-Pathe News, Universal Animated Weekly,* and the *Mutual Weekly.* The topical films listed include *Uncle Sam Awake, War on Three Fronts, America is Ready, How Uncle Sam Prepares, Heroic France, Our Fighting Forces, Tanks at the Battle of Ancre,* and *Manning Our Navy.*

8. These states rights distributors include Hanover Film Company, Heroic France Syndicate, M-C Film Company, Rogson Film Company, Continental Producing Company, and Facts Film Company.

9. *The Story of the Famous Players-Lasky Company* (Museum of Modern Art Archives, dated 1919), p. 65.

10. "Paramount October Releases," *Moving Picture World* 33.12 (22 September 1917): 1869.

11. Advertisement, "At the Front with Fox," *Moving Picture World* 34.2 (13 October 1917): 162–163.

12. "List of Current Film Release Dates," *Moving Picture World* 38.1 (5 October 1918): 130, 132, 134, 136.

13. "Bankruptcy in Pictures Linked to War Conditions," *Variety,* 25 October 1918, p. 32; "How War Affects Pictures," *Moving Picture World* 35.5 (2 February 1918): 648.

14. Epes Winthrop Sargent, "Advertising for Exhibitors," *Moving Picture World* 32.10 (9 June 1917): 1595.

15. "Pictures of War Not Unpopular with Public," *Moving Picture World* 34.4 (27 April 1918): 569.

16. "Essanay Cuts Out Depressing Stories," *Moving Picture World* 32.10 (9 June 1917): 1605.

17. Sargent, "Advertising for Exhibitors," 1595.

18. "Written on the Screen," *New York Times,* 21 July 1918, sec. X. Also, "Universal Latest to Announce That It Will Produce Only 'Cheerful' Photoplays during the War," *New York Times,* 25 August 1918, sec. X.

19. Advertisement, *Moving Picture World* 32.4 (28 April 1917): 650.

20. "Notes and Comments," *Moving Picture World* 35.10 (9 March 1918): 1340.

21. "New Film Plays," *The Milwaukee Journal,* 9 June 1918, sec. 2.

22. Kevin Brownlow, *The War, the West, and the Wilderness* (New York: Knopf, 1979), 131.

23. Charles Reed Mitchell, "New Message to America: James W. Gerard's *Beware* and World War I Propaganda," *Journal of Popular Film* 4.4 (1975): 276.

24. Garth Jowett, *Film: The Democratic Art* (Boston: Little, Brown, 1976), 67.

25. Walter E. Greene, "Artcraft Year Old," *Motography*, 28 July 1917, p. 207.

26. *Federal Trade Commission v. Famous Players-Lasky Company, et al.* Federal Trade Commission Docket 835, in Howard T. Lewis, *The Motion Picture Industry* (New York: Van Nostrand, 1933), 153.

27. Advertisement, *Moving Picture World* 33.6 (11 August 1917): 899.

28. *Story of the Famous Players-Lasky Company*, 21.

29. "List of Current Film Release Dates," *Moving Picture World* 32.1 (7 April 1917): 168, 170, 172, 174.

30. Advertisement, *New York Times*, 25 August 1918, sec. X.

31. Lewis, *Motion Picture Industry*, 240.

32. Advertisement, *New York Times*, 31 March 1918, sec. X.

33. Advertisement, *Exhibitor's Trade Review*, 20 July 1918, p. 594.

34. *Hearts of the World* (D. W. Griffith, 1918).

35. "Written on the Screen," *New York Times*, 29 September 1918, sec. X.

36. Lewis, *Motion Picture Industry*, ix–x.

37. "In the Theaters," Kokomo, Indiana, *Dispatch*, 30 September 1917; Jeanie Macpherson scrapbook, vol. 103, Cecil B. DeMille Collection, Brigham Young University Library (hereafter cited as DeMille Collection).

38. Lasky to DeMille, 5 March 1917, box 240, folder 1, DeMille Collection; *The DeMille Legacy*, ed. Paolo Cherchi Usai and Lorenzo Codelli (Pordenone: Edizioni Biblioteca dell'Immagine, 1991), 62.

39. "Written on the Screen," *New York Times*, 6 May 1917, sec. 10.

40. Tino Balio, "Stars in Business: The Founding of United Artists," in *The American Film Industry*, rev. ed., ed. Tino Balio (Madison: University of Wisconsin Press, 1985), 157–158.

41. Lasky to DeMille, 19 January 1917, box 240, folder 1, DeMille Collection; *DeMille Legacy*, 451.

42. Lasky to DeMille, 11 January 1917, box 240, folder 1, DeMille Collection.

43. Vachel Lindsay, "Queen of My People," *The New Republic*, 7 July 1917, p. 281.

44. Harvey C. Horater to Artcraft Pictures Corporation, 19 May 1917, box 240, folder 1, DeMille Collection.

45. Harry D. G. Robinson to Arthur G. Whyte, 24 May 1917, box 240, folder 1, DeMille Collection.

46. Al Lichtman to Lasky, 26 May 1917, box 240, folder 1, DeMille Collection.

47. Lasky to DeMille, 19 January 1917, box 240, folder 1, DeMille Collection; *DeMille Legacy*, 451.

48. Ibid.

49. Lasky to DeMille, 8 February 1917, box 240, folder 1, DeMille Collection.

50. Lasky to DeMille, 5 March 1917, box 240, folder 1, DeMille Collection; *DeMille Legacy*, 62.

51. Lasky to DeMille, 8 February 1917, box 240, folder 1, DeMille Collection.

52. DeMille to Lasky, 3 February 1917 and 8 February 1917, box 240, folder 1, DeMille Archive; *DeMille Legacy*, 484, 493.

53. Lasky to DeMille, 15 March 1917, box 240, folder 1, DeMille Collection; *DeMille Legacy*, 527.

54. Script for *The Little American*, box 1228, folder 5, p. 20, DeMille Collection.

55. For more discussion of the development of both classical cinema style and the star system, see David Bordwell, Janet Staiger, and Kristin Thompson, *The Classical Hollywood Cinema: Film Style and Mode of Production to 1960* (New York: Columbia University Press, 1985), parts 2 and 3.

56. "Cast and Synopsis, *The Little American*," Motion Picture Division, Library of Congress, LP-11016 (microfilm).

57. Script for *The Little American*, box 1228, folder 5, p. 1, DeMille Collection.

58. Ibid., pp. 2, 4, 5.

59. Ibid., p. 2.

60. Ibid., pp. 2–3.

61. Cyril Fields, *The Great War, 1914–1918* (New York: G. P. Putnam's Sons, 1959) 31.

62. "Lusitania first hand," box 13, folder 13, DeMille Collection.

63. Script for *The Little American*, box 1228, folder 5, p. 64, DeMille Collection.

64. Ibid., p. 94.

65. Lasky to DeMille, 26 May 1917, box 240, folder 1, DeMille Collection.

66. "The Little American," *Exhibitor's Trade Review*, 14 July 1917, p. 410.

67. For more information about Lady Duff Gordon, see Lady Duff Gordon, *Discretions and Indiscretions* (New York: Frederick A Stokes, 1933), and Meredith Etherington-Smith and Jeremy Pilcher, *The "It" Girls: Lucy, Lady Duff Gordon, the Couturiere "Lucille," and Elinor Glyn, Romantic Novelist* (New York: Harcourt Brace Jovanovich, 1993).

68. Although the title "America's Sweetheart" was first used by manager Pop Grauman on the marquee of his theater in San Francisco in 1914, when the Pickford film *Tess of the Storm Country* played there, my research shows it was not used consistently or systematically until the release of *The Little American* in 1917. Mary Pickford, *Sunshine and Shadow* (New York: Doubleday, 1955), 377.

69. "The Little American," *Exhibitor's Trade Review*, 14 July 1917, 410.

70. G. W. Mark, Strand Theater, Grinnell, Iowa, *Motography*, 3 November 1917, p. 907; H. A. Schwahn, Eau Clair Theater, *Motography*, 4 August 1917, p. 229.

71. "Mary Pickford Packs Theater," *Motography*, 18 August 1917, p. 350.

72. Mae Tinee, "Proceeding to Censor the Censor," *Chicago Tribune*, 3 July 1917.

73. "Chicago, July 18," *Variety*, 20 July 1917, p. 29.

74. Tinee, "Proceeding."

75. Tinee, "Let Funkhouser Cast Filmy Eye on This Array! 'The Little American' in other Cities Passed by Censors," *Chicago Tribune*, 4 July 1917, sec. 2.

76. Advertisement for *The Little American*, *Chicago Tribune*, 4 July 1917, sec. 2.

77. "Mary Pickford Film to be Shown Privately Today," *Chicago Tribune*, 8 July 1917, part 1, sec. A.

78. "Citizen Censors Approve 'The Little American' Film," *Chicago Tribune*, 10 July 1917.

79. "Jury Complete to 'Try' Mooted Movie of War," *Chicago Tribune*, 13 July, 1917, sec. 2.

80. "Wants New Censor Board," *Variety*, 13 July 1917, p. 22.

81. "Jurors Say You Can See 'Little American' Film, Only One, Von Moos, Against Forcing Permit," *Chicago Tribune*, sec. 1.

82. Advertisement for *The Little American*, *Chicago Tribune*, 21 July 1917.

83. "The Little American," *Variety*, 20 July 1917, p. 29; "Creel's O.K. of 'The Little American,' Fails to Hold Funkhouser to Promise—Czar May Lose Job," *Exhibitor's Trade Review*, 21 July 1918, p. 532; "Little American Wins," *Moving Picture World* 33.4 (28 July 1917): 625.

84. Frederick Luebke, *Bonds of Loyalty: German Americans and World War I* (DeKalb: Northern Illinois University Press, 1974), 237, quoting Hermann Hagedorn, "The Menace of the German-American Press," *Outlook* 116 (August 1917): 579–581.

85. For more information on the Praeger case and on the problems caused for what came to be known as "hyphenated Americans," see Luebke, *Bonds of Loyalty*.

86. "What the Picture Did for Me," *Motography*, 4 August 1917, p. 229.

87. "What the Picture Did for Me," *Motography*, 25 August 1917, p. 385.

88. "Mary Pickford Urges All Film Stars to Contribute Ambulances to the Red Cross," *Minneapolis Tribune*, 15 July 1917, sec. 13.

89. "Little Mary Patriotic," *Milwaukee Journal*, 12 August 1917, sec. 2.

90. Photograph with caption "Pictorial Weekly, *Chicago Tribune*, 12 August 1917."

91. Gordon, *Discretions and Indiscretions*, 261.

92. "Mary Pickford Doing 'Bit,' " *Motography*, 7 July 1917, p. 33.

93. "Mary Pickford Is Thanked by San Francisco Mayor," *New York Mirror*, 7 July 1917; Robinson-Locke Collection, scrapbook 388, Billy Rose Theater Collection, New York City Public Library.

94. Photograph of Mary Pickford and an ambulance, *New York Times*, 13 July 1917, rotogravure sec.

95. "Film Flashes," *New York Times*, 15 July 1917, sec. X.

96. *Variety*, 17 August 1917, p. 21; "A Christmas Party in September," *Moving Picture World* 34.2 (13 October 1917): 261; "Right Off the Reel," *Chicago Tribune*, 2 December 1917, sec. 7.

97. "It's Colonel Mary Pickford Now," *Motography*, 15 March 1918, p. 494.

98. "Mary Pickford Starts a Fund for the Red Cross," *Toledo Blade*, 9 December 1917, Robinson-Locke Collection, scrapbook 388; "Mary Pickford Takes San Francisco," *Motography*, 2 February 1918, p. 220; "Studio Actors Knit with Mary Pickford," *Motion Pictures*, April 1918, Robinson-Locke Collection, scrapbook 388.

99. Pressbook for *How Could You, Jean?*, June 1918, Motion Picture Division, Library of Congress, LP-12496 (microfilm).

Chapter 3. Programming Theaters and Exhibiting Movies in Wartime

1. "The Motion Picture and the War," *Moving Picture World* 35.5 (2 February 1918): 678.

2. Epes Winthrop Sargent, *Picture Theater Advertising* (New York: Chalmers, 1915), 27.

3. "Rivoli Opens to the Public Dec. 27," *Moving Picture World* 35.1 (5 January 1918): 54–55.

4. *The Modern Musketeer* contains references to the war appropriate to a narrative set in a contemporary time period, but the war itself does not play a significant role in the narrative.

5. "Rivoli Opens to the Public," 55.

6. Harold Edel, "How It Is Done at the Strand," *Moving Picture World* 34.12 (22 December 1917): 1769.

7. Sargent, *Picture Theater Advertising*, v.

8. "Live Wire Exhibitors," *Motion Picture News*, 5 May 1917, p. 2823.

9. "Stanley Sells Tickets Subject to Agreement to Respect Flag," *Moving Picture World* 32. (5 May 1917): 789.

10. Advertisement, "I Am the New Manager of the Broadway Theater," *New York Times*, 23 December 1917, sec. X.

11. "Seattle Film Men Aid Red Cross Drive," *Moving Picture World* 33.2 (14 July 1917): 273.

12. Sargent, "Advertising for Exhibitors," *Moving Picture World* 33.5 (4 August 1917): 789.

13. Sargent, *Picture Theater Advertising*, 4.

14. John F. Barry and Epes Winthrop Sargent, *Building Theater Patronage: Management and Merchandising* (New York: Chalmers, 1927), 183.

15. Edel, "How It Is Done at the Strand," 1767.

16. Advertisement, *Moving Picture World* 32.4 (28 April 1917): 630.

17. United States Food Administration, letter, 2 October 1917, National Archives, record group 4, 12 HC-A4, box 505.

18. "Fairbanks Starts Red Cross Fund," *Moving Picture World* 33.1 (7 July 1917): 64.

19. "Strand Places Dedicatory Tablet," *Moving Picture World* 35.10 (9 March 1918): 1350.

20. *Motion Picture News*, 14 April 1917, p. 2327.

21. "Baltimore Makes Anthem Obligatory," *Moving Picture World* 35.2 (12 January 1918): 272.

22. "Written on the Screen," *New York Times*, 6 May 1917, sec. X.

23. "Buffalo Exhibitors Praised for Patriotism," *Moving Picture World* 34.6 (10 November 1917): 897.

24. J. Seymour Curry, *Illinois Activities in the World War* (Chicago: Thomas B. Poole, 1921), vol. 1, p. 81.

25. Ora Almon Hilton, "The Control of Public Opinion in the United States during the World War" (Ph.D. diss., University of Wisconsin, 1929), 20, quoting the Committee on Public Information, *General Bulletin*, no. 7, 25 July 1917, Division of Four Minute Men (Washington, DC, 1917).

26. Bertram Nelson, "The Four Minute Men," in *What Every American Should Know about the War*, ed. Monteville Flowers (New York: Doran, 1918), 255.

27. James R. Mock and Cedric Larson, *Words That Won the War: The Story of the Committee on Public Information* (Princeton: Princeton University Press, 1939), 113.

28. B. C. Van Wye, "Speech Training for Patriotic Service," *Quarterly Journal of Speech Education* 4 (October 1918): 368.

29. Nelson, "Four Minute Men," 252.

30. Ibid., 253 (quote of Woodrow Wilson).

31. Hilton, "Control of Public Opinion," 21.

32. Curry, *Illinois Activities*, vol. 1, p. 90.

33. Ibid.

34. Carol Oukrop, "The Four Minute Men Became a National Network during World War I," *Journalism Quarterly* 52.4 (winter 1975): 633.

35. Ibid., 633, quoting "A Tribute to Our Allies," *Four Minute Men Bulletin*, no. 46.

36. Van Wye, "Speech Training," 396.

37. George Creel, *The Complete Report of the Chairman of the Committee on Public Information 1917, 1918, 1919* (Washington, DC: Government Printing Office, 1920; rpt. New York: DaCapo Press, 1972), 1.

38. "Four Minute Singing Coming into Use in Patriotic Gatherings," *Forward*, 2.10 (17 October 1918): 3.

39. Advertisement, *Motion Picture News*, 28 April 1917, p. 2692.

40. Advertisement, *Motion Picture News*, 5 May 1917, p. 2876.

41. Sargent, "Advertising for Exhibitors," *Moving Picture World* 35.9 (2 March 1918): 1235–1236.

42. Ibid., 34.13 (29 December 1917): 1939.

43. Ibid.

44. David M Kennedy, *Over Here: The First World War and American Society* (New York: Oxford University Press, 1980), 37.

45. Kevin Brownlow, *The War, The West, and the Wilderness* (New York: Knopf, 1979), 22, quoting Lewis Selznick in *Moving Picture World* 21.7 (15 August 1914): 963.

46. Sargent, "Advertising for Exhibitors," *Moving Picture World* 39.1 (4 January 1919): 79.

47. *The Story of the Famous Players-Lasky Company* (1919), 56–7, Museum of Modern Art Archives.

48. Sargent, "Advertising for Exhibitors," *Moving Picture World* 33.12 (22 September 1917): 1846.

49. "Be Town Figure," *Motion Picture News*, 21 April 1917, p. 2472.

50. Ibid.

51. Barry and Sargent, *Building Theater Patronage*, 32.

52. Elmer Axel Beck, *The Sewer Socialists: A History of the Socialist Party of Wisconsin, 1897–1940* (Fennimore, WI: Westburg Associates, 1982), 196, quoting Daniel Hoan.

53. Hilton, "Control of Public Opinion," 2.

54. Samuel Hopkins Adams, "Invaded America," *Everybody's Magazine* 28.1 (1918): 28–33, 82, 84.

55. Karen Falk, "Public Opinion in Wisconsin during World War I," *The Wisconsin Magazine of History* 25.4 (1942): 399–400.

56. Falk, "Public Opinion in Wisconsin," 390.

57. Beck, *Sewer Socialists*, vol. 1, p. 185.

58. Beck, *Sewer Socialists*, vol. 1, p. 196.

59. Editorial, *Milwaukee Journal*, 1 August 1918.

60. Advertisement, *Milwaukee Leader*, 5 May 1917.

61. The drive for "100 percent Americanism " grew out of the nativist movement soon after World War I began in Europe. In his history of the homefront, David M. Kennedy notes, "That kind of rank nativism, tinged often with

anti-radicalism, seeped deeper and deeper into the American mind as the war progressed, carried by the current of a newly fashioned phrase: '100 percent Americanism.' The 100 percenters aimed to stamp out all traces of Old World identity among immigrants. They visited their worst excesses on German-Americans, which at first glance was scarcely surprising." (Kennedy, *Over Here*, 67). For more information about nativism and 100-percent Americanism, see John Higham, *Strangers in the Land: Patterns of American Nativism, 1860–1925* (New York: Atheneum, 1963).

    62. Fannie Gordon, "Happenings on Stage and Screen," *Milwaukee Journal*, 11 August 1918, sec. 4.

    63. Beck, *Sewer Socialists*, vol 1, p. 186.

    64. "Envelope Admission," *Variety*, 12 July 1918, p. 42.

    65. Advertisement, *Milwaukee Journal*, 14 July 1918, sec. 2.

    66. Advertisement, *Milwaukee Journal*, 12 May 1918, sec. 2.

    67. Advertisement, *Milwaukee Journal*, 21 July 1918, sec. 4.

    68. Advertisement, *Milwaukee Journal*, 28 October 1917, sec. 4.

    69. Gordon, review of *Hearts of the World*, *Milwaukee Journal*, 28 July 1918, sec. 4.

    70. Advertisement, *Milwaukee Journal*, 31 July 1918.

    71. Editorial, *Milwaukee Journal*, 1 August 1918.

    72. Gordon, review of *Hearts of the World*.

    73. Advertisement, *Milwaukee Journal*, 2 June 1918, sec. 2.

    74. Sargent, "Advertising to Exhibitors," *Moving Picture World* 34.12 (22 December 1917): 1775.

    75. *Minneapolis Tribune*, 28 October 1917, sec. 13.

    76. "Theaters Can Open on Idle Mondays," *New York Times*, 20 January 1918.

    77. "Picture Business Satisfied with Garfield Holidays," *Variety*, 8 February 1918, p. 46.

    78. "Blue Tuesdays Mean Good Mondays," *Moving Picture World* 35.6 (9 February 1918): 885.

    79. "Right Off the Reel," *Chicago Tribune*, 27 January 1918.

    80. "The Year in Review," *Exhibitor's Trade Review*, 20 July 1918, p. 539.

    81. "World Correspondents Describe Business Conditions," *Moving Picture World* 35.6 (9 February 1918): 793–798.

Chapter 4. The Film Industry and Government Propaganda on the Homefront

    1. "Industry Subscribes Over 2½ Million to Liberty Loan," *Exhibitor's Trade Review*, 23 June 1917, p. 173.

2. United States Food Administration letter to Crockett Brown, 7 September 1917, United States Food Administration Collection, National Archives, record group 4, 12 HC-A4, box 505.

3. Brown to the United States Food Administration, 11 October 1917, United States Food Administration Collection, record group 4, 12 HC-A4, box 505.

4. "Food Will Win the War," certificate from the USFA, 1917, United States Food Administration Collection, record group 4, 12 HC-A4, box 506.

5. "Slide Campaign on Pledge Card Drive," United States Food Administration Collection, record group 4, 12 HC-A4, box 506.

6. "Film Men Form Temporary Organization," *Moving Picture World* 29.4 (22 July 1916): 612.

7. "Film Men Discuss Organization," *Moving Picture World* 28.13 (24 June 1916): 2210.

8. "Film Men Form Temporary Organization," *Moving Picture World* 29.4 (22 July 1916): 612.

9. George Creel, *How We Advertised America: The First Telling of the Amazing Story of the Committee on Public Information That Carried the Gospel of Americanism to Every Corner of the Globe* (New York: Harper, 1920), 4.

10. Stephen Vaughn, *Holding Fast the Inner Lines: Democracy, Nationalism, and the Committee on Public Information* (Chapel Hill: University of North Carolina Press, 1980), 22.

11. James R. Mock and Cedric Larson, *Words That Won the War: The Story of the Committee on Public Information* (Princeton: Princeton University Press, 1939), 134.

12. "Industry Subscribes Over 2½ Million to Liberty Loan," *Exhibitor's Trade Review*, 23 June 1917, p. 173.

13. "Facts and Comment," *Moving Picture World* 33.6 (11 August 1917): 911.

14. Sam Spedon, "Here We Are Again," *Moving Picture World* 33.1 (7 July 1917): 61; "NAMPI Launches Membership Drive," *Moving Picture World* 35.11 (16 March 1918): 1490.

15. Frederick Elliott to George Kleine, June 1918, George Kleine Collection, Library of Congress, container 66.

16. "Facts and Comment," *Moving Picture World* 35.7 (16 February 1918): 943.

17. "War Achievements of the Motion Picture Industry Set Forth in Brief to Federal Officials by National Association," *Exhibitor's Trade Review*, 20 July 1918, p. 552, quoting Woodrow Wilson.

18. "Industry's Pledge of War Service Given Generous Recognition by Federal Officials When Film Representatives Visit Capital," *Exhibitor's Trade Review*, 21 July 1917, p. 515.

19. Arthur Friend, memo, 8 August 1917, United States Food Administration Collection, record group 4, 12 HC-A4, box 504.

20. "Movies Boom Liberty," *New York Times*, 19 September 1917.

21. "Movies Aid the Cause of Patriotism," *Forward* 1.27 (15 November 1917): 2.

22. Director of Publicity, War Loan Organization, memo to Mr. Cooksey, 22 May 1918, National Archives, record group 53, item 22, box 6.

23. Herbert Hoover to Friend, 9 August 1917, United States Food Administration Collection, record group 4, 12 HC-A4, box 504.

24. Ibid.

25. Ibid.

26. William Clinton Mullendore, *History of the United States Food Administration, 1917–1919* (Stanford: Stanford University Press, 1941), 3, quoting Herbert Hoover.

27. Ibid., 82.

28. Mary Pickford to Hoover, 24 September 1917, United States Food Administration Collection, record group 4, 12 HC-A4, box 504.

29. "We would appreciate that in the future we have our cameraman take the views in order that they may be taken at least at a different angle, and therefore we have a picture which can be slightly different from others." J. A. Berst to Arthur Friend, 27 September 1917, United States Food Administration Collection, record group 4, 12 HC-A4, box 504.

30. Friend to Ben Allen, 24 October 1917, United States Food Administration Collection, record group 4, 12 HC-A4, box 504.

31. "Slide Campaign on Pledge Card Drive," United States Food Administration Collection, record group 4, 12 HC-A4, box 506.

32. Maxcy Robson Dickson, *The Food Front in World War I* (Washington, DC: American Council on Public Affairs, 1944), 131.

33. United States Food Administration letter to exhibitors, 2 October 1917, United States Food Administration Collection, record group 4, 12 HC-A4, box 504.

34. Dickson, *Food Front*, 131.

35. Mullendore, *History*, 87.

36. United States Food Administration to exhibitors, 24 October 1917, United States Food Administration Collection, record group 4, 12 HC-A4, box 505.

37. John C. Flinn to Friend, 17 August 1917, United States Food Administration Collection, record group 4, 12 HC-A4, box 504.

38. R. C. Maxwell, memo, 25 April 1918, United States Food Administration Collection, record group 4, 12 HC-A4, box 504.

39. A. I. McCreary to Lyda Flager, 8 February 1918, United States Food Administration Collection, record group 4, 12 HC-A4, box 504.

40. "Motion Pictures," United States Food Administration Collection, record group 4, 12 HC-A4, box 504.

41. United States Food Administration to J. H. Hecht, 16 May 1918, United States Food Administration Collection, record group 4, 12 HC-A4, box 504.

42. Dickson, *Food Front*, 124, quoting Rufus Steele to Ben Allen, 30 September 1918.

43. "Hoover to Universal," *The Moving Picture Weekly*, 9 February 1918, p. 8.

44. "Making Your Theater a Family Institution with a Permanent Clientele," *Exhibitor's Trade Review*, 20 July 1918, p. 580.

45. Memo from the Office of the Director of Publicity, War Loan Organization to Mr. Cooksey, 22 May 1918, National Archives, record group 53, item 22, box 6.

46. Mock and Larson, *Words That Won the War*, 134.

47. "War Achievements of the Motion Picture Industry," 552.

48. This was just 254 theaters shy of the total number of theaters in the United States, according to a tally made by the Motion Picture Directory Company. "Motion Picture Theaters in the United States and Canada," Motion Picture Directory Company, United States Food Administration Collection, record group 4, 12 HC-A4, box 504.

49. "War Achievements of the Motion Picture Industry," 552.

50. Fannie Gordon, "The Movies," *Milwaukee Journal*, 8 September 1918, sec. 2.

51. *The Bond* (Charlie Chaplin, 1918).

52. Memo to the Secretary of the Treasury, 20 January 1919, National Archives, record group 53, item 22, box 6.

53. Photograph of Mary Pickford, *New York Times*, 24 June 1917.

54. "Liberty Loan Lights," *Chicago Tribune*, 21 October 1917, sec. 1.

55. Mae Tinee, "Right Off the Reel," *Chicago Tribune*, 30 December 1917, sec. 7, quoting Oscar Price to Marguerite Clark.

56. Caption, *Milwaukee Journal*, 14 April 1918, sec. 2.

57. "Written on the Screen," *New York Times*, 27 May 1917, sec. X.

58. Advertisement for *The Bar Sinister*, *New York Times*, 28 April 1918, sec. X.

59. "Written on the Screen," *New York Times*, 28 April 1918, sec. X.

60. Samuel M. Field to Kleine, 8 March 1918, George Kleine Collection, container 66.

61. Advertisement, *New York Times*, 13 October 1918, sec. X.

62. "Motion Picture Industry Aids Pit and Shell Drive," *Forward* 2.9 (3 October 1918): 6.

63. "By Request of the War Department," George Kleine Collection, container 65.

64. Photograph of Pickford, Chaplin, and Fairbanks, *New York Times*, 30 December 1917, rotogravure sec.

65. "In the World of the Movies," *New York Times*, 27 January 1918, sec. X.

66. "Written on the Screen," *New York Times*, 10 February 1918, sec. X.

67. Advertisement, *New York Times*, 19 May 1918, sec. X., p. 10.

68. U.S. Civil Service Commission to Kleine, 23 September 1918; Director General, Department of Labor to Kleine, 16 July 1918; Clarence Crestby, Assistant Secretary of Agriculture, to Kleine, 2 April 1918; George Kleine Collection, container 66.

69. "Written on the Screen," *New York Times*, 17 February 1918, sec. X.

70. "Written on the Screen," *New York Times*, 25 August 1918, sec. X.

71. "Motion Picture Industry Aids Pit and Shell Drive," 6.

72. Advertisement, George Kleine Collection, container 65.

73. Kleine to Priorities Committee of the War Industries Board, 8 November 1918, George Kleine Collection, container 67.

74. Kleine to Kendall Banning, written but not sent, 11 July 1917, George Kleine Collection, container 65.

75. Kleine to I. E. Chadwick, 8 February 1917, George Kleine Collection, container 20.

76. F. K. Elliott, Executive Secretary, NAMPI, to Kleine, June 1918, George Kleine Collection, container 66.

77. Kleine to P. A. Powers, 17 July 1918, George Kleine Collection, container 38.

78. As far as I can determine, the Edison Company did not affiliate with NAMPI either. Their representatives are not included in the "Appointments on War Corporation Committee" or on NAMPI's Board of Directors. While the fact that the company would soon be out of the motion picture business may account for its lack of membership, in George Kleine's case the reasons were clearly ideological.

79. McChesney to Kleine, 24 January 1918, George Kleine Collection, container 66.

80. Mary Raymond Shipman Andrews, "The Three Things," *Ladies Home Journal*, November 1915, pp. 19–20; December 1915, pp. 27–28.

81. Alan Crosland to McChesney, 10 November 1917, George Kleine Collection, container 57.

82. Ibid.

83. Program for *The Unbeliever* from the Auditorium Theatre in Chicago, March 1918, George Kleine Collection, container 57.

84. "Good Advertising and Clever Staging Puts over 'Unbeliever' for a Record Week," *Motion Picture News*, 1 June 1918, p. 3269.

85. Advertisement for *Stella Maris*, *Detroit Free Press*, 3 March 1918, sec. 4.

86. "The Reel Players," *Detroit Free Press*, 7 March 1918.

87. Advertisement, *Detroit Free Press, 10 March 1918.*

88. "The Reel Players," *Detroit Free Press,* 11 March 1918.

89. "See Themselves in Martial Film," *Detroit Free Press,* 12 March 1918.

90. "The Reel Players," *Detroit Free Press,* 18 March 1918.

91. "The Reel Players," *Detroit Free Press,* 11 March 1918.

92. Advertisement for *The Unbeliever, Detroit Free Press,* 31 March 1918, sec. IV.

93. Susan E. Meyer, *James Montgomery Flagg* (New York: Watson-Guptill Publications, 1974), 74.

94. Advertisement, *Detroit Free Press,* 24 March 1918.

95. This poster is in the Social Welfare History Archives Center, University of Minnesota.

96. Circular Letter from Kleine to Managers, Salesmen, and Bookers, 7 June 1918, George Kleine Collection, container 67.

97. L. E. Schaeffer to Kleine, 14 June 1918, George Kleine Collection, container 67.

98. A. S. McLemore to Kleine, 24 October 1918, George Kleine Collection, container 57.

99. Kleine to Elizabeth Rickey Dessez, Community Motion Picture Bureau, 4 September 1918, George Kleine Collection, container 66.

100. McLemore to Kleine, 24 October 1918, George Kleine Collection, container 57.

101. Kleine to the mayor of Macon, Mississippi, 15 October 1918 (quote provided the author by Laurence Suid).

102. D. E. Waterston to Kleine, 24 October 1918, George Kleine Collection, container 57.

103. McLemore to Kleine, 29 October 1918 (quote provided the author by Laurence Suid).

104. Kleine to McChesney, 2 March 1918, George Kleine Collection, container 66.

105. Ibid.

106. Kleine to Hinton Clabough, 16 March 1918, George Kleine Collection, container 67.

107. Kleine to McChesney, 2 March 1918, George Kleine Collection, container 66.

108. Kleine to McLemore, 28 December 1918 (quote provided the author by Laurence Suid).

109. McLemore to Kleine, 27 January 1919, George Kleine Collection, container 57.

110. "War Achievements of the Motion Picture Industry," 552.

111. "Association Meets in Rochester," *Moving Picture World* 41.7 (16 August 1919): 939.

112. Janet Staiger, "Standardization and Differentiation: The Reinforcement and Dispersion of Hollywood's Practices," in David Bordwell, Janet Staiger, and Kristin Thompson, *The Classical Hollywood Cinema: Film Style and Mode of Production to 1960* (New York: Columbia University Press, 1985), 104.

Chapter 5. The U.S. Film Industry at the End of World War I

1. "Bankruptcy in Pictures Laid to War Conditions," *Variety*, 25 October 1918, p. 32.

2. Michael Stevens, ed., *Letters from the Front, 1898–1945* (Madison: State Historical Society of Wisconsin, 1992), 69, quoting Kenneth White.

3. Mae Tinee, "A Great Picture with a Great Man on a Great Day!" *Chicago Tribune*, 12 November 1918.

4. For more information, see John Milton Cooper, Jr., *Pivotal Decades: The United States, 1900–1920* (New York: W. W. Norton, 1990), chapter 11.

5. For more information about social, political, and economic changes or lack thereof following the war, see David M. Kennedy, *Over Here: The First World War and American Society* (New York: Oxford University Press, 1980) and Nell Irvin Painter, *Standing at Armageddon: The United States, 1877–1919* (New York: W. W. Norton, 1987).

6. Douglas Gomery, *Shared Pleasures: A History of Movie Presentation in the United States* (Madison: University of Wisconsin Press, 1992), 60.

7. The editor here is referring to remarks made by George Kleine. "The Patriot and the Businessman," *Motion Picture News*, 12 October 1918, p. 2337.

8. *Variety*, 25 October 1918, p. 32.

9. "Coast Studios Curtail Production Account of Epidemic," *Moving Picture World* 38.5 (9 November 1918): 668; "Producers and Distributors Agree on Four Weeks Shutdown of Industry on Account of Influenza," *Wid's Yearbook 1919*, 3.

10. "U Discontinues Program, Blames War Tax for Move," *Variety*, 19 October 1917, p. 25; "The Year in Headlines: Essanay Announces Discontinuance of Program Releases and Concentration on Special," *Wid's Yearbook 1918*, 89; "The Most Important Event of the Year: An Optimistic Outlook, Fewer and Better Pictures," *Wid's Yearbook 1918*, 93.

It is also important to note that this language, "fewer and better," is similar to the language used in industry discourse when feature-length films were being introduced. See Janet Staiger, "The Central Producer System: Centralized Management after 1914," in David Bordwell, Janet Staiger, and Kristin Thompson, *The Classical Hollywood Cinema: Film Style and Mode of Production to 1960* (New York: Columbia University Press, 1985).

11. "The Old and New Year as Seen by George Spoor," *Motion Picture News*,

11 January 1919, p. 262; W. W. Hodkinson Cuts Out Program System of Distribution," *Moving Picture World* 43.1 (3 January 1920): 79; "First National to Make Superfeatures Instead of Program Releases," *Wid's Yearbook 1919*, 15. For information about the shift to feature-length filmmaking and its attendant discourse, see Staiger, "Central Producer System."

12. "Most Important Event of the Year," *Wid's Yearbook 1918*, 69.

13. Ibid.

14. "Chronology of the Departed Year Points Out Industry's Chief Events," *Moving Picture World* 43.1 (3 January 1920): 79–81; "Incorporation of the Year," *Wid's Yearbook 1919*, 283, 285, 287.

15. "Big Motion Picture Incomes Subject to Heavy War Tax," *Variety*, 20 April 1917, p. 16.

16. "Three Film Stars Get 1,000,000 a Year Each," *New York Times Magazine*, 27 May 1917.

17. "War as an Alibi," *Variety, 18 May 1817, p. 20.*

18. "Written on the Screen," *New York Times*, 20 January 1918, sec. X; "Bad For a Year," *Variety*, 1 February 1918, p. 50.

19. "Chains of Theaters an Important Factor," *Wid's Yearbook 1918*, 66–67.

20. "World Correspondents Describe Business Conditions," *Moving Picture World* 35.6 (9 February 1918): 798.

21. "Tendency Among Theaters to Combine," *Moving Picture World* 35.4 (26 January 1918): 493.

22. "Chicago Newsletter," *Moving Picture World* 35.3 (19 January 1918): 356.

23. Douglas Gomery, "Movie Audiences, Urban Geography and the History of the American Film," *The Velvet Light Trap* 19 (spring 1982): 23–29. For a more complete picture of this trend in Chicago and around the country see Gomery, *Shared Pleasures.*

24. "Chicago News and Comment: Many Darkened Houses Laid to the Daily Change," *Motion Picture News*, 5 May 1917.

25. Sam Spedon, "Why the Falling Off," *Moving Picture World* 35.5 (2 February 1918): 639.

26. The accounting firm of Price Waterhouse had determined that the actual cost to the producer of this new tax would be 16 cents per reel per day. Thus, at least in print, producers felt that they were being generous to the exhibitor in only passing on 15 cents worth of their tax. "War Tax Problems Continue Unsolved," *Motography*, 24 November 1917, p. 1069.

27. "Smaller Theaters Getting Slippery End," *Moving Picture World* 35.6 (9 February 1918): 804.

28. "Sixteen Theaters Go Out of Business," "Smaller Theaters Taxed Out of Existence," and "K.C. Film Trade Notes of the Week," were stories that ran in *Moving Picture World* 34.10 (8 December 1917): 1466, 1530, 1537. Others were

"War Tax Too Much," *Variety*, 11 January 1918, p. 46; and "Many Theaters Near New Orleans Closing," *Moving Picture World* 35.2 (12 January 1918): 266.

29. "Smaller Theaters Taxed Out of Existence," 1530.

30. "The Small House Still the Backbone," *Moving Picture World* 35.2 (12 January 1918): 208.

31. "World Correspondents Describe Business Conditions," *Moving Picture World* 35.6 (9 February 1918): 793–798.

32. Ibid.

33. "Chains of Theaters an Important Factor," *Wid's Yearbook 1918*, 66–67.

34. Spedon, "Chains of Theaters," *Moving Picture World* 33.2 (14 July 1917): 213.

35. Howard T. Lewis, *The Motion Picture Industry* (New York: Van Nostrand, 1933), 337.

36. "Exhibitor, Co-operative Organizations Meet," *Moving Picture World* 36.4 (27 April 1918): 523.

37. "Big Increase in the Number of Theaters under Management of Alfred Hamburger," "Long Strides Forward Taken by Chicago Exhibitors and Film Producers," and "Alliance of Jones Linick and Schaefer with Selznick: Handle Goldwyn Films," all appeared in *Exhibitor's Trade Review*, 21 July 1917, p. 509.

38. "Ruben and Finkelstein Getting There Fast," *Moving Picture World* 32.5 (5 May 1917): 841.

39. "Tendency Among Theaters to Combine," *Moving Picture World* 35.4 (26 January 1918): 497.

40. "Producers Decide to Close Up Shop," *Moving Picture World* 38.4 (26 October 1918): 491.

41. Giebler, "Rubbernecking in Filmland," *Moving Picture World* 38.6 (9 November 1918): 671.

42. James E. Westheider, "No Cause for Alarm: Cincinnati and the Influenza Epidemic of 1918–1919" (master's thesis, University of Cincinnati, 1986), 26.

43. "Producers Decide to Close Up Shop," 491.

44. "Influenza Epidemic Working West," *Moving Picture World* 38.5 (2 November 1918): 571; "Facts and Comments," *Moving Picture World* 38.6 (9 November 1918): 654; "Trade News Brevities," *Moving Picture World* 38.6 (9 November 1918): 684; "Overhauled and Renovated, Atlanta Houses Reopen," *Moving Picture World* 38.7 (16 November 1918): 720.

45. "Use Lobby as Vegetable Market," *Moving Picture World* 38.6 (9 November 1918): 685.

46. For more information about the influenza pandemic, see Alfred W. Crosby, *America's Forgotten Pandemic* (New York: Cambridge University Press, 1989). Also useful is Dorothy Ann Pettit, "A Cruel Wind: America Experiences Pandemic Influenza, 1918–1920" (Ph.D. diss., University of New Hampshire, 1976).

47. Tino Balio, *United Artists: The Company Built by the Stars* (Madison: University of Wisconsin Press, 1976), 18.

48. Advertisement, *Moving Picture World* 38.6 (9 November 1918): 638.

49. "Flu Casualty List," *Indianapolis News*, 17 October 1918.

50. "Flu Casualty List," *Indianapolis News*, 23 October 1918.

51. Advertisement, *Indianapolis News*, 2 November 1918.

52. Front page, *Indianapolis News*, 4 November 1918.

53. Advertisement for *Shoulder Arms*, *Indianapolis News*, 4 November 1918.

54. "How McCormick's Boomed Comedian," *Moving Picture World* 38.10 (7 December 1918): 1068.

55. Front page, *Indianapolis News*, 5 November 1918.

56. Front page, *Indianapolis News*, 6 November 1918.

57. Kennedy, *Over Here*, 231.

58. "Indiana Newsletter," *Moving Picture World* 38.9 (30 November 1918): 981; "How McCormick's Boomed Comedian," 1069.

59. Tinee, "A Great Picture."

60. Guy F. Lee, "The Little Fellow," *Chicago Tribune*, 20 October 1918, sec. 7.

61. Carl Withers, ed., *A Rocket in My Pocket: The Rhymes and Chants of Young Americans* (New York: Henry Holt, 1948), 65.

62. Wes Gehring, *Charlie Chaplin: A Bio-Bibliography* (Westport, CT: Greenwood Press, 1983), 24.

63. "Charlie Sues to Protect His Inimitable Antics," *Moving Picture World* 38.8 (23 November 1918): 816.

64. "Here's the Story of Chaplin's 'Shoulder Arms,' " *Moving Picture World* 38.5 (2 November 1918): 406.

65. Walter K. Hill, "Critical Reviews and Comment," *Moving Picture World* 38.5 (2 November 1918): 621.

66. For a thorough treatment of the evolution of Chaplin's star persona and public reaction to him, see Charles Maland, *Chaplin and American Culture: The Evolution of a Star Image* (Princeton: Princeton University Press, 1989).

67. "Advertising Aids for Busy Exhibitors," *Moving Picture World* 38.5 (2 November 1918): 624.

68. Although at least one film historian has described *Shoulder Arms* as controversial (Gehring, *Charlie Chaplin:* 24), I find no evidence for such a claim.

69. Both reviews are contained in Gerald McDonald, Michael Conway, and Mark Ricci, eds., *The Complete Films of Charlie Chaplin* (Secaucus, NJ: Citadel, 1988), 156, 158.

70. Tinee, "Right Off the Reel," *Chicago Tribune*, 15 December 1918, sec. 7.

71. Homer Croy, "Pictures are Soldiers' Third Requisite, Only Food and

Sleep Outrank Them in Importance–Screen Girl in Gingham Makes the Hit," *Moving Picture World* 38.9 (30 November 1918): 927.

72. Walter K. Hill, "Rambles Around Film Town," *Moving Picture World* 38.11 (14 December 1918): 1229.

73. Staiger, "Central Producer System," 142.

74. For a description of press reaction, see Tino Balio, *United Artists: The Company Built by Stars* (Madison: University of Wisconsin Press, 1976), 32–33, and Scott Eyman, *Mary Pickford: America's Sweetheart* (New York: Donald Fine, 1990), 123–128.

75. Balio, *United Artists*, 24.

76. "Paramounts and Artcrafts to Entertain Peace Party," *Moving Picture World* 38.11 (14 December 1918): 1188.

Chapter 6. The War Film in the 1920s

1. Louis Harrison Reeves, "Our General Flatness," *Moving Picture World* 38.11 (14 December 1918): 1203.

2. "Facts and Comment," *Moving Picture World* 38.8 (23 November 1918): 626.

3. Frank P. Sibley, *With the Yankee Division in France* (Boston: Little, Brown, 1919); Emerson Gifford Taylor, *New England in France, 1917–1918* (Boston: Houghton Mifflin, 1920); Harry A. Benwell, *History of the Yankee Division* (Boston: Cornhill, 1919). For a more complete listing, see Lawrence Stallings, *The Doughboys: The Story of the AEF, 1917–1918* (New York: Harper and Row, 1963).

4. Mary Roberts Rinehart, *Dangerous Days* (New York: Doran, 1919); Rupert Hughes, *The Patent Leather Kid, and Several Others* (New York: Grosset and Dunlap, 1927); John Dos Passos, *One Man's Initiation: 1917* (Ithaca: Cornell University Press, 1969); *Three Soldiers* (New York: Doran, 1921); e e cummings, *The Enormous Room* (New York: Modern Library, 1934); Willa Cather, *One of Ours* (New York: Knopf, 1922); Edith Wharton, *A Son at the Front* (New York: Scribners, 1923).

5. Reeves, "Our General Flatness," 1203.

6. "Rapf Champions War Films Having Good Love Story," *Moving Picture World* 38.13 (28 December 1918): 1550.

7. Advertisement for *The Road to France, Moving Picture World* 38.8 (23 November 1918): 788; advertisement for *To Hell with the Kaiser, Moving Picture World* 38.10 (7 December 1918): 1049; advertisement for *Crashing Through to Berlin, Moving Picture World* 38.10 (7 December 1918): 1009.

8. Advertisement for *The Cavell Case, Moving Picture World* 38.11 (14 December 1918): 1146–1147.

9. Advertisement for *The Greatest Thing in Life, Moving Picture World* 38.12 (21 December 1918): 1273.

10. Advertisement for *The Unpardonable Sin, Moving Picture World* 38.13 (28 December 1918): 1545–1546.

11. "Killing War Advertising," *Variety*, 29 November 1918, p. 44.

12. Thomas H. Russell, *America's War for Humanity: Pictorial History of the World War for Liberty* (L. H. Walter, 1919), title page. I am grateful to Thomas Doherty for pointing out this quote. Frank Freidel, *Over There* (Boston: Little, Brown, 1964), 67, credits Pershing's friend, Colonel C. E. Stanton, with the quote.

13. This figure is based on the categorization of films with war-related content provided in Patricia King Hanson, executive ed., *The American Film Institute Catalog of Motion Pictures Produced in the United States, Feature Films, 1911–1920* (Berkeley: University of California Press, 1988).

14. Reviews from the *New York World* and the *New York Tribune*, cited in "The Four Horsemen Ride on the Screen," *Literary Digest* 68.13 (26 March 1921): 28–29.

15. Review of the *Four Horsemen of the Apocalypse, New York Times*, 7 March 1921.

16. Robert Sherwood, review of *Four Horsemen of the Apocalypse, Life*, 24 March 1921.

17. Review in the *Morning Telegraph*, cited in "The Four Horsemen Ride on the Screen," 29.

18. Ibid.

19. These figures are based on a count of films listed under the subject heading "World War I" in Kenneth W. Munden, executive ed., *The American Film Institute Catalog of Motion Pictures Produced in the United States, Feature Films, 1921–1930* (New York: R. R. Bowker, 1971).

20. For instance, 1927 saw the release of *First at the Front, Hard Boiled Haggarty* (First National), *Buck Private* (Universal), *Two Arabian Knights* (United Artists), *The Gay Recruit* (Fox), and *Rookies* (MGM).

21. These examples all come from films screened in 1994 at the Thirteenth Festival of Silent Cinema in Pordenone, Italy: *A Rolling Stone* (Bulls Eye, 1919, Library of Congress); *The Detectress* (Reelcraft Pictures, Model Comedies, 1919?, Academy Film Archive/David Shepherd, Blackhawk Collection); *Hold Me Tight* (Fox Film, Sunshine Comedies, 1920, Narodni Filmovy Archiv); *The Skipper's Narrow Escape* (Betzwood Film Company, 1921, George Eastman House); *Hold Your Breath* (Christie Film Company, 1924, George Eastman House); *Vacation Waves* (Hollywood Productions, Paramount, 1928, Library of Congress).

22. *The Stolen Ranch*, William Wellman, Universal Blue Streak Western, 1926, Library of Congress, Wyler Collection. I am also indebted to the 1994 Festival of Silent Cinema, Pordenone, Italy, for screening this film.

23. For a discussion of the sexual tensions swirling around Stroheim's character—created by a conflict between contemporary ideological notions of the American and the Foreign—see Janet Staiger, " 'The Handmaiden of Villainy': *Foolish Wives*, Politics, Gender Orientation, and the Other," in Janet Staiger, *Interpreting Films: Studies in the Historical Reception of American Cinema* (Princeton: Princeton University Press, 1992).

24. "Watching the War from an Orchestra Chair," *Literary Digest* 99.10 (6 March 1926): 38–42.

25. These plot descriptions have been taken from Munden, *The American Film Institute Catalog.*

26. "The Stage Capture by a Hard-Boiled War Play," *Literary Digest*, 83.1 (4 October 1924): 30–31.

27. Review of *What Price Glory?*, *The Woman Citizen*, 18 October 1924, p. 11.

28. "The Stage Captured by a Hard-Boiled War Play," 30, quoting Mordaunt Hall, "The Screen," *New York Times*, 24 November 1926.

29. Mordaunt Hall, review of *What Price Glory?*, *New York Times*, 24 November 1926, in George Amberg, ed., *The New York Times Film Reviews, 1913–1970* (New York: Arno Press, 1970), 62.

30. "Watching the War from an Orchestra Chair," 38–42.

31. King Vidor would remember that John Gilbert, his leading actor in *The Big Parade*, went from a carefully made-up romantic lead to a dirty, sweaty actor who refused to wear makeup. A review for *Wings*, 1927, also noted that Richard Arlen "has gone through the picture minus make-up." As a result, perhaps, Arlen, more than Charles Rogers, was cited for the realism of his portrayal. Vidor is quoted in Laurence Suid, *Guts and Glory: Great American War Movies* (Reading, MA: Addison-Wesley, 1978), 23. See also "When War-Planes Flame and Audiences Gasp," *Literary Digest* 95.7 (12 November 1927): 30–38, 40, 42.

32. Review of *What Price Glory?*, *The Woman Citizen*, 11.

33. Harry Behn wrote the screenplay for *The Big Parade*, J. T. Donahue was scenarist for *What Price Glory?* Hope Loring and Louis Lighton wrote the screenplay for *Wings*.

34. Paul Fussell in his seminal work on the British experience on the Western Front in World War I, *The Great War and Modern Memory* (New York: Oxford University Press, 1975), makes the same point about war in general and about the Great War specifically: "Every war is ironic because every war is worse than expected. Every war constitutes an irony of situation because its means are so melodramatically disproportionate to its presumed ends. In the Great War eight million people were destroyed because two persons, the Archduke Francis Ferdinand and his Consort, had been shot" (7–8).

35. Advertisements for *What Price Glory?*, *Motion Picture News*, 28 October 1927, p. 1333.

36. Chanticleer, "Songs of War," *The Independent* 113 (November 1924): 396–371.

37. Lawrence Stallings, "Songs My Mother Never Taught Me," *Colliers*, 4 June 1927, p. 12–13.

38. My discussion of the criticism leveled at the academy and especially academic historians is drawn from Carol S. Gruber, *Mars and Minerva: World War I and the Uses of the Higher Learning in America* (Baton Rouge: Louisiana State University Press, 1975).

39. E. T. Saintsbury, "Memoirs of a Four-Minute Man," *American Mercury* 15.39 (March 1927): 284–291.

40. Mordaunt Hall, "The Screen: The Flying Fighters," *New York Times*, 13 August 1927, sec. X.

41. Advertisement, *Saturday Evening Post*, 19 November 1927, p. 95.

42. "When War-Planes Flame and Audiences Gasp," from the *New York Morning Telegraph*, in the *Literary Digest* 12 (November 1927): 38.

43. Ibid., 36.

44. Ibid., 38.

45. "Pictures and People," *Motion Picture News*, 26 August 1927, p. 573; advertisements for *What Price Glory?*, *New York Times*, 16 August 1927, sec. X, and *The Big Parade*, *New York Times*, 15 August 127, sec. X.

46. "Pictures and People," *Motion Picture News*, 28 October 1927, p. 1317.

47. Joseph Corn, *The Winged Gospel* (New York: Oxford University Press, 1983), 51–2, 115.

48. "Air Film Flood," *Variety*, 17 August 1927, p. 13.

49. "$10,000 Aircraft Beacon Blazes from roof of Keswick Theater," *Exhibitors Herald World*, 2 March 1929, p. 51; "Tie-up for *Flying Fleet* Links Theater, Air Line and Newspaper," *Exhibitors Herald World*, 30 March 1929, p. 53; "Managers Fly High to Exploit Aviation Film Attractions," *Motion Picture News*, 10 November 1928, p. 1476.

50. "Airmindedness and the Motion Picture," *Moving Picture World* 6 October 1928, p. 1158.

51. "What the Movies Did For Me," *Exhibitors Herald World*, 26 January 1929, p. 52.

52. "People and Pictures," *Motion Picture News*, 26 August 1927, p. 573.

53. The fact that this figure appears in a review of the film, suggests that it was released as part of a press book. "When War-Planes Flame and Audiences Gasp," 38.

54. For a more thorough discussion of the interrelationship among Lindbergh, World War I, and aviation, see Modris Eksteins, *The Rites of Spring: The Great War and the Birth of the Modern Age* (New York: Anchor Books, 1989), esp. chapter 8, "The Night Dancer."

55. Both Eksteins and Fussell have noted the medieval basis of much wartime discourse. As Fussell writes, "The language is that which two generations of readers had been accustomed to associate with the quiet action of personal control and Christian self-abnegation ("sacrifice"), as well as with more violent actions of aggression and defense. The tutors in this special diction had been the boys' books of George Alfred Henty; the male-romances of Rider Haggard; the poems of Robert Bridges; and especially the Arthurian poems of Tennyson and the pseudo-medieval romances of William Morris." In this " 'raised,' essentially feudal language," a horse becomes a "steed" or a "charger," and so on (21).

56. Advertisement for *Wings*, *New York Times*, 7 August 1927, sec. X.

57. Advertisements for *Wings*, *New York Times*, 8, 9, 10, 11, 13 August 1927.

58. "The Flying Fighters," *New York Times*, 13 August 1927, sec. X.

59. "When War-Planes Flame and Audiences Gasp," 42.

60. Epes Winthrop Sargent, "In 'Wings' Paramount Writes Cinematographic History, What War Fliers Think of the Technical Achievement," *Moving Picture World* 87.8 (20 August 1927): 525. (There is a fitting printing error in this article. At the top of the page the date is given as 20 August 1917.)

61. The *Variety* review, quoted in "When War-Planes Flame and Audiences Gasp," 42, makes the point that the story is the film's weakest point (Sargent, "In 'Wings,' " 525; Mordaunt Hall, "The Flying Fighters," *New York Times*, sec. X). The collection of contemporary reviews in *Literary Digest* also provides the basis for my claim that critics found the flying sequences spectacular.

62. Sargent, "In 'Wings,' " 524.

63. Ibid.

64. See David Bordwell, Janet Staiger, and Kristin Thompson, *The Classical Hollywood Cinema: Film Style and Mode of Production to 1960* (New York: Columbia University Press, 1985), esp. chapters 1–7 and chapter 9.

65. For more information about these three cameras and their place within the development of the classical Hollywood cinema style, see Bordwell, Staiger, and Thompson, *Classical Hollywood Cinema*, chapter 20.

66. Edwin Schallert, "Wings," *Motion Picture News*, 19 August 1927, p. 510.

67. "Big Advance Sale of Tickets for 'Wings,' " *Moving Picture World* 88.2 (10 September 1927), 104; " 'Wings' to Open at Criterion in Chicago, October 30, To Be First Picture in Erlanger House," *Moving Picture World* 88.6 (8 October 1927): 338.

68. "Unique Los Angeles Premiere for 'Wings,' " *Motion Picture News*, 14 January 1928, p. 130.

69. Advertisement for Paramount, "In Tune with These Changing Times!" *Motion Picture News*, 9 June 1928, unnumbered advertising pages.

70. For more information about the transition to sound in the United States film industry, see Douglas Gomery, "The Coming of Sound: Technological Change in the American Film Industry," in Tino Balio, ed., *The American Film Industry*, rev. ed. (Madison: University of Wisconsin Press, 1985), 229–251.

71. "Sound Device in 'Wings,' General Electric Company Synchronization Machine Provides Airplane, Machine Gun Effects," *Motion Picture News*, 31 March 1928, p. 1029.

72. "Each time an airplane hurtled in flames to the earth there was a doleful hooting behind the screen. When the aviators are about to take-off [*sic*] and the propellers are set in motion, the sound of whirling motors makes these stretches all the more vivid." Hall, "The Screen."

73. Advertisement, *Motion Picture News*, 5 May 1928, unnumbered advertising pages.

74. Richard H. DePew, Jr., in "What War Fliers Think of the Technical Achievement," *Moving Picture World* 87.8 (20 August 1927): 525; Schallert, "Wings," 510.

75. "Pictures and People," *Motion Picture News*, 26 August 1927, p. 573.

76. "Aviation Will Thank Film Industry for Aid at Dinner September 24: Hays Will Deliver Print of Feature Length Film of Lindbergh Flight at Testimonial Event," *Exhibitors Herald and Moving Picture World*, 1 September 1928, p. 28.

77. "What the Pictures Did For Me," *Exhibitors Herald and Moving Picture World*, 16 February 1929, p. 62. Additional corroboration of *Wings* popularity is provided in Richard Kozarski, *An Evening's Entertainment: The Age of the Silent Feature Picture, 1915–1928* (New York: Scribner's, 1990), 33. Kozarski includes previously unpublished data compiled by James Mark Purcell which correlates exhibitors' reports on films, available figures on box-office take, and the popularity of films made in the years 1922–1927. In his listing, *Wings* ranks first for 1927, followed by *The Jazz Singer, The King of Kings, The Kid Brother, The Gaucho,* and *Uncle Tom's Cabin.*

78. "16,000,000 Paramount Famous Lasky Corporation Twenty-Year 6% Sinking Gold Bonds," 14 November 1927, George Kleine Collection, container 21.

79. *Battling Sisters* (Lupino Lane Comedy, 1929), located in Narodni Filmovy Archiv, seen during the 1994 Giornate del Cinema Muto in Pordenone, Italy.

80. Press Book for *She Goes to War* (Inspiration Pictures, United Artists, 1929), United Artists Collections, Center for Film and Theater Research, State Historical Society of Wisconsin.

81. Sargent, "The Box Office Lowdown on the Paramount Spectacle," *Moving Picture World* 87.8 (20 August 1927): 524.

82. "Watching the War from an Orchestra Chair," 40.

Chapter 7. Conclusion

1. Adolph Zukor, "Look into Future with These Men," *Motography*, 15 December 1917, p. 1241.

2. Ibid.

3. Ibid., 1242.

4. Herbert C. McKay, "The Amateur Kinematographer," *Photo-era Magazine* 6 (November 1928), 288.

5. George Mosse, *Fallen Soldiers: Reshaping the Memory of the World Wars* (New York: Oxford University Press, 1990), 181.

SELECTED BIBLIOGRAPHY

Manuscript Collections

Cecil B. DeMille Collection. Brigham Young University Archives.
George Kleine Collection. Library of Congress.
Robinson-Locke Collection. Billy Rose Theater Collection, Lincoln Center, New York City Public Library.
William Gibbs McAdoo Papers, Library of Congress.
United States Food Administration Records, 1917–1918, National Archives.
United States Treasury Department Records, 1917–1918, National Archives.

Trade Journals and Newspapers

Chicago Tribune
Esssanay News ("published in the interest of exhibitors and all newspapers which use news of photoplays and players")
Exhibitor's Bulletin (published by the Fox Film Corporation)
Exhibitor's Trade Review
Forward (issued by the State Council of Defense, Madison, WI)
Milwaukee Journal
Minneapolis Tribune
Motion Picture News
Motography
Moving Picture World
New York Times
Official Film News (Published by the Committee on Public Information, Division of Films)
Variety
Wid's Yearbook

Books and Articles

Allen, Robert C., and Douglas Gomery. *Film History: Theory and Practice.* New York: Knopf, 1985.

Ayers, N. W. *N. W. Ayers and Sons American Newspaper Annual and Directory.* Philadephia: Ayer and Sons, 1917, 1918, 1919.

Balio, Tino. *United Artists: The Company Built by Stars.* Madison: University of Wisconsin Press, 1976.

Balio, Tino, ed. *The American Film Industry.* Rev. ed. Madison: University of Wisconsin Press, 1985.

Barry, John Francis, and Epes Winthrop Sargent. *Building Theater Patronage: Management and Merchandising.* New York: Chalmers, 1927.

Beck, Elmer Axel. *The Sewer Socialists: A History of the Socialist Party of Wisconsin, 1897–1940.* Fennimore, WI: Westburg Associates, 1982.

Blaetz, Robin. "Strategies of Containment: Joan of Arc in Films." Ph.D. diss., New York University, 1989.

Bordwell, David, Janet Staiger, and Kristin Thompson. *The Classical Hollywood Cinema: Film Style and Mode of Production to 1960.* New York: Columbia University Press, 1985.

Brownlow, Kevin. *The War, the West, and the Wilderness.* New York: Knopf, 1979.

Campbell, Craig. *Reel America and World War I: A Comprehensive Filmography and History of Motion Pictures in the United States, 1914–1920.* Jefferson, NC: McFarland Press, 1985.

Chandler, Alfred D. *Strategy and Structure: Chapters in the History of the Industrial Enterprise.* New York: Doubleday, 1966.

Chrislock, Carl Henry. *Ethnicity Challenged: The Upper Midwest Norwegian American Experience in World War I.* Northfield, MN: Norwegian American Historical Association, 1981.

Clark, John Maurice. *The Costs of the World War to the American People.* New Haven: Yale University, Press, 1931.

Clarkson, Grosvenor B. *Industrial America in the World War: The Strategy Behind the Line, 1917–1918.* New York: Houghton Mifflin, 1923.

Conant, Michael. *Anti-Trust in the Motion Picture Industry.* Los Angeles: University of California Press, 1960.

Cooper, John Milton. *The Vanity of Power: American Isolationism and the First World War, 1914–1917.* Westport, CT: Greeenwood Publishing, 1969.

Cooper, John Milton. *Causes and Consequences of WWI.* New York: Quadrangle Books, 1972.

Cooper, John Milton. *Pivotal Decades: The United States, 1900–1920.* New York: W. W Norton, 1990.

Corn, Joseph. *The Winged Gospel.* New York: Oxford University Press, 1983.

Creel, George. *Complete Report of the Chairman of the Committee on Public Infor-*

mation, 1917, 1918, 1919. Washington: Government Printing Office, 1920; reprint, New York: DaCapo Press, 1972.

Creel, George. *How We Advertised America: The First Telling of the Amazing Story of the Committee on Public Information That Carried the Gospel of Americanism to Every Corner of the Globe.* New York: Harper, 1920.

Crosby, Alfred W. *America's Forgotten Pandemic: The Influenza of 1918.* New York: Cambridge University Press, 1989.

Curry, J. Seymour. *Illinois Activities in the World War,* vols. 1–3. Chicago: Thomas B. Poole, 1921.

DeCordova, Richard. *Picture Personalities: The Emergence of the Star System in America.* Chicago: University of Illinois Press, 1990.

DeMille Legacy, The. *Ed. Paolo Cherchi Usai and Lorenzo Codelli.* Pordenone: Edizioni Biblioteca dell'Immagine, 1991.

Dibbets, Karel, and Bert Hogenkamp. *Film and the First World War.* Amsterdam: Amsterdam University Press, 1995.

Dickson, Maxcy Robson. *The Food Front in World War I.* Washington, DC: American Council on Public Affairs, 1944.

Dileanis, Leonard. "Herbert Hoover's Use of Public Relations in the U.S.F.A., 1917–1919." Master's thesis, University of Wisconsin, 1969.

Eksteins, Modris. *The Rites of Spring: The Great War and the Birth of the Modern Age.* New York: Anchor Books, 1989.

Eyman, Scott. *Mary Pickford, America's Sweetheart.* New York: Donald Fine, 1990.

Farrar, Geraldine. *Such Sweet Compulsion: The Autobiography of Geraldine Farrar.* New York: Greystone Pres, 1938.

Flowers, Monteville. *What Every American Should Know about the War.* New York: Doran, 1918.

Fussell, Paul. *The Great War and Modern Memory.* New York: Oxford University Press, 1975.

Gehring, Wes. *Charlie Chaplin: A Bio-Bibliography.* Westport, CT: Greenwood Press, 1983.

Gomery, Douglas. *Shared Pleasures: A History of Movie Presentation in the United States.* Madison: University of Wisconsin Press, 1992.

Gordon, Lady Duff. *Discretions and Indiscretions.* New York: Frederick A. Stokes, 1933.

Greenwald, William Irving. "The Motion Picture Industry: An Economic Study of the History and Practices of a Business." Ph.D. diss., New York University, 1950.

Gruber, Carol S. *Mars and Minerva: World War I and the Uses of Higher Learning in America.* Baton Rouge: Louisiana State University Press, 1975.

Hampton, Benjamin. *A History of the Movies.* New York: Covici-Friede, 1931.

Handbook of Federal World War Agencies and Their Records, 1917–1921. Washington, DC: Government Printing Office, 1943.

Hanson, Patricia King, executive ed. *The American Film Institute Catalog of Motion Pictures Produced in the United States, Feature Films, 1911–1920.* Berkeley: University of California Press, 1988.

Hawley, Ellis. *The Great War and the Search for Modern Order: A History of the American People and Their Institutions, 1917–1933.* New York: St. Martins Press, 1979.

Higashi, Sumiko. *Cecil B. DeMille and American Culture: The Silent Era.* Berkeley: University of California Press, 1994.

Higham, John. *Strangers in the Land: Patterns of American Nativism, 1860–1925.* New York: Atheneum, 1963.

Hilton, Ora Ida. "The Control of Public Opinion in the United States during World War I." Ph.D. diss., University of Wisconsin, 1929.

Hoffman, Frederick J. *The Twenties: American Writing in the Postwar Decade.* Rev. ed. New York: The Free Press, 1962.

Huetting, Mae D. *Economic Control of the Motion Picture Industry: A Study in Industrial Organization.* Philadelphia: University of Pennsylvania Press, 1944.

Inglis, Ruth. *Freedom of the Movies.* Chicago: University of Chicago Press, 1947.

Isenberg, Michael T. *War on Film: The American Cinema and World War I.* London: Associated Universities Presses, 1981.

Jacobs, Lewis. *The Rise of the American Film.* New York: Columbia University Press, 1939, 1968.

Jensen, Joan M. *The Price of Vigilance.* New York: Rand McNally, 1968.

Jowett, Garth. *Film: The Democratic Art.* Boston: Little, Brown, 1976.

Kennedy, David M. *Over Here: The First World War and American Society.* New York: Oxford University Press, 1980.

Kozarski, Richard. *An Evening's Entertainment: The Age of the Silent Feature Picture, 1915–1928.* New York: Scribner's, 1990.

Leuchtenberg, William. *The Perils of Prosperity, 1914–1932.* Chicago: University of Chicago Press, 1958.

Luebke, Frederick. *Bonds of Loyalty: German Americans and World War I.* DeKalb: Northern Illinois University Press, 1974.

Lewis, Howard T. *The Motion Picture Industry.* New York: Van Nostrand, 1933.

Livermore, Seward, *Politics Is Adjourned: Woodrow Wilson and the War Congress, 1916–1918.* Middleton, CT: Wesleyan University Press, 1966.

Lyons, Timothy. "Hollywood and World War I, 1914–1918." *Journal of Popular Film* 1.1 (winter 1972): 15–30.

Maland, Charles. *Chaplin and American Culture: The Evolution of a Star Image.* Princeton: Princeton University Press, 1989.

May, Henry F. *The End of American Innocence*. New York: Knopf, 1959.

McKinley, Albert Edward. *Collected Materials for the Study of the War*. Philadelphia: McKinley Publishing, 1918.

Merritt, Russell. "D. W. Griffith Directs the Great War: The Making of Hearts of the World." *Quarterly Review of Film Studies* 6.1 (winter 1981): 46–65.

Mitchell, Charles Reed. "New Message to America: James W. Gerard's *Beware* and World War I Propaganda." *Journal of Popular Film* 4.4 (1975): 275–295.

Mock, James R., and Cedric Larson. *Words That Won the War: The Story of the Committee on Public Information*. Princeton: Princeton University Press, 1939.

Mosse, George. *Fallen Soldiers: Reshaping the Memory of the World Wars*. New York: Oxford University Press, 1990.

Mould, David. *American Newsfilm, 1914–1919: The Underexposed War*. New York: Garland, 1980.

Mullendore, William Clinton. *The History of the United States Food Administration, 1917–1919*. Stanford: Stanford University Press, 1941.

Munden, Kenneth W., executive ed. *The American Film Institute Catalog of Motion Pictures Produced in the United States, 1921–1930*. New York: R. R. Bowker, 1971.

Nash, Roderick. *The Nervous Generation: American Thought, 1917–1930*. New York: Rand McNally, 1969.

Painter, Nell Irvin. *Standing at Armageddon: The United States, 1877–1919*. New York: W. W. Norton, 1987.

Paxson, Frederick. *American Democracy and the World War*. Vols. 1–3. Boston: Houghton Mifflin, 1936.

Ramsaye, Terry. *A Million and One Nights*. New York: Simon and Schuster, 1926.

Ratner, Sidney. *American Taxation: Its History as a Social Force in Democracy*. New York: W. W. Norton, 1942.

Samuelson, Paul A., and Everett Hagen. *After the War, 1918–1920: Military and Economic Demobilization of the United States—Its Effects upon Employment and Income*. Washington, DC: National Resources Planning Board, 1943.

Sargent, Epes Winthrop. *Picture Theater Advertising*. New York: Chalmers, 1915.

Schafler, Ronald. *The United States in World War I: A Selected Bibliography*. Santa Barbara: Clio Books, 1978.

The Story of the Famous Players-Lasky Corporation (1919). Museum of Modern Art Archives.

Straiger, Janet. *Interpreting Films: Studies in the Historical Reception of American Cinema*. Princeton: Princeton University Press, 1992.

Suid, Lawrence. *Guts and Glory: Great American War Movies*. Reading, MA: Addison-Wesley, 1978.

Susman, Warren. *Culture as History: The Transformation of American Society in the Twentieth Century.* New York: Pantheon Books, 1984.

Thompson, Kristin. *Exporting Entertainment: America and the World Film Market, 1907–1934.* London: British Film Institute, 1985.

Van Wye, B. C. "Speech Training for Patriotic Service." *Quarterly Journal of Speech Education* 4 (October 1918): 366–371.

Vaughn, Stephen. *Holding Fast the Inner Lines: Democracy, Nationalism, and the Committee on Public Information.* Chapel Hill: University of North Carolina Press, 1980.

Waller, Gregory A. *Main Street Amusements: Movies and Commercial Entertainment in a Southern City, 1896–1930.* Washington, DC: Smithsonian Institution Press, 1995.

Ward, Larry Wayne. *The Motion Picture Goes to War: The United States Government Film Effort During World War I.* Ann Arbor: UMI Research Press, 1985.

Warner, Marina. *Joan of Arc: The Image of Female Heroism.* New York: Vintage Books, 1982.

Whitney, Nathaniel. *Sale of War Bonds in Iowa.* Iowa City: State Historical Society, 1923.

Wiebe, Robert. *The Search for Order, 1877–1920.* New York: Hill and Wang, 1967.

Withers, Carl, ed. *A Rocket in My Pocket: The Rhymes and Chants of Young Americans.* New York: Henry Holt, 1948.

INDEX

America Goes Over (Departments of War and Navy, and Eastman Kodak, 1928), 197

American Protective League: and DeMille, 30

Anderson, Maxwell, 172; and *All Quiet on the Western Front*, 173

Andrews, Mary Raymond Shipman, 125

Anti-German films, 36, 37, 43, 46; and Milwaukee, 93

Arlen, Richard, 184

Armistice, 137; and *Shoulder Arms*, 153

Aviation: and 1920s film, 178–82, 184, 185

Baker, Newton (Secretary of War): and George Kleine, xv; and DeMille, 29–30

Bara, Theda: and Liberty Loan Campaign, 120

Battling Sisters (Lupino Lane Comedy Corp., 1929), 192

Big Parade (Metro, 1925): and 1920s war films, 168, 171; role of women in, 172; and realism, 173, 229n31; and *Battling Sisters*, 192; anti-war theme of, 193

Bow, Clara: in *Wings*, 193

Brady, William: and NAMPI, 107, 109, 197

Burke, Billie, 117

Cather, Willa, 160

Catholic Church: and *Joan the Woman*, 24

Censorship: and CPI, 108; and *The Unbeliever*, 132–34; and NAMPI, 135. *See also The Little American*

Chaplin, Charles: and Liberty Loan Campaign, 119, 155–56; and *Shoulder Arms*, 148–57; and popular culture, 154; and Helen Keller, 157

Cheating the Public (Fox, 1917), 116

Chicago: and exhibition, 142–43. *See also The Little American*; Funkhouser, Major

Clark, Marguerite, 115, 119–20

Commission on Training Camp Activities: and NAMPI, 123; and *The Boy Who Kept Fit to Win*, 128–29

Committee on Public Information (CPI): and George Kleine, xv; and official films, 40; and Four Minute Men, 80–84; and censorship, 108; and NAMPI, 109–10, 176. *See also* Creel, George

Cooper, Gary, 186

Courtot, Marguerite, 127

Creel, George (chairman of Committee on Public Information): and George Kleine, xv; and CPI's goal, 107–8; and censorship, 108, 135; and *Four Horsemen of the Apocalypse*, 168. *See also* Four Minute Men

Crowder, General Enoch, 135

cummings e e, 160

Davies, Marion: and Liberty Loan Campaign, 120

DeMille, Cecil B.: and *Joan the Woman*, 5–21; and Lasky Home Guard, 29; and Liberty Bonds, 29; and service at the Front, 29–30; and American Protective League, 30; and spying, 30–33; and *The Little American*, 50–56

Documentary films, 38, 40, 41, 209*n6*
Dos Passos, John, 160, 172

Edel, Harold: 76, 79, 86; and Liberty
    Loan Campaign, 120; and Spanish In-
    fluenza, 150
Essential industry, xvii
Export: at end of World War I, 34

Fairbanks, Douglas: and Liberty Bonds,
    119–20
Famous Players-Lasky: merger, 6, 8, 30;
    and *Joan the Woman*, 7; and scenarios,
    8; ouster of Goldwyn by, 11–12; and
    Romance of the Redwoods, 52–54; and
    Mary Pickford, 54; and U.S. Food Ad-
    ministration, 110; and U.S. Treasury
    Department, 110, 120–21; and vertical
    integration, 138; growth of, in 1920s,
    191–92
Farrar, Geraldine, 6, 10–11; and critical
    reception of *Joan the Woman*, 23–24;
    and Liberty Loan Campaign, 35. *See
    also Joan the Woman*
Ferguson, Elsie, 115
Flagg, James Montgomery, 113, 128, 130
Foolish Wives, 170
Foreign film imports, 4, 34
Four Horsemen of the Apocalypse (Metro,
    1921), 166, 168, 170–71
Four Minute Men, 80–84; in Wisconsin,
    91, 105, 113; and post-war disillusion-
    ment, 176–77
Four Minute Singing, 83–84
Friend, Arthur: and *Joan the Woman*, 7,
    23; and U.S. Food Administration,
    111–16
Funkhouser, Major: and *The Little Ameri-
    can*, 63–69; and *The Unbeliever*, 132–
    33

Garfield, Harry (head of U.S. Fuel Admin-
    istration), 101–2
Gish, Lillian, 47–48
Griffith, David Wark: and *Hearts of the
    World*, 47–48, 95–99, 171; and

NAMPI, 107; and *The Greatest Thing
    in Life*, 163; and *Birth of a Nation*, 171

Hays, Will, 158; and aviation, 190–91
Hearts of the World (D. W. Griffith, 1918),
    47–48; in Milwaukee, 48, 95–99,
    155, 171
Hoan, Daniel, 91
Hodkinson, W. W., 4
Hoover, Herbert (chairman of U.S. Food
    Administration): and Famous Players-
    Lasky, 111–12, 135. *See also* United
    States Food Administration
How Could You, Jean? (Artcraft, 1918),
    71–74, 87
Hughes, Rupert, 160
Hun Within, The (Paramount-Artcraft,
    1918), 46

Independent production, 140–42
Indianapolis, Ind.: and *Shoulder Arms*,
    149, 151–53

Joan of Arc: and *Joan the Woman*, 27,
    204–5*n43*
Joan the Woman (Lasky, 1916), 5–29;
    and the Catholic Church, 26; and Joan
    of Arc, 27

Keller, Helen, 157
King, Henry, 192
Kleine, George, xv; and practical patrio-
    tism, xvi; and theater managers, 88;
    and War Industries Board, 123; as in-
    dustry gadfly, 124; opposition to
    NAMPI, 124; and *The Star Spangled
    Banner*, 125; and *The Unbeliever*, 125–
    34 *passim*
Kleine System. *See* Kleine, George

Lafollette, Robert, Sr., 90
Lasky Home Guard: and Cecil B.
    DeMille, 29; and Mary Pickford, 69
Lasky, Jesse: and Mary Pickford, 8; and
    merger with Famous Players, 8–9, 10;
    friendship with Cecil B. DeMille, 10;
    and *The Little American*, 52, 54, 55

Legion of the Condemned (Paramount, 1928), 186, 187

Liberty Loan Campaigns: and Geraldine Farrar, 35; and Mary Pickford, 70, 71, 119–20; and movie theaters, 76, 78; and Four Minute Men, 81; and Douglas Fairbanks, 92; and Charles Chaplin, 119, 155–56; and Famous Players-Lasky, 120–21. *See also* United States Treasury Department

Lindbergh, Charles: and *Wings*, 180

Little American, The (Artcraft, 1917): 56–63; and censorship, 63–69, 87

Lucile, Lady Duff Gordon: and Mary Pickford, 61, 69

Lusitania, 56; and Rita Jolivet, 58; and timeliness, 94–95

McAdoo, William Gibbs, 119, 120, 135, 158

McKee, Raymond: in *The Unbeliever*, 127; enlists, 128; in *The Boy Who Kept Fit to Win*, 128–29

Macpherson, Jeanie: and *Joan the Woman*, 5; and *The Little American*, 50

Magnascope, 186

Milwaukee, Wis., 90–102

Military recruitment: and *Joan the Woman*, 21

National Association of the Motion Picture Industry (NAMPI): organization, 105, 107; goals of, 107; and President Wilson, 109–10; and U.S. Food Administration, 111–16; and U.S. Treasury Department, 116–22; and War Department, 122–23; and Red Cross, 123; and other governmental departments, 123; and "work or fight" order, 135; and censorship, 135; and propaganda, 195; and Edison Company, 221*n78*

Nativism, 216*n61*

Over the Top (Vitagraph, 1918), 46

Paramount, 4

Parsons, Louella, 13

Pickford, Mary: and Famous Players-Lasky, 8; and Artcraft, 44; and World War I filmography, 49–50; and Zukor, 52; as star persona, 53, 57, 59, 74; and war work, 68–71; and U.S. Food Administration, 112; and Liberty Loan, 119

—*Johanna Enlists* (Artcraft, 1918), 50–51

—*Romance of the Redwoods* (Artcraft, 1917), 52–54

Practical patriotism: definition of, xvi, consequences of, xviii; and *The Little American*, 55, 195–98; source of phrase, 201*n11*

Pressbook, 87

Private Peat (Paramount-Artcraft, 1918), 46

Projection speed, 204*n39*

Propaganda: in Hate-the-Hun films, 36, 37, 43, 134–36; and World War I posters, 165; and NAMPI, 195. *See also* Stereotypes; Committee on Public Information

Red Cross: and *Joan the Woman*, 21; and Mary Pickford, 68, 70; and movie theaters, 78, 96; and Douglas Fairbanks, 79; and Four Minute Men, 81; and NAMPI, 123

Rinehart, Mary Roberts, 160

Roadshow, 46–48; and *The Big Parade*, 169; and *What Price Glory?*, 169; and *Wings*, 182

Romance of the Redwoods (Artcraft, 1917), 52–54

Rothapfel, Roxy, 75–76, 86

Sargent, Epes Winthrop, 77, 78–79, 88–89

Saunders, John Monk: and *Wings*, 173; and *Legion of the Condemned*, 173,

186; and *Dawn Patrol*, 173; as a war veteran, 184

Selective Service Act, 137

Serials, 38, 40

She Goes to War (United Artists, 1929), 192

Shoulder Arms (First National, 1918), 137, 148–57 *passim;* and timeliness, 149, 151–53; in Chicago, 153; and critical reviews, 156

Socialists, 90

Spanish Influenza, 33, 34, 139, 147–48; and Harold Edel, 150

Specials, 44–46; definition of, 202*n10*

Stallings, Laurence, 172

Star Spangled Banner, The (Edison, 1917), xvi

States rights distribution: and *Joan the Woman*, 12; definition of, 13; and war-related films, 38

Stereotypes: in *The Little American*, 56–58; Prussian, 58–59, 196

Stroheim, Erich von, 36, 170

Stolen Ranch, The (Universal, 1927), 169–70

Superpatriotism, 65–68, 91

Timeliness: and *Joan the Woman*, 6, 13, 16, 17, 18, 21, 22, 55; and *The Little American*, 55, 62; and Lusitania Week, 94–95; and *The Unbeliever*, 129, 131–32; and *Shoulder Arms*, 149; and post-war film promotion, 165

Topicality. *See* Timeliness

Unbeliever, The (Edison, 1918): and Marine Corps recruitment, xvi, 128; and Milwaukee, 97–100; collaboration with Marine Corps, 125–34 *passim;* plot of, 125–26; in Chicago, 126; in Seattle, 126; in Detroit, 127–28; and timeliness, 129, 131–32; and Funkhouser, 132, 133

United States Army Intelligence: and DeMille, 31–33

United States Department of Agriculture, 123

United States Department of Labor, 123

United States Food Administration, 76; and movie theaters, 79; and Four Minute Men, 81; and NAMPI, 105, 106, 110; function of, 112; and Mary Pickford, 112; and film censorship, 115–16

United States Fuel Administration, 100–102

United States Marine Corps: and *The Unbeliever*, 99–100, 125–34 *passim;* and *The Star Spangled Banner*, 123, 126

United States Treasury Department: and NAMPI, 110, 116–23; and War Cooperation Committee, 118; and Liberty Loan Campaigns, 118–21. *See also* Liberty Loan Campaigns

United States War Department: and *Wings*, 191; and *She Goes to War*, 192

Unpardonable Sin, The (Harry Garson, 1919), 165

Valentino, Rudolph, 66

Vidor, King, 171

War Loan Organization, 111, 116

War Savings Stamps, 87

War tax, 93, 101; and film stars, 140–41; and independent production, 140–42; and film exhibitors, 143, 224*n26*

Washburn, Bryant, 32–33

Wellman, William: and *The Stolen Ranch*, 169; as a war veteran, 184; and *Legion of the Condemned*, 186

Wharton, Edith, 160

What Price Glory? (Fox, 1926), 169, 171, 174; and women, 172, 175

Wilson, Woodrow: and neutrality, 4; and 1916 election, 18, 205*n53*; breaking diplomatic relations, 20; and Four Minute Men, 82; and Fuelless Tuesday, 102; and homefront mobilization, 107; and NAMPI, 109–10; and Versailles Treaty, 159

Wings (Paramount, 1927): war veterans, 178, 184–85; and aviation, 178, 179, 180–85; as a roadshow, 182; critical reviews, 185; and sound, 189–90, 193; and Academy Award, 190; and U.S. War Department, 191

Work or Fight Order, 135

Zukor, Adolph, 4; and DeMille, 30; and Mary Pickford, 52; and *The Little American*, 52, 54, 55; and NAMPI, 107; and War Cooperation Committee, 111; and U.S. Treasury Department, 118